Lesson Plans Ahoy!

Hands-on learning for sailing children and home schooling sailors

Third Edition

NADINE SLAVINSKI

Rolling Hitch Press

New York

Copyright © 2011 Nadine Slavinski

Twenty years from now you will be more
disappointed by the things that you didn't do
than by the ones you did do.

So throw off the bowlines.
Sail away from the safe harbor.
Catch the trade winds in your sails.
Explore. Dream. Discover.

Mark Twain

Many thanks to Markus and Nicky for their support and contributions. *Lesson Plans Ahoy!* owes much of its inspiration to the crews of *Sea Bright* and *Arearea*, as well as the insights and encouragement of Laura, Brigitte, and Markus. Many thanks to the crews who shared their home schooling experiences and views with the author. May you always have a hand's breadth of water under your keels!

Thank you to teaching colleagues Tonianne Lederer, Cameron Lumsden, Jack McMurtry, Bruce Schultz, and Johnnie Wilson for their valuable feedback, as well as editor Cynthia Sherwood of Second Set of Eyes. A hearty thank you to Markus Schweitzer for technical support and formatting this book. Last but not least, thanks to the Peaks Island kids for testing several of the units that appear in this book.

Cover photo by Markus Schweitzer: approaching Gibraltar under sail.

Table of Contents

Introduction

Cruising offers memorable experiences for adults and children alike. For our children, sailing can be a rich educational experience that exceeds the boundaries of a traditional classroom. However, valuable, transferable learning won't happen on its own. If your children are to gain a new body of knowledge that can be applied to future endeavors in school and in life, you will have to deliver an educational program that is explicit and focused. Whether you are setting off on a short cruise, crossing an ocean, or committing to a year of home schooling, this book will help you capitalize on a rich learning opportunity.

Many home schooling programs are difficult to deliver on a boat. They can be highly prescriptive, or simply irrelevant – why study the Industrial Revolution when sailing in the wake of Columbus? Others can be impractical – just try a science experiment at sea! Some parents design their own learning program instead, but such efforts often stress literacy skills and creativity at the expense of a well-rounded curriculum that includes "technical" subjects like mathematics and science. *Lesson Plans Ahoy!* can complement a packaged home schooling program, provide the foundation for a sound, self-directed curriculum, or simply keep sailing children in touch with the sea through interesting learning experiences.

Directions for differentiating the lessons in this book help parents adapt units to the individual, whether the child is learning alone or within a mixed age group. In addition, enrichment activities and cross-curricular links are suggested. Finally, references to national and state curricula from the United States, Canada, the United Kingdom, and Australia are listed so that students can keep pace with expectations in their home educational systems.

With this program, a busy parent must not squeeze schooling into a rigid schedule, but rather use a flexible approach that allows for dolphin visits, meal preparation, and sail changes. Never fear: given a solid boat, a well-prepared crew, and sensible precautions, the ocean can be a safe place to bring your child. And it can provide an educational experience that lasts a lifetime!

Overview

The units in this guide may be used at quiet anchorages, on day sails, or on blue water passages. They can be completed in any order and either condensed to a few lessons or expanded for in-depth studies. The idea is not to strictly follow the text but rather to use it as a guide for student-driven inquiry.

Lesson Plans Ahoy! opens with three science units. In **Unit 1 - Earth and Space Science,** students collect and analyze data and model the lunar cycle. **Unit 2 - Biology** guides parents and students through a fish dissection. Throughout the dissection and follow-up assignments, students focus on how organs work together in interconnected systems. In **Unit 3 – Chemistry**, students conduct an experiment that allows them to isolate and control variables.

The two mathematics sections that follow include one long and one more compact unit. In **Unit 4 - Data Management**, students collect data on water consumption and learn to create a variety of graphs to visually represent their findings. Data collection can run from one to three weeks; the graphing work itself takes two or more lessons. In **Unit 5 - Measurement**, students take a hands-on approach to area and capacity.

Unit 6 – Writing provides detailed instruction on journal writing, non-fiction writing, and creative writing. The aim of this unit is to help students develop as writers in different genres. While students are encouraged to choose their own writing topics, each section provides a number of prompts and strategies for the young writer to use in expanding their skill set. Tips for publishing student work are also included.

Units 7 and **8** turn to **History**, with a close look at two great voyagers, **Christopher Columbus** and **Captain James Cook**. These units are divided into subsections, each with its own set of activities and assignments. Taking a sailor's point of view, these units emphasize that history can be seen through different perspectives.

Unit 9 – Navigation with Map and Compass partners well with the two history units while also integrating an important mathematics component, coordinate graphing. Combining theory and practice, students will learn to create their own maps and find a given location. Finally, in **Unit 10 - Physical Education**, students study how the body changes with exercise and learn how to measure their heart rate.

Each unit includes **Age-Appropriate Adaptations** to guide parents in personalizing lessons for their children. For example, a family's six, eight, and ten-year-olds can all develop their mathematics skills by graphing water use, each child at his or her own level. This allows parents to deliver a single program to several children without juggling several unrelated programs at once – your very own one-room floating schoolhouse!

All units contain sections on **Enrichment**, with many suggestions for extending the main topic, **Cross-Curricular Links**, with important interconnections between subject areas, and **Resources**, with recommended books and educational websites.

Experience, experiment, and enjoy!

The How-To's of Home Schooling on a Boat

Home schooling on a boat isn't always easy, but it needn't be complicated or stressful. With good preparation and an open mind – the same qualities needed for cruising – you can give your child a solid education, as well as deep impressions that will last a lifetime. But asking sailors about home schooling is like asking about anchoring techniques: twenty sailors will provide twenty different answers. It really is a question of family taste and individual circumstance. Like everything else about cruising, home schooling is full of compromises – and rewards.

This section covers general aspects of home schooling in three sections to help parents get started. *Choosing an Approach* considers the pros and cons of packaged and self-designed programs. *General Strategies for Home Schooling on Board* covers the nuts and bolts of delivering an educational program, regardless of whether you choose a packaged program or not. The final section, *Structuring a Curriculum,* helps parents who choose self-design to work out the details of a solid educational program for their children.

Choosing an Approach

Just as you must become well versed in weather patterns once you embark upon your voyage, you must also research some basic information when it comes to your child's education. Start organizing yourself well before your planned departure date, seeking answers to the following questions:

- What are the curricular requirements for your child's grade level?
- If you plan to move your child to a different school after your voyage, what curriculum does the new school follow?
- Will schools require a transcript to place your child back in school after your voyage?

The answers to these questions will help guide your choice of a program for your children.

There are essentially two extremes in approaches to home schooling. At one end of the spectrum are those who follow strict, packaged programs and at the opposite end are the free spirits who design their own curriculum. In between are a fleet of cruisers, each following their own preferred path. This book can be used to supplement a packaged program or as the foundation for self-made home schooling.

PACKAGED HOME SCHOOLING PROGRAMS: THE PROS AND CONS

Packaged home schooling programs lay out a complete school year in a series of pre-planned units and assignments. Reputable organizations offer parents the confidence that their child will stay on track through a carefully designed curriculum. Additionally, these programs relieve parent-teachers of the need for extensive preparation and shopping for materials; it's all there – home schooling at a glance. For an extra fee, some providers even offer support services such as feedback on assignments or conference calls to professional educators. Finally, accredited programs will reward your child's efforts with a transcript that will be useful – perhaps even critical – when the cruise ends and the student is placed back into a conventional school system.

On the other hand, packaged programs can be irrelevant or difficult to implement, with sensitive science experiments unsuited to a rocking platform or topics like *World Cultures: the Inuit.* Try getting your kids excited about that in, say, the Bahamas! Packaged programs can be very convenient, but be cognizant that they offer exactly the cookie-cutter type education you could have left behind on land. Consider the cost involved as well; what is a worthwhile investment for some may be an unnecessary expense to others.

Families with two or more children should consider what their choice of programs means in practical terms. If you use packaged programs, your children will be following unrelated strands of work. That creates quite the juggling act for the parent-teacher. On the other hand, packaged programs may be the best option for parents who are unsure about their teaching ability; the programs provide the security of knowing a reputable agency is behind the plans, not to mention materials and some degree of professional support. Parents who decide to go with a packaged program should shop carefully for one that is not only reputable and accredited, but also consistent with their own views. The

Calvert School is a popular choice among American sailors; another good option for sailors may be a Montessori home schooling program due to the hands-on, student-centered approach they promote. Families who choose packaged programs will still find *Lesson Plans Ahoy!* useful for supplementary work, thanks to its relevant themes and practical approach.

SELF-DESIGNED HOME SCHOOLING: THE PROS AND CONS

The other extreme observed in home schooling sailors is a free spirited "the world is my classroom" approach in which relevant topics are pursued as opportunities arise. In Italy, students learn about the Roman Empire and Roman numerals. In Panama, they study Spanish and the history of the canal. The advantage of such an approach is that children are fully engaged and turned on to learning.

The greatest pitfall of independent design is the danger of leaving out difficult topics or subjects that don't arise naturally in everyday settings. These might be critical to developing literacy and numeracy skills; omitting topics results in an imbalanced education pocked with gaps. I met one family whose two sons were incredibly well versed in subjects that tickled their fancy (Greek mythology being one) but whose basic literacy and numeracy skills were appallingly behind grade level norms. This is an extreme example, but the danger is there for well-meaning parents who subtly transfer their own passions to their children while sweeping their weaknesses under the rug. You can avoid this by following the standards from your home school district (particularly for your own weak areas), planning them into your lessons, and reviewing periodically: have we covered the depth and breadth of this curriculum in terms of core math, literacy, and science skills?

Self-designed programs can deliver a rich and balanced education if the parent-educator is conscientious about steering toward specific goals and benchmarks in all subject areas. It is a fine tightrope act that many professionals take years to master: creating a learning environment that encourages student responsibility while attending to details that may not fit easily into the puzzle. Parents can run with the teachable moments, but should not forget to sit down and address the less attractive leftovers, too.

With a self-made home schooling program, learning can be completely student-centered, but you will be on your own in terms of materials. Contact school authorities for their advice on curriculum, materials, and a smooth transition back into the system, if that is your plan. The *Structuring a Curriculum* section of this introduction will provide guidance. You will also find many resources to guide you in the appendices in this book, including websites with pre-made lesson plans (see *Appendix B: Resources, Interdisciplinary Links, and Field Trips)*. Completed assignments and written reflections are useful records to later document student work for a school administration in lieu of a transcript.

One of the advantages of a self-made program is that parents can create a one-room schoolhouse if they have more than one child. Rather than teaching unrelated topics to two or more children and thus doubling or tripling their workload, parents can use common topics that all the children work on at once. Each child will then develop the topic and respond to assignments in a way appropriate to his or her own level (see *Age-Appropriate Adaptations*). You will still be managing a circus, but at least all the action is in one ring!

General Strategies for Home Schooling on Board

Regardless of the type of program you choose, how do the nuts and bolts of home schooling work? This section aims to illuminate some practical considerations for parents without being overly prescriptive. There is no single recipe for success!

You can find accounts of home schooling experiences on sailing family blogs (see *Appendix B*); these may help you choose your own approach. Devote one locker to books and supplies so that everything is in one place and easily accessible. Immediately establish a structured routine that everyone can adapt to; you can always loosen up later. Many families follow a consistent, Monday through Friday, nine to noon schedule, devoting a few hours each morning to school before extended recess in the afternoon. In a traditional approach, a morning home schooling session might look like this (see *Appendix A* for details):

09:00-10:00 Science Unit 1, Lesson 3

10:00-10:45 History Unit 7, Lesson 8
10:45-11:00 Break and snack
11:00-11:45 Writing Workshop: Non-Fiction report on Columbus
11:45-12:30 Mathematics
Evening: journal writing and reading.

An alternative is some form of block scheduling: focusing on a single topic in depth over a longer period of time (see *Daily Lesson Plans* later in this section for tips on organizing lessons).

If you find your "class" locked below decks slaving over dull exercises on a regular basis, something is wrong. Move your classroom to the foredeck or the beach occasionally. Take a field trip – a proper field trip – armed with field guides, notebooks, and clear learning goals (see *Appendix B* for an entire section on designing field trips). If you treat learning as a chore, your children will echo this attitude and everyone will suffer. On the other hand, if you can establish a playful yet disciplined spirit and stimulate natural curiosity, learning will become an accepted part of your day and a rich facet of the cruising experience.

Above all, share the load. Many families fall into a pattern where Mom is the chief educator while Dad is the chief engineer. Often, this is a natural division based on personal interests and strengths, but it can put too much pressure on either partner. With both parents sharing the teaching load, children will benefit from different teaching styles and your individual strengths. This will establish education as a valued, whole-family endeavor, just as the cruise should be a whole-family adventure.

Structuring a Curriculum

Parents who decide to create their own educational program must plan carefully. This section guides parents through that process, starting with a broad overview and moving into greater detail by demonstrating how to break long units into manageable, daily chunks. For those who are still anxious about this process, don't worry: it's more a matter of looking up and adapting existing documents than coming up with something entirely new.

THE BIG PICTURE: CREATING AN OVERALL PLAN

The beauty of home schooling at sea is that you can approach subjects in a way that makes sense in terms of your cruising plan and your child's needs. That means you can think outside the box of traditional classroom education. Still, rather than starting from scratch, you should see how schools schedule topics within a grade level. The idea is not to follow this schedule but to identify blocks of work for your own overall plan.

Begin by obtaining complete curricular documents from your current school. If possible, schedule an appointment with a teacher of the grade level in question. Explain your plans and ask the teacher to help you identify the "year overview" and "learning outcomes." A year overview maps out which topics are covered at what point in the school year. Learning outcomes are the skills a student should be able to demonstrate at the end of each grade. Sitting down with an experienced teacher will save you hours of plowing through unfamiliar documents on your own. However, be aware that it is above and beyond the call of duty for a teacher to share detailed lesson plans or to devote hours to your cause.

Now you can begin to make informed choices about your own year overview, dividing curriculum into manageable chunks, step by step. Most schools today identify a number of strands within each subject area. These can help structure your plan. For example, literacy skills can be divided into strands like *Writing, Reading*, and *Listening and Speaking*, while math is typically subdivided into *Number Sense, Geometry, Pattern, Measurement, and Statistics* strands.

Next, study the requirements of each subject area and compare these to your cruising plans. Does any unit lend itself to a particular location? Science and social studies topics can often be linked to specific regions. For example, the science topic of *Air* that my second grade son would normally cover in his school was a good fit with our season in New England (warm/cold air, weather, fog, etc). We slated the *Habitats* unit for Panama (islands, rivers, canal, and human impact, etc). This process helps you begin slotting topics into your plan. Other science units such as *Light* could be done just about anywhere. Core skills in mathematics and literacy must be developed over an extended period of time and can be tied into various subject areas.

Check for links between subjects when working on your year overview. This will help build and schedule a block of related units. For example, the math curriculum that we followed for our son included a unit on fractions. Fractions complemented the prescribed *Nutrition* unit (showing how a healthy diet can be divided into sections). Nutrition, in turn, lent itself well to the literacy skill of *identifying features of non-fiction texts*; in this way, two more pieces of the puzzle fell into place. Nutrition also fit in with a history unit on Captain Cook, who worked to eliminate scurvy on ocean voyages. With this information, we scheduled the entire block of fractions / nutrition / non-fiction texts / Captain Cook into our first two months in the Pacific. In this way, a rough overview gained structure, like a dinosaur skeleton that nears completion as each bone is uncovered and put into place. Of course, there will always be a few unmatched spares at the end of this process, which you can fit in at will.

You can also match topics to the pace of your cruising plan. Two weeks in Malta may lend themselves to a shorter piece of work, while six island-hopping weeks in Greece may be matched to a larger body of work. Set tentative but not overly ambitious plans for your first long passage. Some families find this to be a prime time for learning, while others find it impractical; you won't know for yourself until you try.

PLANNING EACH UNIT

Once you have a year overview, you can flesh out upcoming units as their allotted time approaches. You should have an entire unit outlined before starting the first lesson. Units should be built around learning outcomes – what students should be able to do at the end of each unit in each grade level (see *Appendix C)*. Identify which learning outcomes each unit will address and list important vocabulary words, subtopics, and activities. The ten units detailed in this book include guiding questions, learning outcomes, background information, activities, and assignments. They can serve as a template for any new units you add to your curriculum.

Many teachers follow an "inquiry cycle" when planning a unit:

- First, whet student curiosity by finding a natural entrance point into a topic. Have students brainstorm what they know (or think they know) about a topic, and list questions for what they want to find out.
- Second, guide students in learning about the topic through reading, research, experiments, and hands-on activities. This takes several sessions.
- Third, students should organize and analyze the information gathered. They can start to answer some of their original questions and turn a collection of facts into an interconnected whole. This process will raise new questions and launch further in-depth, focused research.
- Fourth, students should draw conclusions, so they're not just memorizing information, but learning how it all fits together. Challenge students to produce a body of work that connects the pieces of their newfound understanding in meaningful, memorable ways (see the concluding assignments in each unit of this book). Further opportunities for exploration can be found in the *Enrichment* section at the end of each unit.
- Finally, students should assess and reflect. They should be active participants in the learning process. How well have they achieved the originally stated outcomes? Are students satisfied with the answers they discovered along the way? There is a *Self-Assessment and Reflection* section at the end of each unit of this book.

As an example, take a writing unit that calls for the student to "write an imaginative story with a clear and developed beginning, middle, and end." You should allot one session to introducing the topic and having your child brainstorm questions such as *What makes a good story?* Plan for at least three sessions to explore fiction stories. During this exploration stage you can use exercises like using a graphic organizer (see Unit 6), or have the student write a character description in her own words. Another session can be devoted to analyzing the information gathered and then asking the student to brainstorm ideas for her own story. Writing the story will run over two or three sessions. Then it's time for revising and editing, which will take two or more sessions. Having the student compare her finished story to an earlier work and then reflect on the unit will take another session. This adds up to about ten lessons for the unit, each a step toward achieving the overall goal.

Examples on how to break down two units in this book can be found in *Appendix A*. Generally, this book avoids being more prescriptive because its purpose is to guide parent-teachers in designing learning experiences that suit their children and their situation rather than providing a "one size fits all" fix.

How long should each unit be? That depends on its complexity and the degree of depth aimed for. As a rough rule of thumb, schools typically devote eight to twelve lessons (forty-five minutes to an hour each) to a single unit. Another frame of reference is the number of hours per week a school devotes to math, reading, and so on. These formulas can serve as a reference point – but beware of trying to educate by numbers! A class of twenty-five students might devote twelve hours to fractions, but three students will have mastered the topic after only three hours, while another three still struggle as the unit is scheduled to end. Education defies quantification: there is no magic number. *A unit is complete when your child has achieved the targeted outcomes.*

The beauty of home schooling is that you can adjust the pace of each unit to fit your child and not expect the opposite. If a student hasn't mastered a topic within your time plan, you can extend the unit, move on to a new theme while incorporating the same skills, or revisit it later. If you move faster than anticipated, great! Still, beware of speeding ahead through topics with a quick learner; he or she will benefit more from enrichment activities than superficially rushing through subjects as if they were items to tick off a shopping list. Remember that some learning outcomes are year-end goals; while some skills can be completed sequentially, others will only be mastered in stages. Evaluate progress often and adjust your overall plan accordingly.

When planning, use a holistic approach and try to connect subjects. In the real world, mathematics overlaps with science, social studies, and literacy. Even if you devote the first hour of boat school to science (chemistry), you can use an overarching theme to transition to math (learning to graph data) in the second hour, and later move on to writing (a story in which an experiment goes wrong and leads the characters into a series of adventures). Still, there are times when a subject-specific skill must be treated in isolation. Math is often devilishly difficult to integrate naturally with other subjects despite the best efforts of experienced teachers. There is no use creating a tenuous or artificial thread between division of three digit numbers and the voyages of Columbus!

Every month, check that you are on track with the expectations detailed in your foundation curriculum. Make sure you have a valid reason for anything you omit. If you substitute topics, be careful to preserve essential skills they seek to develop. For example, if you decide to insert *the Water Cycle* in place of *Air* for science, make sure your children learn the underlying research skills (hypothesize, observe, record, analyze) from the original unit.

Schools certainly err on occasion and devote valuable time to topics of dubious merit and application. So if you have a good reason for sparing your child the agony of, say, sentence diagramming, throw that unit overboard and substitute something – anything! – more useful. On the other hand, beware of applying a close-minded attitude to your child's education ("Well, *I* never had a use for chemistry…"). Decisions based on emotionally charged experiences could rob your child of an important skill. School curricula go through extensive periods of development and review by a body of qualified, experienced professionals who have far more expertise than you, the amateur teacher, are likely to possess. The problem with schools is often the *how* rather than the *what*, so be cautious about discarding entire units of work.

DAILY LESSON PLANS

Once you have a unit mapped out, you can plan detailed, individual lessons. Start with a plan for two weeks at a time, and at the end of that time, plan the next batch of lessons. Don't plan details too far in advance because you are bound to make changes along the way. The exception is to obtain supplies for a cruise in an isolated area where educational materials will be as hard to find as the correct oil filter for your engine. Remember to glance through the lists of *Materials* for every unit in this book before departure.

Focus on one or two sub-skills or sub-topics per session. If the lesson goes off on a tangent, that is all right – these offshoots are indications of your child's genuine interests and should be pursued. After all, the endeavor of taking a child out of school to provide authentic learning experiences should remain true to its mission. However, keep the target skills in mind and weave them into the educational detour as much as possible. If you don't manage to cover an important point, be sure to pencil it into the next lesson.

Beware of letting critical skills slide on a regular basis. This is where some parents fall short as teachers, slipping into informal learning that does not serve their children well in the long term. It isn't realistic to expect every lesson to be a rollicking good time in which your child is completely tuned in to his real-world classroom. At times, teacher and pupil will simply have to knuckle down and cover more mundane tasks – think of it like polishing brass or oiling teak from time to time!

In an effort to provide parent-teachers with comprehensive background information, most units in this book center on extensive informational texts. These should be culled down to the basics for students and used as reference. Starting a lesson by diving into a lengthy chapter is likely to squash any enthusiasm your child has for learning! Instead, ease into each lesson with a "hook" or "tuning in" exercise: spend a few minutes looking up at the daytime moon for Unit 1 (*Earth and Space Science*) or comparing the view in front of you to a map for Unit 9 (*Navigation*). Each lesson should also review information and questions that arose in the previous session.

Then move on to the main body of the lesson, using a combination of reading, discussion, and activity. Vary the media you use, too: cartoons, picture books, this book, digital resources, and so on. End each lesson by recapping the day's material and then opening a door to the next class with a hint of something to come, like a soap opera that ends with a dramatic new twist. You don't have to lead your children through every minute; give them their own space and allow time for independent work (skill drills, math games, homework, assignments, reading) as long as they stay on task.

The sections above summarize the progression from general yearly overview to detailed daily lessons. Yes, there is a lot of work involved, but your effort can be spread out over time, and the rewards will make it all worthwhile.

The Benefits

Just thinking about taking responsibility for your children's schooling can be intimidating, a little like sailing away to unfamiliar waters. Don't get put off by doubts or land-bound naysayers. For sailing children, school can be interesting, exciting, and absorbing; it is connected to real life and the world around them. These children, learning aboard their floating homes, enjoy the kind of rounded, relevant education that many of their peers can only dream of. Sailing and home schooling draws families together in a common endeavor. Your children will enjoy the experience of a lifetime with the people who count most: you, their parents.

Many sailing families report that their children successfully streamline back into conventional schools, often ahead of their peers. One mother happily reported that her children aren't "plugged into their devices" like other teens and have a world outlook that few of their peers can match. Sailing children draw upon their experiences throughout their lives, not only in school but also in career and other life choices.

There are many parents out there just like you: once anxious about home schooling, these families are now turning their dreams into reality. The hardest part is making the decision to go in the first place; after that, you will find that everything falls into place. I have yet to meet a cruiser or cruising child who looks back in regret!

Unit 1 - Earth and Space Science

Equipped with his five senses, man explores the universe around him and calls the adventure Science.

Edwin Powell Hubble

Nature composes some of her loveliest poems for the microscope and the telescope.

Theodore Roszak

Unit 1 - Earth and Space Science

Materials:
- Moonrise timetable (see *Resources*)
- Flashlight
- Materials to create a small book or game
- Screwdriver, stick, or other object to skewer ball or fruit
- Ball, round fruit, or other objects to represent the moon and Earth

Guiding Questions:
What makes the moon look different at different times?
How does the moon move in relation to the earth and the sun?

Learning Outcomes:
Students will understand the roles of the earth, moon, and sun in the lunar cycle and phenomena such as eclipses.
Students will be able to follow the scientific process: hypothesize, observe/test, analyze, draw conclusions and make predictions.

Introduction

For many urban and suburban children (and adults), the moon is something that is simply "up there." We occasionally notice its shape and position but generally pay little attention to the moon. One of the joys of sailing is how it puts us back in touch with nature and natural cycles. Where better, then, to conduct a study of the moon and practice the scientific method than at sea?

Every state or national science curriculum includes a study of night/day and the earth in space. This unit takes students through that subject matter while honing essential scientific research skills: formulating questions and hypotheses, planning research, collecting and recording data, making observations, organizing and analyzing data, and presenting findings. Students will also build a model to understand scientific concepts, another important scientific tool.

Unit Overview

This unit is divided into two complementary sections. *Part 1: The Lunar Cycle* is an ongoing unit based around the scientific process. It has an extended phase of simple data collection that involves recording the moon's appearance each night. Eventually, students will have enough data to analyze and then draw conclusions from, tasks that take longer to complete.

Part 2: Model the Lunar Cycle and Eclipses is a hands-on experience that uses ordinary materials and can be completed in one or two sittings. This section can be done at any convenient time, preferably after at least one week of data collection for Part 1. Having worked through this unit, students will gain a greater appreciation for the natural world and our place in it.

Part 1: The Lunar Cycle

Before beginning, prompt students to list all the facts they know (or think they know) about the moon, its cycle, and its influence on the earth. They will probably have basic knowledge of the moon's phases, its orbit, its influence on tides, and so on. However, few students can describe the phases of the moon more precisely or explain why it works the way it does. What side of the moon waxes (grows) and what side wanes (fades)? Why isn't there a solar eclipse every month? What surface features can we see on the moon? To conclude this introductory stage, organize your fact list into categories (such as the moon, the sun's role, special events, etc).

FORMULATE QUESTIONS

Students will quickly recognize gaps in their knowledge and can move on to formulating a research question. Try to help your child select one manageable question such as:

- *How and why does the visible shape of the moon change?*
- *How does the moon move in relation to the earth?*
- *How does the moon's movement affect how we see it?*
- *How can I predict the size of the moon and its position?*

A good research question is open-ended, has more than just a simple answer, and will raise other questions.

It will be important to provide some basic information for students, such as the fact that the moon does not light itself; it only reflects the sun's light. The moon moves in orbit around the earth and both together orbit the sun. This will be best understood in *Part 2: Model the Lunar Cycle and Eclipses.*

Some questions are difficult to address at sea: What does the far side of the moon look like? What is the moon made of? These are best saved for a time when you have more resources readily available; then, your child's curiosity about such issues can and should be pursued.

IDENTIFY YOUR AIM & MAKE A HYPOTHESIS

What is the purpose of this study? Encourage students to summarize their aim in one or two sentences, such as: *The aim of this study is to understand why the moon looks different at different times.* Or: *I want to find out about how the moon is lit up.*

Students should also make a prediction, or hypothesis, about what they will see and how it works. One beginner's example might be: *I think that the moon will grow and then shrink again because it goes around the earth and hides.* A more advanced example (using *if ... then ... because* format) could be: *If the moon orbits the earth, then it will show different phases because the earth sometimes blocks the sun's light.*

PLAN RESEARCH / METHODS

Once students have a research question and hypothesis, they can plan their research. Obviously, it will be necessary to make visual observations of the moon. Together, decide the following: Over what period of time will they make observations of the moon? What information will be important to record? Where and how will they record their data? Starting data collection at a time when the moon is visible during part of the day will be helpful.

Help your child create a data collection **notebook** so all their information will be in one place. Make a checklist for observations on the front page. The tricky part is to guide students toward potentially important details without dictating every aspect of what should be their own work. One goal of this study is to give students the independence to design and follow through with their own project and their own data collection. If that means they do things in a different way than you would, that's all right. At the end of the project, students will evaluate their work; that is a good time to help them consider other points and to help them be more thorough in their next lab experience. They might even consider doing another cycle of lunar observations that take new factors into account.

The basic points to address include the date, shape of the moon, time/height in the sky, and direction of moonrise/set. Dedicate one notebook sheet or half a sheet to each date. Assist very young students by drawing circles into their notebooks that they can then color according to what they see.

Older students might invent a way to measure brightness and relative size of the moon using readily available objects. For example, they could use a coin held at arm's length and note whether the moon is about this size, or bigger or smaller. Students could compare the moon's brightness to that of an unlit playing card on deck. If children don't think of measuring the moon size or brightness from the outset, wait until a few days of data collection go by and see if they take note of this aspect. Then you can help them review and possibly expand their data collection checklist.

Students should consider how long their data collection phase will be. One night? One week? Some students will know that the lunar cycle lasts about a month and will plan their observation phase accordingly. Others may leave this aspect open and (with your help) simply conclude that observations will have to take place for at least as long as it takes for the moon to complete one cycle. Even if your passage or cruise will not be this long, students can continue their observations back on shore, or analyze the data they have collected over one to two weeks and make predictions about the rest of the cycle.

What will students do if it is too cloudy to see the moon? It will be important to record problems such as this in the data collection process. How long will each observation take? Making observations means having a good, thorough look. Don't just peek through the hatch and sketch a crescent! What features can be seen with the naked eye? What features can be seen through binoculars? How will this information be recorded in a standardized way? Crew members can help make observations; in fact, that's a good thing, since it challenges young scientists to find ways to standardize data collection. How will Dad know whether the moon is big, medium, or small? How bright is it to him? Clearly, Dad will need to be trained by his offspring if he is to be a useful research assistant!

OBSERVATIONS: COLLECT AND ORGANIZE DATA

The lines are cast off, the sails raised: now your trip and data collection can begin at last! It may take a few days to establish a routine, but you will find that data collection is a relatively quick and straightforward daily task. After a few days, ask students to review their data collection checklist and make any necessary adjustments. It is at this early stage that you might prompt them to consider recording the moon's brightness, size, or other important points they did not originally foresee.

Within a few days, a trend will become clear and students may already be able to make predictions about the moon's appearance over the next few days. Students should take special notice of the **moon's features**, many of which are evident to the trained eye. The moon's craters are best viewed at the quarter phase when they are emphasized by long shadows.

Sailors can also compare the height of the moon relative to the mast at a fixed time on successive days. Try predicting moonrise times based on the pattern observed without using a moonrise table. Then set a lookout for the predicted moonrise time and direction to see if the student's calculations were correct. This can be a fun way to punctuate quiet days at sea and certainly helps to cement impressions of the sea and sky into the young mind.

Ideally, you would undertake Part 2 of this unit at some halfway point of the data collection process in order to understand the interaction of moon, Earth and sun more fully.

ANALYZE DATA & DRAW CONCLUSIONS

With at least two weeks of data (but ideally, a full twenty-nine day cycle), students can make a formal analysis of their findings. What answers to their questions became apparent? What details of the moon's appearance did they observe? What **predictions** are they now able to make and are these predictions accurate? One way to test predictions is to make your own chart of moonrise times and phases for the following month. What can students conclude about how and why the moon's appearance changes? Do their observations help them explain phenomena and draw conclusions? Students can be reminded that a good scientist will admit errors and make suggestions for improvement in future studies.

PART 1 ASSIGNMENT: PRESENT FINDINGS

Scientific knowledge is not useful if it is not shared with others. To conclude this unit, students have several choices of summative tasks. These include:

- Creating a lunar cycle flip book
- Producing a computer-generated animation
- Making an oral presentation
- Writing a formal laboratory report.

Details of different ways to achieve this assignment are listed in the *Age-Appropriate Adaptations* section of this unit. Students should appreciate that science is not a static field but one that is constantly being extended by research shared with others.

Part 2: Model the Lunar Cycle and Eclipses

It is extremely interesting, not to mention good fun, to model the lunar cycle. This experience works well after a period of observing the moon: a real-world introduction to the topic. The lunar cycle may seem self-evident, but it is actually the result of an interplay of celestial bodies that is not immediately observable from the perspective of one human being. That is why modeling the lunar cycle is an excellent complement to the research / data collection experience.

This section includes a wealth of information that is best divided over two or more sessions.

SET UP YOUR MODEL

Setting up the model does not take long. It is easiest to work with the model in dark conditions, either in a dim cabin or after sunset. What an experience it is to model the motion of the moon and then go on deck to observe the real thing, now ever so relevant!

Students will need a flashlight or lamp to model the sun, and two round objects, large and small, to model the earth and moon. Ideally, the model Earth should have basic geographical reference points marked on it, such as the poles and equator. Your position on the earth should also be clearly marked, using a sticker, ball of clay, or pin. Mark a second point on the model Earth for comparison, such as your home on land, or a faraway place of interest to the child (Australia, Africa). Find a way to place the earth on a stand (such as a small bowl) to leave your hands free; it can be turned as necessary later.

The moon should be a smaller ball like a lime or ping pong ball. Find a way to suspend or skewer the moon (taped to a string, or stuck on a screwdriver) in order to keep its shape free of a hand's obstruction.

MODEL DAY / NIGHT / TIME ZONES

At this point, students will only need a light source and model Earth. Start with a simple animation of day and night at your point of the earth. Rotate the model earth gradually so that your position marker falls into darkness and then into light again. Take your time to dwell at dawn and dusk for a better appreciation of how light first breaks over the horizon and later fades gradually.

Then consider why there are **time zones** on Earth. When it is dawn at your point on Earth, where is the sun setting? For orientation, you can place two signs, "east" and "west," near your globe. Make sure the earth is orbiting in the correct direction (toward east, allowing the sun to rise there and set in the west). Have students do simple time zone calculations (+/- two hours) so they understand why places west of you are behind in time (the earth hasn't revolved into daytime position there yet) and vice versa.

MODEL THE LUNAR ORBIT AND PHASES OF THE MOON

Next, model the **lunar orbit** around the earth without bringing in the sun. Start with an oversimplification by moving your moon around your point on Earth. Now we see it, now we don't; the moon rises and sets just like the sun (from our Earth perspective, that is. Of course, we know that it is the earth that turns around the sun and not the sun circling the earth).

How long does the moon take to orbit the earth? There are two answers. The moon takes 27.3 days to complete a full circle. This is called a **sidereal month**. However, the earth has also moved along its orbit at the same time, so that the moon has to travel more than 360° and catch up a little. This means that the time from one full moon to the next full moon is 29.5 days: a **lunar (or *synodic*) month**. When working with very young students, simplify things by using the lunar month; only introduce the concept of a sidereal month to older students. Since nearly every calendar month is longer than 29.5 days, it is possible to see two full moons in a single month, but it doesn't happen very often. That is where the term "blue moon" comes from, although the moon's color doesn't change!

Now model the moon's orbit in better detail. One side of the moon always faces the earth while another side is always out of our sight. The latter is called the **far side** (or the **dark side**) of the moon. Though the moon does make a complete turn on its axis, it does so slowly (in 29.5 days), matching the time the moon takes to complete a full cycle around the earth. Thus, the moon and Earth are "locked" together. That is why we never see the far side. It is useful to mark a point (such as a crater) or a half of the model moon to keep it aligned correctly. The term "dark side" is misleading because all parts of the moon have day and night just like Earth, but we cannot see the moon's far side without traveling into space and achieving a new viewpoint. That is why "far side" is a better term.

Picture two people on skates, holding hands, leaning back, and spinning in circles. Each sees the other's face and each completes a full rotation, but neither sees the other's back. This is how the moon and Earth move and why we cannot see the far side of the moon.

Phases of the Moon (Northern Hemisphere View)

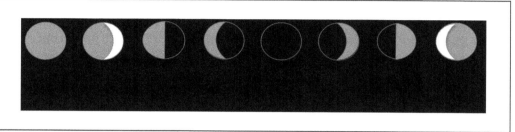

Now bring the sun back into the model. Hold the moon between the earth and sun (for now, keep the moon far away enough from the earth to avoid modeling an eclipse). From our earth perspective, no part of the moon is lit up; this is the phase we call the **new or empty moon**. As the moon orbits to one side, a thin slice of light becomes visible on one edge (the right side for an observer in the northern hemisphere). This thin slice (the **waxing crescent**) gradually spreads as the moon moves to a position beside Earth (first quarter). For older students, it could be instructive to discuss why the **quarter moon** is not called a half moon; that is because the moon has completed a quarter of its orbit at this point (alternatively, you can think of it as a quarter of the whole moon, including the far side).

The phase in which the moon looks fat (more than a quarter, but not quite full) is called the **waxing gibbous**. When the moon is behind the earth and far from the sun, it looks full because its entire visible surface reflects the sunlight (again, keep the moon far enough away from Earth to avoid making a lunar eclipse). Next, the moon circles to the other side of the earth, diminishing through the **waning gibbous** to its last quarter. At this point, the moon's left side is lit. Finally, we see a **waning crescent** (letter C shape) until the moon moves to the "front" and completes its cycle, empty (or "new") again. Think of the C shape as "see you later" as a way to tell at a glance whether the moon is waxing or waning.

If we return to the skater analogy, imagine a spotlight shining from one side. As the skaters spin around, they will be lit from different angles: from the back, from the side, from the front (if not "eclipsed" by the partner), and so on. This is why the moon shows different phases throughout its cycle.

An observer in the northern hemisphere sees the phases as described above. From the **southern hemisphere**, the phases are opposite: a first quarter moon is lit on its left side; a waning gibbous moon is lit on the right side. It is easy to illustrate this effect: simply draw a crescent moon (for example, a waxing northern hemisphere moon with the right side lit) and look at it from a short distance. Now turn your back to it and look again from upside down between your legs. From your new perspective, the moon's left side is lit. At the **equator**, a crescent moon appears to lie on its side when low on the horizon, then "stands up" as it arcs across the sky, only to lie down again on its opposite edge when it descends. In *Resources*, you will find links to animations of the lunar cycle from different points on Earth.

The **full moon** is the only time that the moon rises just as the sun sets and stays in the sky until the sun rises again. At other times in the cycle, the moon is visible for part of the day and part of the night. Challenge students to try to pinpoint the moonrise times for each of the major phases: first quarter, last quarter, and new moon.

This lesson helps students understand what they observe in their daily data collection. It does not provide any information, however, on the length of the lunar cycle or details of the exact position of the moon. That is why the two halves of this unit ("real life" observations and modeling) complement each other well. With older students, you should discuss using models as a scientific tool. In this case, what are the advantages of learning from a model? What are the limitations?

THE MOON AND TIDES

Use the model again in the same way to understand **tides**. Both the moon and the sun exert a gravitational pull on Earth, but the moon, being much nearer, has a stronger pull. The gravity of the moon pulls the earth's water, creating a bulge on that side of the earth. Thus, that location on Earth experiences a high tide. This bulge is balanced by another bulge on the opposite side of the earth where there is a high tide at the same point in time. This effect also means that there are low tides in the points in between.

Sailors know that tides vary, both in the time they occur and in their height. Roughly speaking, there are two tides a day (two highs and two lows). High tide occurs a little later each day; for example, if high tide occurs at noon on Monday, it will occur at about 12:40 on Tuesday. That is because the tide "follows" the moon around the earth, and the earth takes a little longer than twenty-four hours to spin one time.

As stated above, a full moon rises exactly as the sun sets once a lunar cycle. You can best appreciate this effect when sailing at night from east to west. As the moon moves above and then ahead of your boat in the second half of the night, you might even observe your speed increasing slightly, thanks to the tide's pull!

Since the moon does not orbit in a perfect circle, the moon is sometimes closer to Earth and sometimes farther away. When the moon is close to Earth, its gravitational pull is stronger, making tides rise higher (and lows drop even lower). Ask students to orbit the model moon around model Earth in an elliptical path to make this point. Far away = weak tides; close moon = strong tides.

However, the sun has a role to play in the earth's tides, too. When the sun and moon are perfectly aligned, we experience exceptionally high **spring tides** (named for the way the water springs up, not for the season). Conversely, the sun's gravitational pull can also counteract the moon's, pulling in the opposite direction and therefore creating lesser **neap tides**. Though it is difficult to model the earth's surface water bulging, one can easily show the sun and moon in and then out of alignment. Use a tug-of-war comparison to describe the contrary or compound effect produced.

In addition to the influence of the moon and sun, the local geography of a shoreline also affects tides, as do the contours of the ocean floor.

MODEL A SOLAR ECLIPSE

A **solar eclipse** occurs when the new moon slips exactly between your position on Earth and the sun, partially or totally blocking the sun for a few minutes. Until the day that you are perfectly located for this spectacular event, you can model it for better understanding. A solar eclipse of one type or another (you will learn about the different types below) occurs at least twice a year in varying locations.

Continue orbiting the model moon around model Earth. Pause it between the sun and the earth so that the moon casts a shadow over some position on the earth. This is a solar eclipse. Move the moon back and forth to see how it creates a false sunset and later dawn at the marked position. A person wearing special **protective glasses** would observe something like a small bite being taken out of the sun, a bite that grows until the entire sun is swallowed up, only to gradually appear again in the reverse process.

Advanced students can use proper terms for the two parts of the moon's shadow. The faint, outer shadow is called the **penumbra**; a person standing on Earth in the penumbral shadow of the moon sees a partial eclipse. That is, the sun starts to get nibbled at, but never gets gulped away. One only sees a full solar eclipse if positioned in the **umbra**, or dark, inner shadow. (From Latin: *umbra* means shadow, and *paene* means "almost," making penumbra "almost a shadow," the same way a peninsula is "almost an island.")

So, if the moon travels between the sun and the earth during its normal cycle, why isn't there a solar eclipse every month? That is because the moon is relatively small and its shadow usually "misses" the earth. Try this with your model: find a position in which the shadow of the new moon, positioned between Earth and sun, does not darken any point on Earth. Now find a position where it casts a shadow over one position and observe how this shadow moves over part of the earth. That narrow line is called the **Path of Totality** and is less than two hundred kilometers wide. The moon's orbit is tilted at a slight angle to the earth so it does not always move over the same part of Earth; that means that solar eclipses are only visible from the narrow Path of Totality, a path that changes with every eclipse.

At totality, the sun is entirely blocked by the moon and the earth goes dark, like night. Only a blazing **corona**, or halo of fire, is visible around the edges of the moon. This effect lasts for only a few minutes before the earth and moon orbit slightly and no longer line up the same way. It is safe to watch a solar eclipse only with special glasses or pinhole projectors; anyone trying to look directly at the sun will sustain serious eye damage. However, it is safe to look at the corona during totality.

Many ancient cultures revered the sun and had their own explanations for what they witnessed. It could be an interesting research project to study a specific culture and its interpretation of a solar eclipse. Often, ancient people were terrified during the rare event and thought gods were threatening the earth: after all, a solar eclipse occurs at the same location only every 375 years on average!

Since the moon's orbit is elliptical, the moon is sometimes nearer and sometime farther from the earth. When the moon is near, it looks large, and when it is far, it looks slightly smaller. If a solar eclipse occurs when the moon is at the far end of its orbit, the moon's umbra does not reach the earth at all and there is not a full eclipse. However, a faint **antumbral** shadow does reach the earth and creates an **annular eclipse**. In this case, the moon appears too small to completely blot out the sun, though there is still a ring effect of sunlight around the moon (*annulus* means ring; it does not refer to a yearly cycle). The sky remains light and one must use eye protection to view an annular eclipse.

MODEL A LUNAR ECLIPSE

A **lunar eclipse** can only occur when the moon is full and behind the earth. If it is in exactly the right position, the earth blocks the light of the sun from reaching the moon. This process takes several hours and follows the patterns of a solar eclipse. First, a thin slice of the moon grows dark, then the shadow extends to cover more and more of the moon until it goes completely dark, and then it "grows" again from the other side. Unlike solar eclipses, lunar eclipses can be seen by everyone on the side of the earth that faces the moon. You can model a lunar eclipse by holding your skewered moon behind the earth. Try several runs to achieve an example of a total eclipse, a partial eclipse, and no eclipse (when the moon is full but not in the earth's shadow).

The terms **umbra** and **penumbra** are also used to describe the earth's full or partial shadow upon the surface of the moon. Like solar eclipses, there are full and partial eclipses of the moon, occurring as often as three times a year (some years, however, there are no partial or total eclipses, just a barely noticeable **penumbral eclipse**). It is safe to observe a lunar eclipse with the naked eye because, just like looking at the moon on any night, we only see the reflection of the sun's light.

Theoretically, the moon should be invisible during totality because the earth is blocking sunlight from reaching it. However, indirect light does filter through the earth's atmosphere and reaches the moon; this can give the moon a faint brown or even red tint, depending on the state of the atmosphere at the time of the eclipse.

PART 2 ASSIGNMENT

Going through the lunar modeling is a significant accomplishment in itself! However, it is important to finish this activity with a summative task. Option one is to make an **illustrated book** or a **movie** (using computer technology like *iMovie* or *Windows Movie Maker;* see *Enrichment*) that explains the phenomena you have explored (day/night, eclipses, or time zones). This can be a non-fiction work that explains the phenomena scientifically, or a work of fiction such as an informative storybook. For a low-tech approach, students can use a blank notebook or work from scratch to turn a packet of folded papers into a book. Some might even choose to include all the features of a published book, together with cover art, back cover summary, author's profile, and so on. Option two is to **design a board or card game** based on facts about the lunar cycle.

In either case, students must find a way to summarize and express what they have learned. They should aim their work at a specific audience, such as a certain age or interest group.

Age-Appropriate Adaptations

In this section, you will find guidance on how to differentiate, or adapt, this unit for your child. Start with the correct age group, but also glance through the notes for one level younger or older, then mix and match as appropriate.

Self-assessment and reflection are valuable learning tools. They encourage students to think back upon their work and store their new body of knowledge in a meaningful and memorable manner. To that end, a number of self-assessment and reflection questions are listed for each age group. It is not necessary to address all the questions; substitute others as you see fit. Completed assignments and written reflection are useful records to later document student work for a school administration.

Ages 4-6

Young children are fully capable of going through the activities described in Parts 1 and 2 above. Their assignments, however, should be modified.

Part 1 Assignment: *Present findings.* Young children can make a flip book or a circular moon table that can be rotated to show different phases of the moon. Ideally, each image should be labeled with the name of the phase even if that means asking an adult to do the labeling. With help, young students could even prepare a presentation for their peers, such as classmates back at home or other sailing children.

Part 2 Assignment: *Make a space science book, movie, or game.* For this age group, a book will be easier to create than a movie or game. A book can be nonfiction that explains the phenomena, or a work of fiction such as a storybook with characters on their way to lunar adventures. Students should dictate text to a parent or older sibling to accompany their art. Even at this age, it is important to aim the book or game at a specific target audience.

Self-Assessment and Reflection: Young children should orally review the works produced (Part 1 flip book and/or Part 2 illustrated book or game), answering questions like:
- *What is the main idea you tried to show in your work?*

- *Does your work inform other people about what you have learned?*
- *Are you pleased with the result? What could you have done better?*

Ages 6-8

Students ages six to eight are fully capable of going through all the activities as detailed in Parts 1 and 2 above. Their assignments can be modified:

Part 1 Assignment: *Present findings.* Students can make a flip book or a circular moon table that can be rotated to show different phases of the moon. Phases should be labeled with the name and the day of the cycle. Students can add another wheel behind the others that shows dates of the upcoming month. In this way, their table can be used as a predictive tool. Alternatively, students could prepare a presentation for their peers, such as classmates back at home or other sailing children.

The most advanced students of this age group can start to use scientific vocabulary (such as prediction/hypothesis, results, and conclusion) and might even prepare a modified laboratory report (see next level).

Part 2 Assignment: *Make a space science book, movie, or game.* Students ages six to eight could choose to create a nonfiction fact book or movie, write a creative story or script, or create a game based on the lunar cycle. The central aim is a work that reflects their new body of knowledge and communicates it to a specific audience. Students should challenge themselves to produce the highest possible standards of art and text appropriate to their age and ability level. They should draft ever more detailed versions before completing a final product.

Self-Assessment and Reflection: The student should critically examine the book, movie, and/or game created by discussing it.
- *What was the central idea you wanted to convey? Is that clear in your work?*
- *What are the strengths of your product? What are the weaknesses?*
- *How did you overcome any difficulties?*
- *What resources did you use to solve any problems? (computer, books)*

Students in this age group are fully capable of going through all the activities as detailed in Parts 1 and 2 above. Assignments can be adapted as follows:

Part 1 Assignment: *Present findings.* Children in this age group would enjoy making a circular moon table as explained above, but that should only be part of their work. Like scientists who present their findings, these students should choose a means to share what they have learned with others. They can create a detailed presentation in written or oral form that includes illustrations and lists the steps in the scientific process that have been followed. Students can follow lab report style and organize their work under the following headings: aim of the study, prediction (hypothesis: What do you think will happen?), method, materials, results (What happened? What did you observe?), and conclusion (Was your prediction right? Why or why not?).

Part 2 Assignment: *Make a space science book, movie, or game.* Whatever their chosen format, students must be sure to summarize and express what they have learned, and aim at a specific target audience. The work should go through a draft process before arriving at a final product.

Self-Assessment and Reflection: This could be started as a discussion, but some written reflection should follow.
- *Does your book, movie, or game and/or presentation convey its message clearly to the intended audience?*
- *What are the strengths of your work? What are the weaknesses?*
- *How did you overcome any difficulties?*
- *What resources did you have available to you? Which was the most useful and why?*
- *What advice would you give another student doing the same exercise?*

Ages 10-12

Students ages ten to twelve should use scientific vocabulary and formal reporting style when completing their unit assignments.

Part 1 Assignment: *Present findings.* Students ages ten to twelve should see themselves as scientists throughout this unit and conscientiously use proper scientific methods. Their assignment is to complete a formal laboratory report, organized under these headings: aim of the study, hypothesis (what we expected to happen), apparatus (materials used), method (how the study was conducted), observations and results, conclusion based on evidence found, and evaluation (listing weaknesses of the study and suggestions for improvement). Finally, the student should pose further research questions that have arisen in the course of their field study.

Part 2 Assignment: *Make a space science book, movie, or game.* Students usually choose to work in areas of strength to complete such projects. On the other hand, they might consider working in an area of weakness in order to strengthen it. Parents can assist in this decision-making process. The work should be aimed at a specific audience and go through a draft process before arriving at a final product. Students should strive to produce a work filled with detailed, relevant facts presented in a neat and interesting manner.

Self-Assessment and Reflection: Students should write a formal reflection on the scientific process of Part 1. Review what steps were taken, from early preparation through observations and analysis.
- *What went well in your work? What did you overlook?*
- *Did you have to make adjustments as you went through your study?*
- *What could you have done better or differently?*
- *What would be the differences between our study of the lunar cycle and a controlled, laboratory experiment?*

Next, students should examine their final product (an informative book, movie, or game) from Part 2.
- *Did you meet your goals in creating an interesting and informative product?*
- *What did you do especially well and what could you improve?*
- *What parts of the creation process did you particularly enjoy or feel challenged by?*

Enrichment

Students who enjoyed this unit could follow up by studying the moon in more detail. Many of its surface **features** (craters and *maria*, the smooth areas of the moon) are visible to the naked eye or through binoculars. On the other hand, students may decide to follow another interest, such as the sun, other **planets**, or constellations. **Constellations** make for good cross-curricular links into **Social Studies** since many are named for mythical characters and are interrelated with other constellations. It would also be interesting to research the stories of constellations from other cultural viewpoints; for example, what shape did the ancient Chinese see in the Great Bear?

We did not study **seasons** in our modeling exercise. That can be done by orbiting the tilted earth around the sun and measuring how long certain points in the northern and the southern hemispheres stay lit up: hence, long summer days and long winter nights. Similarly, students can study the disparity between a lunar month (approximately 29.5 days) and a solar year (365 days). Twelve 29.5 day months would only add up to 354 days, when the earth has not yet completed its orbit around the sun to start a new cycle of seasons.

Cross-Curricular Links

History and Social Studies: In Unit 7, students study the voyages of Christopher Columbus and their consequences. Students can link this science unit to history by focusing on one episode of Columbus' fourth journey. When marooned in Jamaica, Columbus managed to extort an ongoing food supply from local people by making use of a lunar eclipse. Knowing a total eclipse of the moon was to occur, Columbus told the natives that it was a sign from God, who wanted the visitors fed, or else! The trick worked, and Columbus' men were fed until they could be rescued a year later.

Students could go on to study perceptions of the moon and calendars in different cultures (for example, the origins of our month names and calendar, or other systems such as the interesting Maya calendar).

Mathematics: Studying phases of the moon can support the concept of fractions for young students. What is a quarter moon? Why is it called that?

Technology: If power and computer availability permit, students will likely enjoy making a movie for the Part 2 assignment. While this may seem like a daunting task for some, software like *iMovie* or *Windows Movie Maker* are surprisingly user-friendly and will put students in step with modern tools of technology. Likewise, the Part 1 presentation could be completed with *Keynote* or similar software.

Writing: The Part 2 Assignment (create an illustrated book) is an excellent opportunity to follow the writing cycle (plan / draft / revise / edit / publish) and incorporate age-appropriate topics such as "writing convincing and informative non-narrative texts."

Resources

Even though modeling the lunar cycle will provide students with an excellent understanding of the moon, it helps to have a well-illustrated nonfiction book at hand. One recommended book is *The Sun and the Moon* by Patrick Moore. It is compact and filled with fine illustrations. Another good book for young readers is *Why is Night Dark?* by Sophy Tahta, an Usbourne Starting Point Science book, also compact in size.

A clear, easy to read and understand astronomy book is H.A. Rey's classic, *The Stars*. In it, the author of Curious George uses illustrations to describe our solar system and its features. He also redraws the constellations so that they make sense. A must for every sailor!

In carrying out the modeling section, my son and I found our own lime / globe / flashlight system to be extremely informative and fun, and far more effective than any animation. However, having a look at Internet animations of the moon orbiting the earth could reinforce learning, especially in watching the exact path of the moon's orbit around Earth. When you have Internet access, try http://science.howstuffworks.com/dark-side-of-moon.htm for its animation of the lunar cycle. An outstanding animation of the lunar phases for the northern and southern hemispheres as well as at the equator can be found at: http://www.ilovemedia.es/en/resources/moon_phases.html.

One website animates the difference between a sidereal and synodic month: http://www.sumanasinc.com/webcontent/animations/content/sidereal.html.

The time of the moonrise can be found under: www.timeanddate.com. Several websites provide solar and lunar eclipse calendars with dates and locations. Nothing beats seeing the real thing if you can! The web authority is Mr. Eclipse (astronomer Fred Espenak), who has created a comprehensive, easily navigated website that includes everything under the sun, so to speak: www.mreclipse.com.

Another interesting website critiques artwork in illustrated children's books. Is the moon shown correctly for the given situation? Students can test what they have learned by looking at the examples and correcting the artwork: http://analyzer.depaul.edu/paperplate/Bad%20Moons%20Rising.htm.

Several interesting activities related to this unit can be found under *At Home Astronomy* which includes *Finding the Size of the Sun and Moon,* and *Meteoroids and the Craters They Make*. NASA also lists several interesting activities on an educational website, among them, an interesting *Lunar Landform Identification* lesson for advanced students. See:
http://cse.ssl.berkeley.edu/AtHomeAstronomy/index.html   http://lunar.arc.nasa.gov/education/activities/index.htm#9

A great resource for hands-on science is www.fossweb.com, a research-based science curriculum developed for teachers and parents by UC Berkeley. It features fully developed science modules (units) including *Sun, Moon, and Stars* (Grades 3-6), and *Planetary Science* (Middle School), among others.

Unit 2 - Biology: Fish Dissection

Science is simply common sense at its best.

Thomas Huxley

I have never let my schooling interfere with my education.

Mark Twain

Unit 2 - Biology: Fish Dissection

Materials:
- Bony fish
- Sharp blade
- Pencil, paper
- Sharp scissors (optional)
- Magnifying glass (optional)

Guiding Questions:
How do organs work together in systems?
How are fish similar to and different from mammals?

Learning Outcomes:
Students will be able to identify organs in a fish and explain how organs work together in systems.

Introduction

Next time you catch a fish, don't be too quick to filet it for dinner. First take the time to dissect the fish and conduct an interesting lesson in biology. This study explores comparative fish and mammalian anatomy. The experience will open a student's eyes to more than just the fish they work on; students will also gain new appreciation for the myriad adaptations they see in fish while sailing or snorkeling.

Some sailors do not like to catch or kill fish. Alternatives include buying a fish at a market, catch-and-release fishing, or simply observing live fish while snorkeling (see *Enrichment*). Students can address some points of the exterior examination without handling a fish and then go over the dissection on paper.

Overview

Fish are divided into three classes: bony fish, cartilaginous fish (such as sharks and rays), and jawless fish (such as lampreys). All are cold-blooded. This unit studies bony fish, the biggest of the subdivisions. Any bony fish of reasonable size will do.

The dissection (Part 1) will take approximately thirty minutes depending on the student's age and level of detail undertaken. Begin with a thorough exterior examination before moving on to the innards. Students will identify various organs as they work. Afterward, the fish can still be eaten and the Part 2 concluding activity, including body systems, can be completed during later sessions.

Part 1: Dissection

Before beginning the dissection, look ahead to the assignment and think about how to make illustrations. Students can sketch what they find or take digital pictures (or use both) to later produce a lab report or dissection guide.

EXTERIOR EXAMINATION

First, students should study the exterior of the fish. They can already identify many parts of the fish and their functions. Does this seem to be an especially fast or slow species? Is this a young fish or an adult? Have students touch and extend the fins. How many fins are there? How are they different? Some are more fragile or flexible than others. Why? How can this fish defend itself? (The spines of fins can lift to make the fish look bigger and also make it harder for a predator to swallow.)

How much of the fish's body is taken up by its head? Trunk? Tail? Note the scales and surface features. How is it adapted to life in the sea? Does the color vary? Does the fish have any camouflage? Often fish are darker on top, to make them difficult to see from above, with a white belly, making them difficult to see from below against light filtering through the surface.

Next, look at the eyes. Are there eyelids? Can the student find the nostrils? Look in the **mouth** and check the teeth. Mammals only have teeth on their jaws, whereas fish can also have teeth on their tongues and the roof of the mouth. What can teeth tell us about an animal's diet?

Now students should formulate a **hypothesis** about what they expect to find in the upcoming dissection. Some examples of appropriate hypotheses are: *If an animal lives in the water, then I expect to find some special adaptations because the animal will need different ways to move, breathe, etc. Or: Since a fish is an animal, I expect to find many of the organs I know from the human body because a fish also needs to breathe, eat, and reproduce.* A more basic hypothesis would be: *Some of the fish's insides will look like a person's but some parts will be different because fish live in the water.*

Fish Exterior Diagram

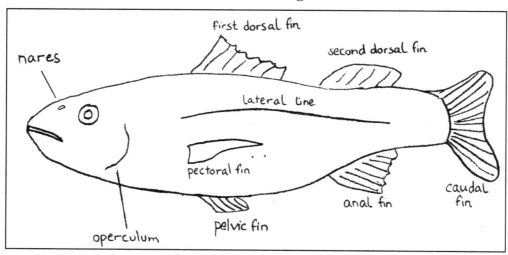

Then students can sketch the external side view of the fish. Students can draw their own fish or label parts on a drawing completed by parents. They should measure the fish and record this on the diagram. Features like the eye and fins should be sketched with care.

The **fins** are used for propulsion, turning, and maintaining stability in the water. The caudal fin (tail) provides forward push for the fish. Most steering is done by the pectoral fins on the sides of the body. The dorsal, pelvic, and anal fins keep the fish's position in the water stable. Record the fins' positions and shape carefully and also note which are soft and which are spiny.

Students should look carefully for the **lateral line**. This is a sensory organ that detects vibrations in the water, allowing a fish to coordinate its movements within a large school or to find prey. Have a close look at the lateral line with a magnifying glass. Does it differ from the surrounding area?

The **gills** are one of the most interesting parts of a fish. Mammals have lungs, fish have gills; both need oxygen. Fish do not breathe water: they take in oxygen through water, which passes over the gills (see below). Some fish must swim constantly to keep water flowing over the gills; others are able to take in water while motionless. The **operculum**, or gill cover, protects the gills.

The visible "nostrils" of a fish are part of its olfactory (smell) system. These **nares** detect chemicals in the water. Fish can taste with their mouths and some have whisker-like **barbels** that also contain taste structures.

DISSECTION

One of the aims of this activity is to understand how organs work in systems: be careful not to simply go on a treasure hunt for organs without considering how they connect to the rest of the body. Have two interior fish diagrams ready: the identification diagram and a blank page where students can fill in their own findings. Students can make their own blank to match the shape of their fish, or parents can provide one for young children. Don't fret if you don't identify all the organs listed (spleen, gonads, and gall bladder can be tricky); the most important structures for our study (intestine, heart, liver, gills) are easy to identify.

Using a sharp blade or scissors, slit open the underbelly of the fish, cutting from the anus forward toward the gills. Be careful to make only a shallow cut of the surface muscles. Ideally, one should completely cut away one side of the fish to fully expose the body cavity. In practicality, this is hard to do with a meaty fish. It is also possible to find all the organs through a long slit in the underside. As you work, you will find **membranes** (mesenteries) holding organs in place, and thin blood vessels running throughout the body.

Find the **anus** (where excrement is released) and behind it, the **urogenital opening** (where urine and eggs or sperm are released). The **gonads**, or reproductive organs, can be difficult to identify unless the fish is about to reproduce. Not all fish reproduce in the same way. Most fish are **oviparous**, meaning they produce eggs that hatch outside the body (most are fertilized externally, fewer internally). However, other fish (**ovoviviparous**) allow their offspring to develop internally to a certain degree: the young emerge as larvae. **Viviparous** fish give birth to fully developed young.

Fish Dissection Guide

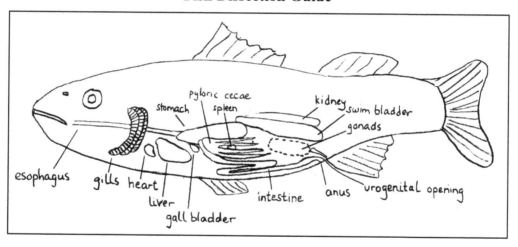

Above the anus and along the backbone, students will find the long, dark **kidney** (made up of two difficult to distinguish sections). This organ "cleans" blood of waste products.

Many fish species have an **air or swim bladder** that is filled with gas for buoyancy. This is located above the other organs, near the spine. The fish can vary the amount of gas in the bladder for more or less buoyancy. Other fish, like mackerel, do not have a swim bladder at all and use body oil for buoyancy instead. Sharks rely on their oily livers for buoyancy. Bottom dwelling fish have no swim bladder.

Working forward from the **anus** makes it easy to locate the **intestine**, where nutrients are absorbed into the bloodstream. Herbivorous fish have longer intestines than carnivorous fish (long intestines maximize nutrient absorption). You should be able to find **pyloric cecae**[1] near the stomach end of the intestine. Cecae are finger-like pouches that connect to the intestine and produce digestive juices. Some fish species have only a few cecae, while others have thousands.

Students should try to locate the small **spleen** (it functions as part of the immune system and in blood regulation) and then the stomach. The **stomach** is more pronounced in carnivorous fish and it could be small or large depending on how recently the fish ate. Next, trace the digestive system backward from the intestine and stomach to the **esophagus**[2] and the mouth. The mouth sends food to the stomach through the esophagus while sending water to the gills through another opening. Sketch these organs on your diagram. Truly inquisitive students can attempt to open the stomach and study its contents.

Locate the dark heart and the liver (close to the head). The **liver** is much larger than the heart and is part of the digestive system; its function is to clean the blood and produce bile to digest fat. In some fish species, the liver also stores fats and vitamins. Students should look for connections between the liver and other organs. Another (small) organ located nearby is the **gall bladder**. This stores bile and is part of the digestive system.

The size of a fish's **heart** depends on whether it is a fast or slow swimming species. The heart functions as a pump for the circulatory system, moving blood from the heart to the gills, the rest of the body, and back. Look for how the heart is connected to the rest of the body. A fish heart has only two chambers (human hearts have four). One major difference is that a fish heart pumps blood in a simple circuit around the body, while a mammalian heart has a double circuit (first pumping blood to the lungs to get air and back to the heart,

[1] Other forms commonly found: *caeca (caecum), ceca (cecum)*.
[2] British: *oesophagus*.

then on a second circuit around the rest of the body). Don't be shocked if the fish heart seems to beat intermittently during your dissection; moving the fish can cause blood to pulse through the heart.

Now students can turn their attention to the **gills**, another part of the respiratory system. Use scissors to carefully remove the operculum. There are several gill layers supported by stiff **gill arches**. How many can the student count? Students should cut one out and draw its feathery structure (gill filaments, also called *lamellae*). It will help to put the gill arch in a dish of water to suspend (or "float") and spread out the lamellae. Blood circulates over their large surface area in the opposite direction of the water flow. Discuss why this method of water flow over the gills is advantageous. (It creates an area for gas exchange that allows the fish to get the oxygen it needs while releasing carbon dioxide.) Gas exchange in a mammal's lungs works in a similar fashion. Fish suffocate out of water because the gills are no longer supported and spread out (as we can see by suspending them in a dish); the area for gas exchange therefore becomes inadequate to effectively supply the fish with oxygen.

Careful examination of the **eye** will show that it has a round lens, unlike a human lens, which has a disc shape. A round lens works better to focus light rays under water. It is harder to get a clear look at a fish's **brain** because of the protective skull; if you have had enough of fish innards, skip this section! Otherwise, use scissors to cut back from the nares (nostrils) toward the top of the head. You will have to cut or chip away bone to expose the brain, which is covered in fat cells. Much of the fish's brain mass is taken up by sections devoted to smell and sight.

Once all organs are removed from the body cavity, students can study the **muscle** tissue. Use a magnifying glass if you have one. Muscles make up most of the body of a fish, and most is fast twitch muscle fiber for speed and explosive movement (rather than slow twitch). Students should be able to make out the V shape pattern in the muscle fibers.

Some fish have **fatty tissue** next to the inner organs; this may appear as a large, grey mass that fills much of the posterior end of the body cavity.

The **assignment** for Part 1 is to dissect a fish and make a labeled diagram. This will eventually form part of the final assignment (below).

Part 2: Understanding Body Systems

Part 2 serves as a brief review of the dissection with a more focused look at body systems working together. We will concentrate on three systems: digestive, circulatory, and respiratory. Students should review each of these systems and list their function(s). Then, each student should use colored pencil or highlighter to shade all organs of one system on his or her sketch in the same color.

The digestive system breaks down food into small parts to extract energy for use by the body. Unlike humans, most fish do not use their teeth to chew food ("mechanical digestion") but only to hold and position it for swallowing. Fish teeth show this as they lack a grinding surface; instead, they are sharp for grabbing and holding. Like humans, fish send food to the stomach through the esophagus (a tube with no digestive juice). The stomach, intestine, pyloric cecae, liver, and pancreas all work together to digest food (the fish pancreas is difficult to identify as it is scattered through the mesentery). All these organs should be marked in the same color to highlight the digestive system within the dissection sketch.

The same process should be followed using another color to highlight two systems that work closely together. First, students can trace the circulatory system. This is composed of the heart and blood vessels that move blood throughout the body, delivering oxygen and nutrients and taking away carbon dioxide. Secondly, they can color the respiratory system, composed of the fish's gills and gill arches (in mammals: lungs, plus mouth, nose and trachea).

Finally, students should consider how each system depends on others. Why is the circulatory system important to the digestive system, or to the respiratory system? The circulatory system can be seen as a delivery person who carries important products to customers. For example, nutrients absorbed by the digestive system are carried around the body by the circulatory system. In the same way, oxygen supplied by the respiratory system is transported around the body. This delivery person also plays the role of garbage collector, carrying away waste products such as carbon dioxide.

There are many other body systems but they are outside the scope of this study. Other body systems common to fish and humans include the skeletal (supports the body), muscular (moves the body), reproductive (produces young), excretory (removes wastes), endocrine (produces regulatory chemicals for the body), integumentary (covers and protects the body with scales or skin), and nervous (sends signals through the body) systems.

If students are working toward a national curriculum that covers all body systems, you should extend the unit to study those formally (see *Enrichment*). Take note that US and UK texts describe some systems in slightly different terms (for example, the terms *cardiovascular* and *circulatory* systems differ slightly in usage).

Final Assignment: Writing a Lab Report

In Part 1, students dissected and sketched a fish. In Part 2, students color-coded all organs of certain systems and described their function and interdependence with other systems. Now, students can choose one of two concluding activities for this unit.

One is to write a complete lab report. An advanced lab report should follow each of the following points:

- Aim of the study
- Student's hypothesis (prediction)
- Apparatus (materials used)
- Method (how the study was conducted)
- Observations (sketches and notes)
- Conclusions based on evidence found
- Evaluation of the study (listing difficulties or weaknesses and suggestions for improvement).

The conclusion should refer back to the hypothesis and should also discuss how organs work together in systems (focusing on the three systems covered above). All students should make some comparisons between fish and mammalian anatomy. Of course, most organs are arranged differently in a fish but the functions correspond closely to human organs. Students should not shy away from admitting problems, such as the failure to find certain organs; this is part of a thorough evaluation.

The second option is to create a fish dissection guide using annotated sketches, artwork, or digital pictures. The dissection guide should be aimed at a specific audience, including age range. For example, it could be created for a friend on another boat or a classroom at home. This should also discuss how organs work together in systems and how the systems work as a "team."

Age-Appropriate Adaptations

In this section, you will find guidance on how to differentiate, or adapt, this unit for your child. Start with the correct age group, but also glance through the notes for one level younger or older, then mix and match as appropriate.

Self-assessment and reflection are valuable learning tools. They encourage students to think back upon their work and store their new body of knowledge in a meaningful and memorable manner. To that end, a number of self-assessment and reflection questions are listed for each age group. It is not necessary to address all the questions; substitute others as you see fit. Completed assignments and written reflection are useful records to later document student work for a school administration.

Ages 4-6

Students in this age group are fully capable of going through the activities described in Parts 1 and 2 above. Their assignments, however, should be modified.

Part 1 Activity: *Dissect a fish.* Very young students will be fascinated by the dissection and can go through all parts of the body, focusing on basics such as organs of the digestive, circulatory, and respiratory systems. One constraint is working with a sharp cutting tool; parents will have to open the fish, but should allow students to examine the organs themselves. Parents can provide the outline of a fish body and even draw in the organs for the youngest students.

However, even students who are in the early stages of literacy can label the organs themselves in simple words ("fin," "liver"); this will introduce them to the basics of a formal study.

Part 2 Activity: *Understanding body systems.* The idea that organs work together in systems is an important one that even young students should address, although in abbreviated form. Cover (and color) at least the digestive system.

Assignment: *Write a lab report* or *Create a fish dissection guide.* Young students could complete the lab report in its most basic form by simply reviewing and listing all the steps they took in the dissection. It is not necessary to follow strict lab report style. A parent could act as scribe to record the student's description. Alternatively, students could use their art skills to make a cut-and-paste guide to fish organs from colored paper and glue them in to the correct locations while discussing them. The most important thing for this age group is to reinforce what was learned and express that in their own terms. Check the *Enrichment* activities listed below, or seize the next teachable moment to further reinforce the lesson. At your next meal, for example, talk about the digestive system. Where is your food going first? Next? Which organs will be at work?

Alternatively, preschool children can make a basic fish dissection guide with help. They can use photos, sketches, or paper cut-outs for organs to make a colorful illustration representing the innards. Their work could be annotated by a parent or older sibling, or they can copy single word labels provided for them onto their work ("stomach," "heart"). This work could also be completed using technology (using photos of the child at work in each stage).

Self-Assessment and Reflection: Children should orally review their experience with questions such as:
- *What did you enjoy about the unit? What didn't you enjoy?*
- *Did the inside of fish look like you thought it would?*
- *Could you find most of the organs?*
- *Are your notes or sketches clear and useful?*
- *What do you now know about how bodies work that you didn't know before?*

Ages 6-8

Students in this age group are fully capable of going through all the activities as detailed in Parts 1 and 2 above. Their assignments can be modified.

Part 1 Activity: *Dissect a fish.* By dissecting a fish, students will gain a better understanding of how organisms work. Some will need help drawing the outline of the fish. Parents should judge if their children are ready to work with cutting tools; otherwise, allow students to work as independently as possible. Students should explore what they discover and make guesses about what they see before a parent provides guidance in identifying each organ and its function. Emphasize the digestive, circulatory, and respiratory systems but also look for others.

Be sure to take note of adaptations the fish shows to its marine environment and make basic comparisons to mammals. However, students in this age group will likely be so fascinated by the fish in front of them that it will be hard to detour into more abstract connections!

Part 2 Activity: *Understanding body systems.* Students in this age group can easily color code the three systems suggested and discuss the topic of how organs work together in systems to a good level of detail.

Assignment: *Write a lab report* or *Create a fish dissection guide.* Students in this age group can complete either of these assignments in basic form (meaning a list of steps for the lab report or a simple step-by-step dissection guide). The central aim is a work that reflects and communicates students' new body of knowledge in their own words. Students can choose pencil and paper format or could work on a computer if resources permit. The most advanced students of this age group can start to use scientific vocabulary (such as prediction / hypothesis, results, and conclusion) and might even prepare a beginner's laboratory report (see next level).

Self-Assessment and Reflection: Students should reflect on the process they went through by answering questions such as:
- *What did you know about organs before the dissection?*
- *How were you able to identify each organ?*

- *What was especially difficult?*
- *Are you pleased with the results of your work?*
- *What could you have done better?*
- *Does your lab report or dissection guide clearly show what you have learned?*
- *What resources (parents, computer, books) did you use to complete your work?*

Ages 8-10

Students in this age group can follow the entire unit as detailed in Parts 1 and 2 above. Assignments can be adapted as follows:

Part 1 Activity: *Dissect a fish.* Students can take the lead during the fish dissection. They can follow all steps of the outlined dissection. They should devote considerable effort to thinking about fish adaptations to a marine environment. It is also important to spend time comparing and contrasting fish to mammals in discussion.

Part 2 Activity: *Understanding body systems.* Simply color coding systems is too simplistic for students at this level; be sure to spend time talking through the digestive system, organ by organ. How does a fish's digestive system differ from a mammal's? Students should also undertake a thorough study of the respiratory system, focusing on how gills work.

Assignment: *Write a lab report* or *Create a fish dissection guide.* Whichever product students choose, it should be completed with clear illustrations and attention to detail. Students should use scientific terminology in organizing a lab report (use headings listed), or a step-by-step dissection guide aimed at a particular audience. All students should strive to work independently, make multiple comparisons between fish and mammalian anatomy, and discuss how organs work together in systems.

Self-Assessment and Reflection: Students should complete a short written reflection with points such as:

- *What did you know about organs and body systems before the dissection? What do you know now?*

- *How were you able to identify organs?*
- *What was especially difficult?*
- *Is everything of importance included in your lab report or dissection guide? Does it clearly show what you have learned?*
- *What are the strengths of your work? What are the weaknesses?*
- *What resources did you have available to you? Which was the most useful, and why? How did you overcome any difficulties?*
- *What advice would you give another student doing the same exercise?*

Ages 10-12

Students ages ten to twelve should take on this project in its full scope and work very independently. This age group should use scientific vocabulary and formal reporting style when completing unit assignments.

Part 1 Activity: *Dissect a fish.* Students in this age group will enjoy sharing the experience but should take the lead, with parents taking an advisory role only as needed. Students should make every attempt to find all organs and to trace how organs are connected to other parts of the body. Any parts that are difficult to identify or locate can be mentioned in the lab report's evaluation section. Students should pause often to make comparisons to mammalian anatomy and consider special adaptations to the marine environment.

Part 2 Activity: *Understanding body systems.* This topic appears in most middle level science curricula so it is important to do it justice. Do not simply list the organs in a system; study each in depth. How do gills work? Why is the intestine as long as it is? Which organs correspond to mammalian organs, and which do not? Students may also add other systems such as the nervous or reproductive system to their study.

Assignment: *Write a lab report* or *Create a fish dissection guide.* Students ages ten to twelve should see themselves as scientists throughout this unit and conscientiously use proper scientific methods. Their experience will connect directly to formal schoolwork if they write a lab report. Students should not only make comparisons between fish and mammal organs but also fish and mammal body systems. The conclusion and evaluation sections should be extensive and thorough. Students should critically examine their own experience in listing weaknesses of the study, suggestions for improvement, and posing questions for further research.

Self-Assessment and Reflection: Students should write a formal reflection on the scientific process. Review what steps were taken, from the exterior examination through observations and analysis. Consider points such as:

- *What went well in your work? What did you overlook?*
- *Which aspects of the dissection did you find particularly interesting or challenging?*
- *Did the organs match expectations? For example, was the heart as big or as small as you imagined it would be?*
- *Is a fish dissection a good way to learn? What are the problems of using fish dissection to make generalizations about other animals? What other ways can we learn about animals?*

Enrichment

Follow this lesson with a snorkeling field study of live fish in their natural habitat at your first opportunity (another option is to visit an aquarium). What different types of fish can you find? What specific adaptations do different fish show? How are these adaptations evident when one sees the fish in action? Look closely, for example, at how a fish uses its fins to control its movement in the water. If possible, observe how the gill covers move while the mouth opens to take in water (and oxygen).

This unit focuses on the anatomy of a bony fish. This is just one of three types of fish, which also include cartilaginous fish (sharks and rays). Since many children are fascinated by sharks, this unit could easily be extended to types of sharks and their particular adaptations.

Whales and dolphins, or **cetaceans**, are sea mammals and therefore a completely different group of creatures. However, they have developed many of the same external features as fish. A good enrichment exercise would be to study the similarities and differences between cetaceans and fish. Although cetaceans have developed fins similar to fish fins, all have tails held horizontally, unlike the vertical tails of fish. Some whales have no dorsal fins. How do they remain stable in the water? What marine adaptations are different in cetaceans and fish? What do you know about cetacean respiration?

Students may also broaden their study to include **food chains**, another subject common to many school curricula. Another enrichment project would be to study overfishing and the plight of many endangered marine species around the world.

Cross-Curricular Links

Physical Education: In Unit 10, students observe how heart rate changes with exercise. These two units could complement one another since the dissection gives students a look at organs involved while the PE lesson provides a "feel" for the heart's work.

Technology: If resources allow, students can develop their technology skills by creating a digital lab report or fish dissection guide. They could combine text and digital images (even video) for the lab report or to create an audio-visual dissection guide.

Writing: Students who choose to create a fish dissection guide as their assign-ment have an excellent opportunity to follow the writing cycle (plan / draft / revise / edit / publish) and incorporate age-appropriate topics such as "write simple explanations and short reports across all content areas."

Resources

A Quick Course in Ichthyology, by Jason Buchheim, is a very detailed guide to fish (including detailed anatomy and an extensive section on sharks): http://www.marinebiology.org/fish.htm. This site is useful for all age groups thanks to its illustrations. Another good web guide is *Biology of Fish* by Dr. Robert Moeller, Jr. This is a helpful resource for advanced students as it de-votes some time comparing fish to mammals and details all fish body systems thoroughly: http://www.cichlid-forum.com/articles/biology_of_fish.php.

An excellent Internet resource is http://www.biology4kids.com/files/systems_main.html. There, body systems and the connections between them are explained in child-friendly terms. A good resource for hands-on science in general is www.fossweb.com, a research-based science curriculum developed for teachers and parents by UC Berkeley. It features fully developed science modules including *Plants and Animals* (US Grades K-2), *Living Systems* and *Human Body* (Grades 3-6), and *Diversity of Life* (Middle School), among others. Nancy Clark's www.nclark.net is another useful resource for middle and high school level science.

Young students can learn more about human anatomy through Joanna Cole's *The Magic School Bus Inside the Human Body* (illustrated by Bruce Degen). This book tells an educational and fun story, surrounded by fact boxes filled with supporting details and illustrations that help bring systems to life. It takes an inside look at cell structure and organs of the respiratory, circulatory, nervous, and digestive systems. Published by Scholastic Books, New York, 1989.

Unit 3 - Chemistry

Chemistry ought to be not for chemists alone.

Miguel de Unamuno

The universe is full of magical things patiently waiting for our wits to grow sharper.

Eden Phillpotts

Unit 3 - Chemistry

Materials:
- Baking Soda[1]
- Vinegar
- Small funnel (Experiment 1)
- Hose to fit to funnel - 30cm or longer (Experiment 1)
- Thermometer (Experiment 2)

This is a partial list. Most of the materials required for these experiments are ordinary household items and are listed in the relevant section.

Guiding Questions:
What is chemistry? How can I recognize a chemical reaction?
How can I explain what happens when an acid and an alkali are mixed?

Learning outcomes:
Students will be able to conduct a controlled experiment and draw conclusions from their observations.
Students will be able to recognize and describe a chemical change using age-appropriate scientific vocabulary.

Introduction

The problem of conducting a meaningful chemistry experiment at sea is solved in this experiment thanks to the benign substances involved, their easy availability, and flexible setup in your onboard chemistry "lab" – in other words, the cockpit or galley! In this classic experiment – mixing baking soda and vinegar – bubbling, overflowing liquids excite and amuse children again and again. But it's more than just special effects and fun: this is a real lab experiment in which students control variables, collect data, repeat their observations over a series

---

[1] Baking soda (sodium bicarbonate) is also sold as *Natron*. Baking powder can be substituted as necessary, although it may not react as strongly as baking soda.

of trials, and draw conclusions. In this way, they will personally put the scientific process into action.

Overview

A detailed introduction, *Chemistry Basics*, covers all relevant points needed to understand the experiment; pick and choose the sections appropriate to your child's age level. Action-oriented students might jump ahead to the *Preview* before covering the basics, and then go on to the complete experiment.

Directions for two versions of the same experiment are described in this unit. Each measures a different outcome of the same reaction. Experiment 1 measures the volume of gas produced by the chemical reaction, while Experiment 2 measures the resulting temperature change. Experiment 1 is slightly more thrilling than 2 but is more complicated to set up. Students can do one or both of the experiments. If you have more than one child, one can conduct Experiment 1 while the other child runs Experiment 2; they can then compare results. While both experiments have the potential for minor spills, the chemicals will do no harm and students who are reasonably careful will not see any negative effects on their results. It is perfectly feasible to conduct either experiment at anchor or while sailing over calm waters.

Although the materials are all easily obtained, plan ahead and gather exactly what you need before heading away from civilization. The materials might drive your decision to choose Experiment 1 or 2. Each section includes a list of materials and directions, followed by notes that guide students through writing a lab report. Graphing and data analysis are also practiced in this unit (therefore linking in to Unit 4).

One full experiment can be done in about an hour, but the entire unit should be completed over several sessions. Start with a few lessons devoted to basics like states of matter, the *Preview* activity, and defining molecules / elements / atoms and acids / alkalis before moving on to the experiment. Follow-up and the lab report will require another two to three sessions.

Chemistry Basics

Using **scientific vocabulary** like the words in bold below will help students understand the subject and later apply their experiences to school or other situations. This will also create the setting for a serious scientific endeavor rather than simple entertainment. Even very young students can be introduced to basic terms like solid, liquid, gas, chemical, acid, and alkali.

STATES OF MATTER

Unless your children are older students who have had some exposure to matter and materials, you should begin by discussing **states of matter**. For very young students, this section is very important and can be made into its own unit (see *Age-Appropriate Adaptations*). The idea is not to read this text to a student but to discuss the main ideas and try the activities described (freeze water / melt ice, mix substances, let salt water evaporate, etc).

Begin by examining everyday materials with your child. Water is a logical starting point: it is a **liquid** that can be frozen into a **solid** or heated into a **gas**. This illustrates the principle that materials can undergo a **physical change** but later revert to another state of matter given the proper conditions (in this case, temperature). The chemical properties of the water are unchanged: it remains H_2O regardless of the state. Another example is lava: molten lava is a liquid but cools to a solid. It is important to recognize how **temperature** plays a role in changing the state of a substance in these cases.

Have students examine other materials. Water is a **liquid**; it is runny. But what about honey? It flows, but less fluidly than water. This leads to a discussion of **viscosity**, or the "thickness" of a liquid. Students should formulate and write down a working definition of a liquid (for example, *a liquid is fluid and takes the shape of its container*). **Solids** also seem obvious: *solid as a rock. A table is solid wood.* Then examine sugar together to help students form a more sophisticated definition of a solid. Sugar can be poured and it takes the shape of its container like a liquid, but the crystals are actually solids with small particle sizes. Students should write a definition of a solid (for example, *a solid is something firm that does not change shape*). Advanced students might turn their attention to Jello to help them understand that a **colloid** is a solid suspended within a liquid.

Gas is more difficult for children to define because it is usually invisible. You can make air, a gas, more tangible for children by blowing up a balloon or a plastic bag; now they can feel and "see" the air. They can even weigh the bag and discover that air has **mass** (or, very simplistically, weight). Unlike solids and liquids that have a definite volume, gases can expand or be condensed. A beginner's definition might be: *A gas is usually invisible. It can move and fill up space freely.*

ELEMENTS AND COMPOUNDS

An **element** is a pure substance; it can't be broken down into any other substance. Elements can be compared to letters, the building blocks of all written words. The most common elements on Earth are oxygen, hydrogen, carbon, and silicon. Elements have **properties**: they may be metals or non-metals, and can be found as solids, liquids, or gases. Even though elements are pure, they can still be broken down into **atoms**: tiny, uniform parts of an element. At age ten or above, students are introduced to the structure of an atom, a subject beyond the scope of this unit. (In brief, an atom is made up of a nucleus with protons and neutrons, surrounded by electrons.)

The Periodic Table of Elements provides an overview of all known elements. Students are usually introduced to the Periodic Table of Elements and chemical notation at about age twelve, but basic, illustrated versions also exist for younger students (see *Resources*). Details of the Periodic Table can be explored through follow-up activities (see *Enrichment*).

Elements can co-exist alongside other elements or they can chemically combine into **compounds** such as water (H_2O) or carbon dioxide (CO_2). Groups of chemically joined atoms are called **molecules**. Molecules are the smallest subset of any compound or element that still retain its unique properties (or "behave" in a way characteristic for that substance), such as a molecule of water. Looking at states of matter through the eyes of a chemist, students can imagine how molecules are arranged. In solids, molecules are held closely together by strong attractive forces. Molecules in liquids are also close, but they slide and flow around each other. Fast-moving gas molecules are so weakly attracted that they rarely touch.

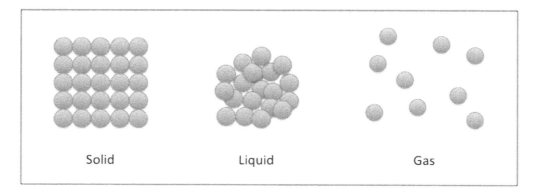

Older students can study the **Particle Theory** of states of matter with the help of the diagram above. This is a model based on experimental evidence. Like all models, it helps our understanding of the natural world even though the exact arrangement of particles cannot be directly observed.

Raising the temperature of ice weakens the bonds between water molecules, and the ice melts into water. Each molecule remains a threesome (H+H+O), but slides loosely around other, identical molecules. If water is heated, the molecules speed up, collide against each other, and expand into more space, becoming a gas. Each individual molecule retains a steady ratio of two hydrogen atoms to one oxygen atom. Imagine a bumper car game in which a car/driver pair moves around a closed course. In this analogy, each car and driver pair is a molecule that may come close to others, then moves away again, but always remains a twosome. Molecules work in the same way, with varying numbers of components.

CHEMICALS AND CHEMICAL REACTIONS

Elements and compounds mix with others in unique ways, depending on the composition of each. Mixing substances does not always result in a chemical reaction. For example, if salt is mixed into water, nothing happens – or, more accurately, the salt **dissolves** in the water and can no longer be seen. This is merely a **physical change.** The salt is still there, and it can return to its original state – just leave a shallow dish of salt water in the sun and let the water evaporate; a salty crust will be left behind. Other materials, like oil, will **suspend** in water: they do not mix but simply float separately. Such exploratory experiments can be very valuable in understanding chemistry.

When substances mix and make something new, a **chemical reaction** has occurred. Combining vinegar and baking soda sets off a chemical reaction in which the original materials combine into entirely new substances. A chemical reaction can be identified when **heat, smoke, or light** is produced (an energy change), or when colors change (for example, leaves changing color). Other indications of chemical reactions are gases bubbling (**effervescing**) or solids separating out within a liquid (**precipitating**). Many chemical reactions are benign – for example, cooking an egg – but some reactions can be unsafe (such as explosions). Some chemical reactions are very fast (burning a match), while others are slow (metal rusting over time).

ACIDS AND ALKALIS

In this unit, students will combine two special groups of chemicals: **acids** and **alkalis**. Weak acids and alkalis can be found in everyday items and aren't dangerous, but concentrated forms can dissolve or "eat away" other objects. Think of James Bond squirting acid at jail bars to escape – not the most scientifically correct example, but a strong image!

Lemon juice is an acid: it tastes sour, reacts strongly with certain materials, and in concentrated form can corrode other materials. Another example is vinegar (acetic acid). Our stomachs use their own acid to help in digestion. Tomatoes and fizzy sodas contain acids, too. There is even acid in the venom of bees and ants, which causes their bites to sting. These examples will remind students that chemistry is all around us in the real world, not just confined to laboratories.

The opposite of an acid is a **base**. A base that dissolves in water is called an **alkali**. Common examples are baking soda, baking powder, and ammonia. These are often used in soap and household cleaning agents because, similar to acids, they can be corrosive, breaking down other substances like the minerals that build up in a teapot. Alkalis such as baking soda have a bitter taste –

but please don't have students taste any unknown substances to sample what they are! Instead, use an **indicator** (see *Enrichment*).

Acids or alkalis can be **diluted** or **concentrated**. They are measured on a **pH scale**: very acidic solutions have a pH of 1 (such as the acid used in batteries), while the most basic solutions have a pH of 14 (such as drain cleaner). In the middle, at pH 7, are neutral substances such as water or alcohol. Like the Richter scale used to measure earthquakes, the pH scale is not linear; pH 4 is not just twice as much as pH 2, but many times more.

It is important to emphasize that not all chemicals are as benign as baking soda and vinegar. **Safety** is an important consideration in chemical experiments, which often involve protective gear such as goggles and gloves. This experiment is exceptional because it does not require special safety equipment, but common sense should be exercised: keep substances away from the eyes and mouth! Do not substitute any other acid or alkali when conducting the experiments described below!

Getting Started

The previous sections introduced important information for home schooling sailors to use in covering the topic of chemistry. By now every child will be raring for action, so start with a simple "preview" activity.

PREVIEW: HAVING FUN WITH CHEMISTRY

For an informal preview, have students pour a small amount of vinegar into a cup and see what happens when a teaspoon of baking soda is added (with some dishwashing liquid for extra effect). Cool! A big, bubbling eruption ensues. Once students calm down from their excitement, you should point out the hallmarks of a chemical reaction: bubbling (showing that a gas was produced) and temperature change (by touching the cup, students will notice that the mixture gets cold very quickly).

Then try another experiment. Take another liquid, like water, and throw in the baking soda. Nothing happens! Follow up by mixing other common kitchen liquids and powders (lemon juice, milk, sugar, flour) and observing the results:

magic potion? Or boring letdown? Why do some substances react while others just sit quietly? You can explain that some substances are more reactive than others depending on their chemical makeup. Acids and alkalis, as opposites, set off dramatic chemical reactions.

IDENTIFY AN AIM AND FORM A HYPOTHESIS

Now that your child is poised to launch into a proper scientific experiment, have her formalize her work. What is the purpose of the upcoming experiment? Encourage the student to summarize her aim in one or two sentences, such as *The aim of this study is to find out more about the chemical reaction between an acid and an alkali.* A young child might state *I want to find out what really happens when the ingredients mix.*

Based on her observations in the preview and background information gained in introductory lessons, the student should be able to formulate a **hypothesis**. A hypothesis is a prediction of what will happen. A beginner's hypothesis might be: *When I add baking soda to vinegar, they erupt because they're opposites. Adding more vinegar will make a bigger reaction.* An advanced student might hypothesize: *If acids and alkalis are opposites, then a chemical reaction will occur and result in measurable changes.* It might take several attempts to form a "good" hypothesis, so let the student brainstorm different variations before choosing the best.

Experiment 1: Volume of CO_2 Gas Produced

In this experiment, students use a consistent amount of vinegar and add varying amounts of baking soda, then measure the volume of carbon dioxide gas produced in the ensuing chemical reaction. Since gas is invisible, students must use a system to "reveal" it. This is accomplished by trapping the gas and having it displace water in a bottle. The change in water level shows the amount of carbon dioxide (CO_2) produced. Plus, the underwater bubbling is a fun "special effect" that is very pleasing to young scientists!

Complete Materials List for Experiment 1:
- Baking soda

- Vinegar (approx. 5% acid)
- Small funnel
- Hose that fits funnel (30cm or longer)
- Measuring cup
- Teaspoon and tablespoon measure (or medicine cup)
- Transparent bottle (1L or more)
- Wide rubber band
- Strong cup
- Masking tape
- Bucket
- Water

SETTING UP

It is fun to play the mad professor by setting up and tinkering with this experiment. First, the student should prepare a small **funnel** to hold upside down over a cup, where the chemicals will be mixed. In order to make a **tight seal** and prevent any gas from escaping, stretch a wide rubber band around the top edge of the cup. Next, attach one end of the **hose** to the narrow neck of the funnel. The other end will lead into the bottle.

Setting Up Experiment 1

Run a strip of **masking tape** along the length of the bottle (for marking the water level change). Fill the **bottle** with water, close it, and place it upside down in a **bucket** two-thirds full of water. Now the lid can be removed (water pressure will keep the bottle full) and the end of the hose can be pushed into the bottle. When the student mixes baking soda and vinegar in the cup and quickly clamps the funnel over it, the gas produced will travel through the hose and begin to force water out of the bottle. In this way, the student can see and measure how much CO_2 is produced.

PROCEDURE FOR EXPERIMENT 1

Next, students must prepare a **table** for their observations. It should include a place for the amount of baking soda (variable) and vinegar (constant) used in each attempt. Another column will show the volume of gas produced. Since scientists must be able to confirm their results, include space for two repeat tests. Students can decide whether to run through every trial twice in a row, or go through the entire procedure once, then repeat.

Experiment 1: Sample Observation Table

Baking Soda	Vinegar	Volume of Gas	
½ tsp	4 tbsp	test 1:	test 2:
1 tsp	4 tbsp	test 1:	test 2:
2 tsp	4 tbsp	test 1:	test 2:
3 tsp	4 tbsp	test 1:	test 2:
4 tsp	4 tbsp	test 1:	test 2:

Now everything is ready for the first trial. The student should pour the standard amount of vinegar (four tablespoons) into the cup, then carefully measure the correct amount of baking soda for the first trial. If possible, use flat-topped measuring spoons (in half and full teaspoon sizes) to get an exact measure. If not, do your best with a conventional teaspoon and scrape off any excess with the flat side of a knife.

For the first trial, the student should use half a teaspoon of baking soda. He should toss this quickly into the cup containing the vinegar and immediately clamp the funnel over it. The substances will react almost instantly and gas will bubble into the bottle, forcing water out. When the action quiets down, he can make a mark on the tape to show how much gas was produced. Then he can pull the hose out, close the bottle, and remove it from the bucket. The student can measure the volume by pouring water from a measuring cup into the bottle and noting the amount. This can be done after each trial or all in one go when all trials are complete.

The student should repeat the experiment with different amounts of baking soda (0.5, 1, 2, 3, and 4 teaspoons of baking soda in five separate trials) and a constant amount of vinegar. It is important to discuss why scientists use only one **variable** (this isolates the influence of each factor). Remind the student to refill the bottle and completely clean and dry the cup each time. When working with larger amounts such as two teaspoons of baking soda, first measure the required amount into a separate cup. Do not throw the first teaspoon into the vinegar before the second; otherwise, a partial reaction will begin and some of the gas will escape.

Soon a trend should emerge: the more baking soda used, the more carbon dioxide produced. However, the trend is not linear; in other words, four teaspoons of baking soda will not produce twice the carbon dioxide as two teaspoons did. Graphing the data will make this effect clear. The amount of carbon dioxide gas produced levels off quickly after the trials using two to three teaspoons of baking soda. Ask the student to brainstorm why this might be. This will form part of the lab report.

A good scientist should be able to reproduce results in separate tests. For example, if one teaspoon of baking soda created 350 ml of gas, then a second test should show approximately the same amount. If not, help the student consider any errors he might have made. Did he measure the chemicals very carefully each time? Did he capture all the gas or did some escape? Such considerations will form an important part of the lab report. On a boat, it is hard to get identical results, but they should be relatively close.

Experiment 2: Temperature Change

This experiment focuses on the temperature change that results from the chemical reaction of an acid and an alkali. All materials are easy to find, but you should ensure that you have a thermometer with an appropriate range.

Complete Materials List for Experiment 2:
- Baking soda
- Vinegar (approx. 5% acid)
- Thermometer
- 2 cups
- Teaspoon and tablespoon measure (or medicine cup)

Experiment 2 is easy to set up and manipulate since there is no issue of escaping gas. Even if a small amount of the mixture should spill, this should not affect the temperature change. However, it is important to have a **sensitive thermometer** that measures in the range of room temperature. Fever thermometers are inadequate because they only measure a narrow range at around 37°C (98°F). A **graduated thermometer** that shows fractions of degrees can usually be obtained by special order from a pharmacy.

Experiment 2: Sample Observation Table

Baking Soda	Vinegar	Temp. Before °C or °F	Lowest Temp. After	Total Temp. Change
½ tsp	4 tbsp	test 1: test 2:	test 1: test 2:	test 1: test 2:
1 tsp	4 tbsp	test 1: test 2:	test 1: test 2:	test 1: test 2:
2 tsp	4 tbsp	test 1: test 2:	test 1: test 2:	test 1: test 2:
3 tsp	4 tbsp	test 1: test 2:	test 1: test 2:	test 1: test 2:
4 tsp	4 tbsp	test 1: test 2:	test 1: test 2:	test 1: test 2:

Help your child create a table of observations with two columns for the amount of baking soda and vinegar, plus three temperature columns: temperature before the reaction, temperature after the reaction, and total temperature change (see previous page).

If the thermometer reads 22°C beforehand and drops to 20°C after the reaction, the total temperature change is 2°C. Since every trial should be repeated, students should leave space for a second set of observations. Remind students to fill in the table carefully, using units of measure such as teaspoon/tablespoon or degrees (in Celsius or Fahrenheit).

PROCEDURE FOR EXPERIMENT 2

Place the mixing cup in a baking pan or bowl to catch any spillage. The student should measure four tablespoons of vinegar into the cup and hold the thermometer in it for at least one minute. She should wait until the reading has stabilized to write down the temperature of the vinegar. Then, she can measure half a teaspoon of soda and dash it into the vinegar. Now the exciting part begins, with the mixture frothing in a bewitching manner and, like magic, the temperature dropping within a few seconds. The temperature should only be recorded when it has reached its absolute low.

Then the student can conduct further trials with different amounts of baking soda added to the same amount of vinegar (use 0.5, 1, 2, 3, and 4 teaspoons of baking soda in five separate trials). Just as in Experiment 1, it is important to discuss why scientists use only one **variable** (this isolates the influence of each factor). Be sure that the student cleans and dries the cup between each trial. When using amounts such as two teaspoons of baking soda, she should first collect the baking soda in an extra cup. Do not throw the one teaspoon of soda into the vinegar and then follow with the second because this will stagger the chemical reaction and affect the results.

Successive trials should reveal a trend: the more baking soda used, the greater the resulting temperature drop. However, the trend is not linear; in other words, four teaspoons of baking soda does not produce twice the temperature change that two teaspoons did. In fact, the temperature change will level off quickly after the trials using three to four teaspoons of baking soda. Ask the student to consider why. This will form part of the lab report.

Students should be able to reproduce their results in separate tests. If one teaspoon of baking soda mixed with four tablespoons of vinegar created a temperature drop of 3°C, then a second test should show approximately the same temperature change. If not, the student must consider possible sources of error. Did she measure the baking soda carefully? Did she wait for the temperature to stabilize fully? Such considerations will form an important part of the lab report. Don't expect perfectly matching results for repeated tests – but if the results vary significantly, the student must try to identify the source of the error, correct it, and repeat the test. On the other hand, recognize that experiments in informal lab settings rarely turn out exactly as theory predicts they "should."

Understanding the Chemical Reaction

What exactly happened in this chemical reaction? In each experiment, the amount of CO_2 produced and the temperature change leveled off after successive trials because there is an optimal ratio of acid to alkali. Once this optimal ratio is exceeded, the extra baking soda cannot all be used up. Think of watering a plant: after a certain amount of water is absorbed, the excess goes unused and runs out the bottom of the flowerpot.

In Experiment 2, the temperature dropped because heat energy is **absorbed** during the reaction (an **endothermic** reaction). The same effect is used in first aid cold packs used to treat injuries. A cold pack is activated by a blow that bursts an internal bag, allowing two chemicals to mix. This produces a cooling effect in a chemical reaction similar to the one observed in the student's experiment. Other chemical reactions, like the small explosions that take place in an engine, **release** heat energy (called **exothermic** reactions).

ADVANCED CONCEPTS

Older students can be introduced to the **Periodic Table of Elements** and **chemical notation**. These topics are usually only introduced at about age twelve and then expanded on in later school years. The formula for baking soda, or sodium bicarbonate, is $NaHCO_3$. This tells us that each molecule of baking soda is made up of one sodium atom, one hydrogen atom, one carbon atom, and three oxygen atoms. It is the bicarbonate (HCO_3) that is active in this experiment. In vinegar (CH_3COOH), the hydrogen (the final H in that long notation) is active in this experiment.

Scientists represent chemical reactions through **chemical equations** like the one below. On the left are the **reactants** and on the right are the resulting **products**. This acid-alkali reaction is called a **neutralization reaction** because the products are neither acid nor basic; they are neutral. The full chemical equation for the baking soda / vinegar reaction looks like this:

$$NaHCO_3 + CH_3COOH \rightarrow CO_2 + H_2O + CH_3COONa$$

You will notice that the number of atoms is equal on both sides of the equation. We start with five hydrogen atoms on the left, and end up with five on the right. Chemical reactions should end in a **balanced equation** because nothing disappears; the chemical bonds simply change and rearrange. This is called **conservation of matter**.

In fact, two reactions occur in quick succession in these experiments: first, an acid-alkali reaction (in which hydrogen from the vinegar reacts with baking soda to make carbonic acid) followed by a decomposition reaction (the carbonic acid just formed quickly breaks down into carbon dioxide and water). This accounts for the slight delay in seeing the chemicals bubble and produce measurable changes in temperature or amount of CO_2 produced. We can isolate the active ingredients to show the most important parts of our acid-alkali reaction in a chemical equation like the one here.

Acid-Alkali Reaction				**Decomposition Reaction**		
(reactants)				(products)		
HCO_3 +	H	$\rightarrow$	H_2CO_3	$\rightarrow$	H_2O +	CO_2
from baking soda	from vinegar		carbonic acid		water	gas

Assignment: Writing a Lab Report

The principal learning experience in this unit is the experiment itself. However, the lab report is an important follow-up that challenges students to articulate their findings. This report serves to reinforce the learning outcomes for the student. Even the youngest students can be guided through a basic form of lab report that will consolidate what they have observed and learned (see *Age-Appropriate Adaptations*).

A thorough lab report should include each of the following points:

- Aim of the study
- Student's hypothesis (prediction)
- Apparatus (materials used, sketches)
- Method (how the study was conducted)
- Observations (measurement, notes, and graphs)
- Conclusions based on evidence found
- Evaluation (difficulties, weaknesses, and ideas for improvement)

Much of the lab report has already been prepared and simply awaits compilation. Students identified the aim and a hypothesis before the experiment. It is perfectly all right for students to find a flaw in their original hypothesis as long they address it in the conclusion. Summarizing the apparatus and method should be easy. Then students can write out their notes and graph the data from their tables to present as observations. Students who do both experiments should plot both data sets on one graph to see how they parallel each other.

The main task left for students is to write a conclusion and evaluation. The **conclusion** should refer back to the hypothesis and tie the entire study together. What predictions can they now make about certain chemical reactions? What has the student learned about chemistry and chemical reactions?

Finally, the student should **evaluate** the experiment. A frank appraisal is important; good scientists admit their errors and learn from them. What went well, or what went wrong? Did the student observe any unexpected or unexplainable phenomena? What sources of error were identified? What advice does the student have for other scientists attempting similar experiments?

SOURCES OF ERROR

Recognizing potential sources of error is an important part of a thorough science experiment. Both of the experiments in this unit have room for error. Can students guess what these may be? (Take some time to brainstorm sources of error together before the text below gives them away.)

Both experiments are prone to human error in measuring the amounts of baking soda and vinegar, especially in small quantities, or errors in measuring gas volume or temperature change. Since common kitchen ingredients are used rather than carefully controlled laboratory supplies, there is bound to be some irregularity in the outcomes of these experiments.

Experiment 1 is open to error in several ways. If students don't achieve a tight seal around the cup, some gas will escape. Some gas will always escape before the funnel can be clamped over the cup; this is an unavoidable procedural error, but the amount of gas lost can be kept to a minimum. The principal source of error in Experiment 2 is misreading the thermometer or using one that does not reflect small temperature differences accurately. On the whole, however, both experiments provide an excellent, authentic chemistry experience for junior chemists working in informal settings.

Age-Appropriate Adaptations

In this section, you will find guidance on how to differentiate, or adapt, this unit for your child. Start with the correct age group, but also glance through the notes for one level younger or older, then mix and match as appropriate.

It is important to stress safety with all age groups: just because we are able to conduct the experiment with certain chemicals doesn't mean that the student can safely experiment with any others!

Self-assessment and reflection are valuable learning tools. They encourage students to think back upon their work and store their new body of knowledge in a meaningful and memorable manner. To that end, a number of self-assessment and reflection questions are listed for each age group. It is not necessary to address all the questions; substitute others as you see fit.

Ages 4-6

Very young students should begin by learning about states of matter and do the simple activities mentioned in the *Chemistry Basics* section before starting the main experiment. They can be introduced to basic concepts and vocabulary such as solid / liquid / gas, and acid / alkali.

Activity: *Experiments.* Young children are fully capable of completing either experiment, acting as lab assistant to a parent. They can help measure the observations and record results; this will reinforce basic literacy skills and introduce students to the basics of a formal study. Limit the number of trials to three rather than five (with 1, 2, and 3 teaspoons of baking soda), because the excitement can wear off and turn a fun learning experience into a chore. Alternatively, let one parent supervise the first trials with the student, and then bring in the second parent, asking the student to show them what to do. Young students *love* showing hapless parents how to do something and this can help squeeze a few more trials out of the experiment.

Assignment: *Write a lab report.* Young students can complete the lab report in very basic form by reviewing the experiment verbally. They should form a simple hypothesis and briefly consider obvious sources of error. The most important thing is for students to reinforce what they learned and to express it in their own terms. What happened when we mixed baking soda with vinegar? Why doesn't that happen with sugar and vinegar?

Self-Assessment and Reflection: Children should orally review their experience with questions such as:
- *What did you enjoy about the experiment? Why?*
- *Did the chemical reaction have surprising results?*
- *What helped you understand the new ideas you learned?*
- *What went well in your experiment? What could you have done better?*

Ages 6-8

Students ages six to eight will benefit from learning about states of matter and take the lead in the simple activities described in the *Chemistry Basics* section. Students can be introduced to vocabulary such as solid/liquid/gas, elements, and acid/alkali. They can consider the difference between physical change and a chemical reaction.

Activity: *Experiments.* Students should be capable of conducting either experiment, taking the lead with adult guidance. The student should work as independently as possible, exploring and summarizing what she observes. If she raises questions, prompt her to consider possible answers before supplying them yourself. The student can measure and record observations. Consider limiting the number of trials to three rather than five (using 1, 2, and 3 teaspoons of baking soda) to keep the activity stimulating, or work over two separate sessions. Alternatively, let one parent supervise the first few trials with the student, and when it starts to wear thin, the second parent can step in as a new lab assistant and ask the student how to continue. Students *love* showing hapless parents what to do and this can help squeeze a few more trials out of the experiment.

Assignment: *Write a lab report.* Students in this age group can write a brief lab report with guidance, listing the steps followed and drawing basic conclusions such as *The more baking soda I added, the more gas came out because there were more ingredients to react with.* The aim is to produce a work that communicates the student's new body of knowledge in his own words. Advanced students should use the terms *hypothesis*, *results*, and *conclusion*.

Self-Assessment and Reflection: Students should reflect on the process they went through by answering questions such as:
- *What did you enjoy about your experiment? Why?*
- *Did the chemical reaction have surprising results?*
- *What did you know about chemistry before? What did you learn?*
- *What was especially difficult to do or understand?*
- *What could you have done better? What advice would you have for another student getting ready to try the same experiment?*

Ages 8-10

Young students should cover states of matter before moving on to the main experiment. Talk through the basic concepts of chemistry (elements, physical change versus chemical reaction) and use terms like acid, alkali, and pH. Advanced students can look at simple chemical notation.

Activity: *Experiments.* Students should work quite independently once the experiment is set up. Use three to five trials in either experiment.

Assignment: *Write a lab report.* Students can follow formal lab report style and use scientific terminology. All students should strive to work independently, drawing conclusions without help.

Self-Assessment and Reflection: Students should complete a short written reflection with points such as:

- *What did you know about chemicals before this experiment? What do you know now?*
- *Is everything of importance included in your lab report? Does it clearly show what you have learned?*
- *What are the strengths of your work? What are the weaknesses?*
- *What was especially difficult to do or understand?*
- *What advice would you give another student doing the same exercise?*

Ages 10-12

Students in this age group should quickly review states of matter. Discuss basic concepts (elements, physical change versus chemical reaction, acid / alkali / pH), explain the idea of atoms, and introduce chemical notation and the Periodic Table of Elements. Advanced students can learn terms such as compound and molecule.

Activity: *Experiments.* Students should work very independently; they will enjoy sharing the experience but can take the lead, with parents taking an advisory role only as needed. Students should see themselves as scientists throughout this unit and conscientiously use proper scientific methods.

Assignment: *Write a lab report.* Students should write a full lab report and work independently by completing a draft of the lab report alone (they can make revisions later with parental guidance). The conclusion and evaluation should be thorough and use appropriate scientific terms. Students should critically examine their experience in order to list weaknesses of the study, make suggestions for improvement, and pose questions for further research.

Self-Assessment and Reflection: Students should write a formal reflection on the scientific process. Think about points such as:

- *What did you know about chemicals before this experiment? What do you know now?*
- *What went well in your work? What problems did you experience?*
- *Which aspects of the experiment did you find interesting or difficult?*
- *Is everything of importance included in your lab report? Does it clearly show what you have learned? What could be improved?*
- *What advice would you give another student doing the same exercise?*

Enrichment

This chapter started with an investigation into **states of matter**. Very young students should make a whole unit out of this subject before launching into the acid/alkali experiment. One way to do this is to heat or freeze water to observe physical changes, or to place a bowl of salt water in the sun for an extended period of time. The water will evaporate, leaving behind a salt crust.

To further study acids and alkalis, students can make an **indicator** and test various liquids for pH. To do so, collect the liquid from a boiled red cabbage. Add a spoon of this indicator to a cup of an acidic substance (such as vinegar, "white" grape juice, or lemon juice) diluted in water. A chemical reaction occurs that turns the mixture red-pink, indicating acid. On the other hand, baking soda (an alkali) diluted in water is an alkali; it will turn blue-green when the indicator is added. Neutral substances will not show a color change.

Acid-alkali chemical reactions can be found in everyday examples; just bake some muffins! Small holes will appear in the dough. That's because the recipe's baking soda reacts with an acidic ingredient (like lemon juice) and releases carbon dioxide, pushing bubbles through the dough. The result is a light, fluffy muffin. Recipes that lack acidic ingredients use baking powder, which is a blend of baking soda plus an acidic ingredient (such as cream of tartar). The ingredients react when activated by moisture and heat.

Older students can make an entire unit out of studying details of the Periodic Table of Elements, such as atomic number. Elements that share certain properties are grouped together: for example, metals toward the left side and "noble" gases on the far right. Find more at www.nclark.net/PeriodicTable.

Students can compare this experiment to the other science chapters in this book. They can consider questions such as: What are the different methods scientists use to gain knowledge? When is a controlled experiment (like this one) appropriate, and when are other methods useful (such as observation or modeling)? What are the limitations of these different methods? How have scientific methods and knowledge changed over time?

Cross-Curricular Links

History: A study of medieval alchemy would provide an interesting historic perspective to this unit. It was once believed that all matter was made up of only four "elements": earth, air, fire, and water. Alchemy was not a disciplined science, and scientists later developed a more methodical approach to studying the natural world (this can in turn tie in to the Renaissance). Science has evolved – and continues to evolve! For example, the Periodic Table of Elements has been gradually expanded to include new, man-made elements. Who knows what scientists will discover next?

Mathematics: This unit can be linked to Unit 4, *Data Management*, by graphing the volume or temperature observations. Another connection can be made to Unit 5, *Mathematics: Measurement*, by mathematically calculating the volume in Experiment 1. Of course, volume can simply be measured by pouring from a measuring cup. However, advanced students can use the formula for the volume of a cylinder (the bottle) for the same purpose.

$$\pi r^2 h \quad \text{(in which r= radius and h=height)}$$

It is not necessary to measure the volume of the entire cylinder; just use the "height" of the gas in the bottle for *h*. For example, if the gas filled 7cm of a bottle with radius 4cm, the volume of gas produced is

$$\pi r^2 h = \pi (4)^2 (7) = \text{answer } 352 \text{ cm}^3$$
(rounded to the nearest cm and using $\pi = 3.14$)

Since volume is usually measured in liters and milliliters, 352 cm^3 should be converted to 352ml (see Unit 5).

Space and Environmental Science: Did you know that the atmosphere of Venus contains a high percentage of sulfuric acid? This chemistry unit could provide a good lead-in to space science by comparing the planets of our solar system. Alternatively, you can link into environmental science by studying acid rain; this happens when pollutants create excessive sulfuric acid in the atmosphere. Polluted precipitation makes soil and water systems too acidic to support normal plant and wildlife. Acid rain can even damage stone buildings, a problem for historic sites.

Writing: Completing a lab report is a form of procedural writing and can link in with age-appropriate benchmarks from writing strands. Students may draw from their own lab experience to write a fictional story about a science experiment leading to unintended, comical results (turning the boat pink, shrinking a crewmember, or another minor catastrophe which the hero or heroine must solve).

Resources

Students who particularly enjoy hands-on science can find a number of simple experiments in books such as *The Usborne Big Book of Experiments* (London: Usborne Publishing, 1996). This excellent book describes science experiments that are easy to carry out. Most are aimed at young elementary students. Make sure you have all the materials beforehand. Many Internet sites list science experiments that can be conducted without full laboratory equipment. One is Tim Hunkin's http://www.hunkinsexperiments.com/ and another is Eric Muller's www.doscience.com. Nancy Clark's www.nclark.net is another rich resource for middle and high school level science.

Tina Seelig's *Incredible Edible Science* lists many interesting chemical experiments based around cooking and even includes recipes so that your end product is a tasty treat! In-depth sidebars describe the science behind the cooking at a level appropriate for ages ten and above, but they can be simplified for younger students (New York: W.H. Freeman and Company, 1994). John Daniel Hartzog's *Everyday Science Experiments in the Kitchen* also lists a number of science experiments. The explanations use basic vocabulary and are aimed at an audience ages five and above (New York: Rosen Publishing, 2000). Other titles by the same author include *Everyday Science Experiments in the Backyard* and *Everyday Science Experiments at the Playground*.

To find a Periodic Table of Elements, look in a middle level science textbook or download one. Excellent beginner's versions can be found under http://elements.wlonk.com. These use pictures and words to convey the basics of each element. A fully detailed Periodic Table can be found at www.nrc-cnrc.gc.ca/images/education/pte-poster_e.jpg.

A wonderful resource for hands-on science is www.fossweb.com, a research-based science curriculum developed for teachers and parents by UC Berkeley. It features fully developed science modules such as *Solids and Liquids* (U.S. Grades K-2), *Mixtures and Solutions* (Grades 3-6), and *Chemical Interactions* (Middle School), among others.

Unit 4 - Mathematics: Data Management

Do not worry about your difficulties in Mathematics.
I can assure you mine are still greater.

Albert Einstein

A child educated only at school is an uneducated child.

George Santayana

Unit 4 - Mathematics: Data Management

Materials:
- Graph paper and a computer graphing program (optional)
- Stickers for very young students (dots or other to represent bottles)

Guiding Questions:
How can I show numbers in picture form?
What information can pictures give me that a number cannot?

Learning Outcomes:
Students will be able to interpret and create graphs appropriate to their level.

Introduction

Representing data in the form of graphs is a basic skill that students of all ages can begin to master; in mathematics, the topic is often referred to as *data management*. Even the youngest children will enjoy the challenge of visually representing numbers, while older students will gradually move in the direction of comparing and analyzing data from graphs. By collecting and analyzing data at sea, your child will learn age-appropriate data management skills and can practice fundamental mathematical operations (addition, subtraction, multiplication, division) according to their level.

Students can draw graphs by hand or use a computer graphing program. If you opt for the latter, make sure you are familiar with the program and keep graph paper as a backup in case power supply or laptop availability becomes unexpectedly limited.

Unit Overview

Before you can graph, you need numbers, or raw data. Sailing provides countless opportunities for data collection. This lesson is based on one data set (water consumption on board during one passage or cruise) but you can easily substitute or add further subjects to practice graphing (such as fuel consumption or nationalities of boats in the anchorage). A study of water consumption provides an opportunity to create graphs, from the simplest bar graphs to line graphs or more elaborate pie charts.

This is an extended unit that you should cover gradually over the course of several cruising weeks or an extended passage. For the first week or so, the student can simply collect data. Over the next week, he or she can begin graphing. After data collection is complete, it will be time for comparative graphing and data analysis. Many aspects of data management support the field of science in terms of systematic collection, presentation, and analysis of data.

Graphing Water Consumption on Board

Studying water consumption on board is not only a convenient means to practice graphing; it is also an excellent vehicle to teach children the value of precious resources. Involve older children with water calculations from the very beginning: How many liters (or gallons) of water do you use per person, per day? Liters are handy simply for their smaller volume and ease of subdivision (3.79 liters make one US gallon; 4.55 liters make one imperial gallon). Young children can measure how much water they drink in a day; older students can approximate how much water the crew will need for drinking, cooking, and washing, and then multiply by number of days.

The principal goal is to create graphical representations of water consumption on board over the course of a cruise or passage (therefore, units consumed per time). Some crews are very consistent in their water use while others notice variations due to outside influences (drinking more in warmer latitudes) or perceived resources (some crews conserve more strictly in the beginning of their passage, and later allow themselves greater water privileges when they see their supply will easily last, while others are just the opposite).

Students should measure or closely calculate water consumption on board in up to three categories each day:

- Drinking water (and juice, etc.)
- Galley (water used for cooking and dishwashing)

- Hygiene (washing body and hands, brushing teeth, laundry)

To track water use, students will need a data sheet like the one below. Make your own version of this table with fewer categories or different headings as needed. Older students can generate the categories themselves. Note that the table here already has a heading and specifies the units used, two important details of data management.

Sample Data Collection Sheet

Water used over time (in liters)

	Drinking	Galley	Hygiene
Day 1			
Day 2			
Day 3			
Day 4			

During long passages on our sloop, each crewmember had his or her own bottle that was refilled as necessary. This allowed each person to track his or her intake, both in terms of keeping within reasonable rations as well as hydrating adequately. Cooking and washing water are easy to track as long as running water is avoided. (Fill the sink with a stopper to rinse dishes after a salt water wash; half fill a cup to brush teeth.) Anyone using running water is likely to have a water maker and can track his consumption by the amount of water produced, or can estimate water consumption.

PICTOGRAPHS AND BAR GRAPHS

When enough data has been collected, start collating it into a pictograph or bar graph. In every case, make sure both axes are labeled (including units used) and the graph has a title. Pictographs are the simplest form of graphing, using pictures instead of data points. For example, a pictograph may be a stack of bottles piled high for each day (place stickers on axes drawn and labeled by parents). Stress the fact that stickers should be lined up neatly from the bottom up so that the water used from day to day can be easily compared.

Bar graphs are especially useful for **comparing groups of data**. The examples provided here (including simple, grouped, and composite bar graphs) will give students some idea of what their results might look like. Students can use one type of graph first (for example, water use in week 1 as a composite bar graph), then another format for a different set of data (week 2, or another passage, as a grouped bar graph). Discuss with your child how a bar graph is useful (comparison, information at a glance).

Simple Bar Graph (Age 6 Student)

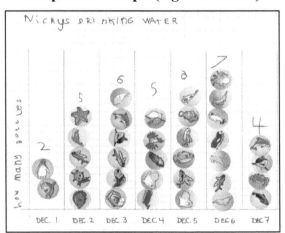

Building from a simple bar graph, students can create even more informative graphs by creating composite or grouped bar graphs. These show several categories of information simultaneously. Therefore, a first analysis can be made at a glance. Which category used the most water? The least? Where might we save water?

A **composite bar graph** stacks categories to represent totals by day. A **grouped bar graph** depicts categories side by side for easy comparison. Samples of both graph types are on the following page.

Composite Bar Graph (Age 8 Student)

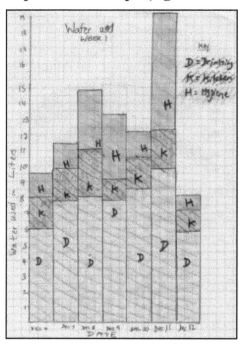

Grouped Bar Graph (Age 10 Student)

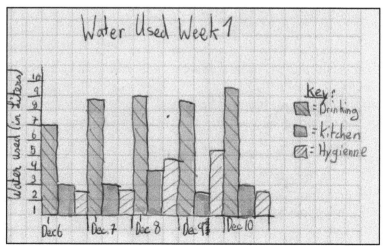

LINE GRAPHS

In the final third of your trip, try plotting water consumption on a line graph for another representation of use over time. This can be done in one of three ways:

- Plot total water consumption in all categories as one figure.
- Plot a single category (such as drinking water only).
- Plot each category in its own color line, one above the other.

Line graphs are particularly useful for showing **change over time** and allow the "reader" to extrapolate future water consumption.

Line Graph (Age 12 Student)

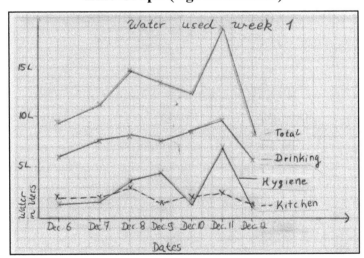

STEM AND LEAF PLOTS

Another way of representing data is through a stem and leaf plot. Think of a plant with several small leaves branching off the same stem. In a data set that includes the numbers 8.0, 8.3, and 8.5, the stem is 8 and the leaves that branch off it are 0, 3, and 5. If the same data set includes 9.2 and 9.8, the next stem of the same "plant" is 9 and the leaves are 2 and 8. These examples make up the bottom two rows of the table below. Stem and leaf plots are useful because they **preserve the original data** while providing a quick **overview**.

If a crew records the amounts of water used each day for drinking, these values could be represented in a stem and leaf plot. Let's say our records show the following liter amounts used each day for drinking: 6.0, 7.7, 8.0, 7.7, 8.5, 9.8, 5.7, 7.2, 9.2, 8.3, 7.8, 8.5, 6.9, and 7.5. Putting the whole number in the "stem" column and the decimals in the "leaf" column, we can produce the following stem and leaf plot for our two-week long data set:

Stem and Leaf Plot: Drinking Water Used

Stem	Leaf
5	7
6	0, 9
7	2, 5, 7, 7, 8
8	0, 3, 5, 5
9	2, 8

Key: 9|2,8 means 9.2 and 9.8

Notice that this plot has a title and a key. It shows that the most frequently occurring value is between seven and eight liters of water used for drinking each day. The bar and line graphs above show the same data (condensed to one week sets). In fact, if you turn this stem and leaf plot sideways you can see the resemblance to a bar graph. The advantage of this stem and leaf plot is that exact values are conveniently listed at a glance. The original data is not lost in an average or hidden among bars.

Advanced students can use stem and leaf plots to learn about mean, median, and mode values. **Mean** is the average calculated by adding all figures and dividing by the number of units; **median** is the middle number in an ordered list; **mode** is the number that appears most often. Using a stem and leaf plot, a student can quickly identify the mode in a data set.

We could even draw a **back to back** stem and leaf plot to show two data sets at a time. The tricky thing is that the left side must be read backwards. For example, the top left values of 5 in the plot below lines up with stem 1, and indicate 1.5 and 1.5 liters used.

Back to Back Stem and Leaf Plot

Water consumption on board

Galley	Stem	Hygiene
5, 5	1	0, 5, 7
0, 0, 0, 5	2	0
0	3	8
	4	8
	5	
	6	
	7	0

Key: 0|3 reads 3.0 and 3|8 reads 3.8 liters

Many students find back to back plots confusing at first but a practiced eye can read the data easily. Stem and leaf plots are simply another way of showing data in graph form. There is no single "best" graph type; each fulfills a different purpose. The main advantage of stem and leaf plots is that they keep all the original data points. This system is usually introduced to students at age ten or older.

PIE CHARTS (CIRCLE GRAPHS)

Pie charts (or more correctly, circle graphs) are useful for showing **parts of a whole** and making **comparisons**. Depending on the total units to be depicted, a pie chart can be very easy or very complicated for a young student to create. If the student uses a computer graphing program (such as Excel), the process is easy since the computer calculates everything and instantly creates a nice pie chart. Without a computer, the process requires several steps and is a task usually only introduced at age ten or above. However, this process allows the student to understand how values are converted rather than letting computer magic take that experience away. The steps in doing this "manually" are listed here. This multi-step process is not terribly difficult but it does get abstract quickly for young students.

First, convert water values into daily averages, and calculate what percent each subset is of the whole. This will yield a decimal that will then have to be converted into a percent. The following section breaks this process down in a step-by-step approach. The table below lists sample calculations.

For example, when crossing the Atlantic, our thrifty crew used an average of 7.6 liters (drinking), 2.07 liters (galley), and 3.01 liters (hygiene) per day.

Converting to Degrees

Liters	Percent as a decimal	Percent converted	Degrees
7.6	0.603	60.3%	216.0
2.0	0.159	15.9%	57.6 (round to 58)
3.0	0.238	23.8%	86.4 (round to 86)
12.6 total	1.000	100.0%	360.0

1. First, **round** the averages to the nearest unit appropriate to the student's level (for example, to the nearest tenths place).
    * Round 2.07 to 2.0L, and 3.01 to 3.0L. Do not change 7.6L.

2. Then, calculate the **percentage** of water use that each category represents.
    * Calculate total liters used: 7.6+2.0+3.0=12.6L
    * Divide each category by the total amount to find its percent. 7.6L out of 12.6 = 0.603, or 60.3% of the total. Round to 60%.
    * Check that all add up to 100%.

3. Now, convert % to **degrees** for use on a circle.
    * Multiply the % by 3.6
    * 60% x 3.6 = 216°. This means that drinking water (7.6L) was 60% of total water consumed and this takes up 216° of a 360° circle.
    * For advanced students only: Where does the 3.6 formula come from? Set up an equation and insert each known percent at the % symbol to find the corresponding number of degrees (x):

$$\frac{\%}{100} = \frac{x}{360}$$

Now, use a **protractor** to divide a circle into appropriate sections. Colored sections allow the audience to clearly distinguish different categories. Be sure to label your pie chart and each of its sections. Discuss with your child what a pie chart is useful for (seeing relative parts of a whole).

Pie Chart (Age 10 Student)

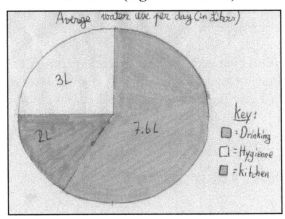

ANALYZE DATA

In the final third of your trip, extend your bar graph and re-draw your pie chart to include your latest data. Compare these to the line graph. Use these questions to guide students in analyzing data:

- *What patterns of water use did you observe?*
- *What explains those patterns?*
- *What are the advantages of each type of graph?*
- *Is one type of graph best for representing water consumption? Why?*
- *What predictions can you make from your graph(s)?*
- *How accurate are your measurements? What are some sources of error? How could you estimate and reduce the error?*
- *Does measuring water consumption affect your habits? How?*

ASSIGNMENT: PRESENT FINDINGS

Having analyzed their data, students should complete a summary of their work in the form of a written report (see *Age-Appropriate Adaptations*). They should sum up the points from their analysis. Then, ask students to consider what predictions they could make using the graph. For example, how much more water would have been needed for a longer journey or how much water will be needed for the next passage?

Ideally, students could even extend their record keeping of water consumption after arriving at their destination in order to compare water use on land and offshore. This would also be a powerful lesson, and it connects to current news topics, such as use of natural resources.

Age-Appropriate Adaptations

In this section, you will find guidance on how to differentiate, or adapt, this unit for your child. Start with the correct age group, but also glance through the notes for one level younger or older, then mix and match as appropriate.

Self-assessment and reflection are valuable learning tools. They encourage students to think back upon their work and store their new body of knowledge in a meaningful and memorable manner. To that end, a number of self-assessment and reflection questions are listed for each age group. It is not necessary to address all the questions; substitute others as you see fit. Completed assignments and written reflection are useful records to later document student work for a school administration.

Ages 4-6

On first thought, one might be tempted to dismiss very young children as incapable of graphing. On the contrary, pictures – graphical information – are a powerful means of communicating ideas of quantity (both absolute and relative) for young students.

Assignment: *Graph Water Consumption and Present Findings*. Parents of young children should simplify both the measurement units and the number of data points. Record only how much water the child himself drank in one day and ignore galley/hygiene use. Parents can first provide measurements and gradually help the child to measure independently. Measurement need not be in formal units like liters or gallons; students can use non-standard units, such as how many bottles were emptied in a day rounded to the nearest whole (in which case, always use the same, small sized bottle so you have multiple units to work with rather than partial units). Then make a simple pictograph using the data. Pie charts and line graphs are not appropriate for this age level. This age group does not have to present their findings, but should use self-assessment to review their work.

Young students will not complete any written work but should be encouraged to discuss their graphs and even interpret other pictographs in simple terms. Use terms like "graph" and "data." Parents could label the students' work with numbers so that students can begin to read and perhaps write their own numbers.

Self-Assessment and Reflection: This entails discussing the student's completed graph, touching on points such as:
- *What was it you were recording? Did you do that clearly?*
- *Can another person "read" your graph?*
- *What part of your graph came out really well?*
- *What can your graph tell you about your water use?*
- *How is a graph useful?*

Ages 6-8

Assignment: *Graph Water Consumption and Present Findings*. Most students in this age group will be able to draw bar graphs with guidance. They can track water use in more than one category. The goal is for students to be able to draw and interpret a variety of graphs, and to make predictions from trends revealed in the graph. Instead of presenting findings in a written report, substitute verbal discussion and prompt your child to be thorough in his or her explanations and analysis. Creating line graphs, stem and leaf plots, or pie charts are not skills usually asked of this age group. However, students ages six to eight can use a computer to generate pie charts in order to see a different style of data management.

Children ages six to eight should begin to move from non-standard units of measure (six full bottles) to standard measures (liters or gallons; the latter is much more complex to break into subgroups). Round to the nearest unit as appropriate unless you specifically want to work on decimals or fractions. Students can produce a simple bar graph to record and then predict water consumption. For example, *By the end of day X, we should have used no more than Y liters of our supply.* Then students can check if water consumption is indeed within range as the passage unfolds. The older end of this age group can begin to deal with an input factor: *We started with X liters, used Y, and added Z back in through water made or collected underway.*

What if Dad spilled his bottle and needed a refill? What if we had twice as many people on board? What if a yellow submarine appeared and sprayed us with fresh water? Children in this age group *love* to play "what if" in increasingly improbable versions, which could be your ticket to fun math practice.

Self-Assessment and Reflection: Have the student dictate all the important points of a good graph to a parent or older sibling, who acts as scribe. This will create a checklist for a good graph. Then have the student apply the checklist to his or her own work. Finally, conduct a short discussion in which the student looks back on what was difficult or easy for him throughout the entire process.

- *Is your work neat and clearly labeled?*
- *Is the information presented easy to understand?*
- *Can the graph be used to make predictions?*
- *Was there something that was difficult at first that you can now do more easily?*
- *How did you overcome any difficulties?*

Ages 8-10

Students in this age group can do much of the above unit as described.

Assignment: *Graph Water Consumption and Present Findings.* Students should be responsible for drawing and labeling axes. They can attempt bar graphs, line graphs, simple stem and leaf plots, and pie charts. These students can also present their findings in brief written form, and write a short answer to the question: What are the advantages of each type of graph? Is one type of graph best suited to represent water consumption? Why?

These students should practice multiplication and division as much as possible (the water consumption data lends itself to this well). If we have four people on board and each drinks three liters per day, how much drinking water will we need for our ten day passage? What if the passage takes twelve days? Or, estimate how much water remains in your tanks in mid-passage and divide per person. How much can we use now if there are four days to go?

Calculating averages is another mathematical operation this age group can practice. What is our water consumption per day on average? Does the average change over the course of our trip? Why? What average speed do we have to maintain to reach our destination in a week's time?

Self-Assessment and Reflection: Students should complete a written reflection, considering questions such as:

- *What was hard for you to understand at first? What helped you better understand that over time?*
- *Are your graphs neat and easy to understand? Can you make predictions from them?*
- *Are you satisfied with your final graphs? Be specific in explaining why.*
- *Which type of graph is most useful for which purpose, and why?*

Ages 10-12

These "oldest" students can work through the unit assignments in unmodified form.

Assignment: *Graph Water Consumption and Present Findings*. Students ages ten to twelve can calculate water consumption in a number of categories and plot their own bar graphs, line graphs, stem and leaf plots, and pie charts with minimal assistance (paying attention to details like labeling axes and units). They can learn to manipulate decimal units. Written reports presenting findings should be approached quite seriously.

Compare your water consumption pie chart and bar graph to your line graph. What are the advantages of each type of graph? Is one type of graph best suited to represent data on water consumption? Why? Challenge students to produce a thorough and detailed response, always supporting statements with reasons. Students should extend their report to suggest what other types of data might be valuable and how that might best be represented in graph form.

Students ages ten to twelve should be challenged to apply more advanced multiplication and division whenever possible. They can work through word problems (use water, fuel, or cookies consumed daily) and find mean, median, and mode values (see *Stem and Leaf Plots*, above). Many students in this age group will be able to work with decimals and might practice converting liters to gallons or the reverse.

Self-Assessment and Reflection: Students should complete a written reflection, considering questions such as:
- *Which type of graph do you enjoy making the most, and why? The least?*
- *Did you handle units like liters or gallons well?*
- *What was hard for you to understand at first and what helped you better understand that over time?*
- *Are you satisfied with the quality of your graphs? Be specific.*
- *Which type of graph is most useful for which purpose, and why?*

Enrichment

After learning the basics of graphing, students can be encouraged to collect data of various types and graph each set in different ways. They can analyze and critique graphs found in the press (or see www.junkcharts.typepad.com for some examples). A natural extension of this unit is the subject of **coordinate graphing**, covered in *Unit 9: Navigation*. Students can also carry out the graphing exercise detailed in this unit with different data. Collect information on dolphin visits and present it in a bar graph by location/number of visits or behavior (number of dolphins swimming in the distance, swimming alongside the boat, leaping in the bow wave, surfing off the stern, etc).

Cross-Curricular Links

History: Imagine life on an ocean-going ship 500 years ago. How did Columbus' crews store water and how much did they consume? Did they have different needs than we do?

Physical Education: Students completing the heart rate "lab" in Unit 10 can use their graphing skills to visually represent and analyze changes in their heart rate during and after exercise.

Science: Graphing is an important tool in science. Many of the steps involved in this unit (data collection, presentation, and analysis) parallel the scientific method addressed more explicitly in Units 1, 2, and 3. Students interested in science can also research why humans can't drink salt water, or how to desalinize ocean water.

Credits

Many thanks to students Nicky, Keri, Charlotte, Jack, and Anuschka for creating the graphs used in this unit.

Unit 5 - Mathematics: Measurement

It is nothing short of a miracle that the modern methods of instruction have not yet entirely strangled the holy curiosity of enquiry.

Albert Einstein

Education is not the filling of a pail, but the lighting of a fire.

William Butler Yeats

Unit 5 - Mathematics: Measurement

Materials:
- One to three identical cereal boxes (or similar boxes)
- Material to fill boxes with (sand, rice)
- Scissors
- Ruler
- Tape

Guiding Questions:
What is capacity? What is it useful for?
How can I change a container so that it holds more?

Learning Outcomes:
Students will understand the concepts of area and capacity.
Students will be able to manipulate a container's shape to alter its capacity.

Introduction

How big is this container? How much does it hold? Through a hands-on, problem-solving experience, students will define the concepts of area and capacity for themselves. While older students can study the concepts of area and capacity explicitly, younger children will develop their mathematical awareness and lay the groundwork for future studies through a playful approach to the same subject matter.

Unit Overview

Area and capacity are concepts that are usually introduced to students ages eight and above. However, we can and should lay the foundation for these concepts much earlier. *Part 1: Basics* does exactly that. Young students will enjoy and benefit from filling, emptying, and measuring containers. By finding ways to compare containers, they explore the concept of capacity. Older students who have already had an introduction to area or capacity can skip this section.

Part 2: Redesigning a Container is a fun and educational activity for all age groups. Instead of simply memorizing a formula or filling in worksheets, students will take measurement into their own hands in a much more meaningful manner.

Some basic definitions are provided here to refresh the parent-teacher:

Perimeter is the length around the sides of a two dimensional object. For example: A worm's tunnel goes around a rectangular yard with sides six and eight meters in length. How far does the worm have to travel to check the whole length of his tunnels? Answer: 6m+8m+6m+8m = 28 meters.

Area is the space inside a two dimensional shape. For example: How much space does Fluffy the dog have in her yard if it is 6 meters wide and 8 meters long? Answer: 6m x 8m = 48 m^2. It is important to note that units are now square meters.

Capacity is the space within a three dimensional shape (or, the amount a container can hold). For example: The rectilinear water tank in a cargo ship is 5m wide, 4m deep, and 5m long. How much water can it hold? Answer: 5m x 4m x 5m = 100m^3. Note that units are now cubic meters. To convert to liters, a more common unit used in daily life, note that 1m^3 =1000 liters (see *Age-Appropriate Adaptations* for ages 10-12).

The term **capacity** is sometimes confused with **volume**, which is the amount of space a three dimensional object takes up (more often used with solid shapes than containers). Volume can be calculated in the same way as capacity. Older students should learn to differentiate between these related concepts.

Part 1: Basics

Part 1 is for very young students or those with minimal exposure to formal measurement. Older students can start directly with Part 2.

This playful "warm up" activity explores the concept of capacity. Materials can be easily found at the beach or in your galley. Line up three different containers and a material to fill them with (sand, water, or dry rice). Ask students to work out a way to determine which container holds the most. They can begin by comparing two containers and later a third, finally organizing the collection into order of capacity. If possible, use two containers that have different shapes but similar capacity, such as an empty jar and a small box.

Very young students will find this activity challenging and will typically go through several false starts. Let them play uninterrupted until their attention wanders or they are tempted to give up. Then encourage them to work from small to big. Fill the smallest-looking container to the top, and then pour the contents of the small container into what appears to be the next biggest container. If it all fits with space left over, which container is bigger? What about the next container?

The student should draw conclusions from the experience. What container holds the most? How does shape affect how much a container can hold?

Part 2: Redesign a Container

This section is the heart of this unit and can be completed by all students from ages four to twelve. The difference will be the extent to which mathematical terms like area and capacity are used, emphasis on detail, and degree of independence in student work.

Students should start with two to three identical cereal boxes (or any box that is easy to cut). Students will change the shape of one box and use the other for comparison at the end of their work. If you only have one box, you can still do the activity but will have to compare by using recorded measurements.

First, calculate the surface area and capacity of the box and write them down. The perimeter of each side is unimportant to this exercise but could be calculated to emphasize the difference between these three terms. Younger students will go about this in a different way than older students (see *Age-Appropriate Adaptations*). Now students are ready for the challenge: Change the shape of the box so that it holds more (using standard units, like cm^3, or non-standard units, like more rice or sand). Mathematically speaking, we could say: "Using the same area, create greater capacity."

Students must use all the parts of the original box and therefore maintain the same area. It must be a completely closed shape when complete with no leftovers. These directions are brief; the project might take an hour or more.

When finished, measure the capacity of the redesigned box and compare this to the original. Have you succeeded in creating a bigger container? What type of shape has a greater capacity in general?

Students will discover that the more uniform the sides of their container are, the greater capacity or volume they will be able to achieve. In other words, a cube has greater capacity than a rectangular box of the same surface area. A sphere has even greater capacity per area but is a difficult shape to achieve.

Age-Appropriate Adaptations

In this section, you will find guidance on how to differentiate, or adapt, this unit for your child. Start with the correct age group, but also glance through the notes for one level younger or older, then mix and match as appropriate.

Self-assessment and reflection are valuable learning tools. They encourage students to think back upon their work and store their new body of knowledge in a meaningful and memorable manner. To that end, a number of self-assessment and reflection questions are listed for each age group. It is not necessary to address all the questions; substitute others as you see fit. Completed assignments and written reflection are useful records to later document student work for a school administration.

Ages 4-6

Part 1 Activity: *Basics*. Very young students should begin with the warm up activity. Considering the problem of how to measure the capacity of different containers is the main exercise for them. Students can invent playful means of measuring, such as filling a container with water, sand, or rice. It is not necessary to use standard units or a ruler.

Part 2 Activity: *Redesign a Container.* Young students should fill their original container with sand (capacity), then re-work their second box into a new shape (great, hands-on fun) with help. They do not have to specifically aim for greater or lesser capacity, but just re-shape the same materials into a new box. Next they can measure the capacity of their new container using the same filling method as before. Challenge them to find answers to questions such as: How can we compare the contents of each box? How do we know that it held more (or less)?

Young students can also break down the three dimensional box into two dimensional shapes – literally. Cut open the box along its edges to see what shapes are found. Identify these shapes by name: rectangle, square, etc.

Self-Assessment and Reflection: This can be a simple matter of reviewing the student's work orally with questions like:

- *Did you have any problems when comparing containers?*
- *How can you tell if one container is bigger than another?*
- *What would you do differently?*

Ages 6-8

Part 1 Activity: *Basics.* Very young students are hardly ready to master formulas and multiplication, but they can explore measurement concepts on a basic level. Students can invent playful means of measuring, such as filling a container with water, sand, or rice. After some experimentation, students in this age bracket can move on to using standard measures (cups or milliliters) and may be introduced to the terms perimeter, area, and capacity.

Part 2 Activity: *Redesign a Container.* These students can work with a ruler to measure the sides of their box. The most advanced can use addition to calculate perimeters and perhaps even multiplication for area and capacity. Be careful, however, not to lose the student in the details of measurement at the expense of understanding the overall concept of what capacity really is and how that relates to area.

Working with some help, students should re-work their second box into a new shape and measure the capacity of their new container using standard or nonstandard units. Does the new shape have a greater or lesser capacity? Challenge students to summarize their findings. How can we compare the contents of each box? Which shape holds the most? How do we know that it holds more?

Older students in this age group should explore the fine differences between the terms *capacity* and *volume*. They can compare boxes that contain materials (capacity) to bricks that take up a certain amount of space (volume). What other examples can you think of? What is volume useful for?

An extension for students enjoying this activity would be to calculate area by drawing various shapes on graph paper and simply adding up the squares within each shape. This prepares them for the concept of square feet or square meters. You can prepare your student for multiplication by counting in batches. For example, draw a rectangle with one side of two, such as 2 x 5. They can count the boxes in ones, then in twos. Move on to a rectangle with one side of five, or of ten, to count by 5's or 10's.

Self-Assessment and Reflection: Students should reflect on the process they went through. Consider points such as:
- *How did you measure the capacity of your containers? Did it work?*
- *Did you stay with your first idea or change to a new approach?*
- *What did you discover when you changed the shape of your second box?*
- *What is capacity? What can we use area and capacity for?*
- *What is volume and how is it different? What can volume be used for?*

Ages 8-10

Part 1 Activity: *Basics.* It is not imperative for this age group to do Part 1, but it could provide a fun focusing activity on the topic of measurement. Although this age group should use standard measures when moving into Part 2, it can be stimulating for them to design a method of non-standard measures through Part 1 first. Alternatively, they can lead into the activity by measuring a variety of boxes and calculating area and capacity, practicing addition and multiplication.

Part 2 Activity: *Redesign a Container.* Students should create a table in which to record the area and capacity of the original box and the new design. Students at this level should be able to accomplish much of the project work independently, though they will need encouragement and guidance at key points of their investigation.

Students in this age group should explore the fine differences between the terms *capacity* and *volume*. They can compare boxes that contain materials (capacity) to bricks that take up a certain amount of space (volume). What other examples can you think of?

Students can also become more familiar with the concept of area by drawing various shapes on graph paper. Then, simply add up the squares within each shape to calculate the area. This reinforces the concept of square feet or square meters. Students who still struggle with multiplication tables can count in batches. For example, draw a rectangle with one side of two, such as 2 x 5. They can count the boxes in ones, then in twos. Move on to a rectangle with one side of five, or of ten. What patterns do you observe when calculating the areas of rectangles with one side = 2cm? Or with one side = 5m? This exercise helps students move on to calculating areas of shapes without needing graph paper to imagine the squares within a shape.

Self-Assessment and Reflection: Students should complete a short written reflection based on the following points:
- *What did you first try when you started changing the shape of the box? Did you stay with your first idea or change to a new approach?*
- *What did you discover about area and capacity?*
- *How is capacity different than volume? What is volume used for?*
- *Why is it helpful to understand area and capacity? List examples important on a boat.*
- *What advice would you give another student doing the same exercise?*

Ages 10-12

Part 1 Activity: *Basics.* Not necessary for this age group.

Part 2 Activity: *Redesign a Container.* It is one thing for a student to memorize the simple formulas for area and capacity, and another thing to actually understand the concepts and how they relate to each other. Students ages ten to twelve should be ready to take on this project in its full scope and work very independently. Advanced students can go on to explore area and capacity of non-quadrilateral shapes, such as circles / cylinders or triangles / prisms. (Hint: A right triangle is a rectangle cut diagonally into two. Hence the formula: Area= ½ base x height).

It is important for students in this age group to explore the fine differences between the terms *capacity* and *volume*. They can compare boxes that contain materials (capacity) to bricks that take up a certain amount of space (volume). What other examples can you think of? What is volume used for?

A mathematical skill that can be pulled into this exercise is **unit conversion**. You might start by going back to perimeter with examples on paper. The perimeter of a square with four sides each = 25 cm is 100 cm. 100 cm equals 1 meter. What about a square with sides of 50cm? (Answer: 200cm or 2m.) Converting square units is more complicated. The area of a square with sides of 1m is (1m x 1m) $1m^2$. This is not $100cm^2$ but rather, $10,000cm^2$! Why? 1m=100cm; therefore, 100cm x 100cm = $10,000cm^2$. Another example is the area of a rectangle with sides of 30cm and 40cm. 30cm x 40cm = $1200cm^2$. In terms of meters, this is 0.3m x 0.4m= $0.12m^2$. Volume and capacity follow the same pattern. A liter is $1000cm^3$ or $0.001m^3$. A tricky topic, indeed!

Self-Assessment and Reflection: Students should complete a written reflection about their work. Encourage them to consider the following points:
- *What did you first try when you started changing the shape of the second box? Did you later decide on a new approach? Why?*
- *What type of shape has a greater capacity?*
- *What is the relationship between area and capacity?*
- *What is volume and what is it useful for? List boating examples.*
- *What containers do we have aboard? Can you measure their capacity?*

Enrichment

After completing Part 2, students can go on to create a third box with a shape that is more extreme or the opposite of the previous two containers. (One box can be re-used once its dimensions are noted, but it is handy to see three containers of different shapes next to each other at the end of the experiment.)

Advanced students could broaden their investigation of area and capacity / volume by working with more complex, compound shapes. Real life links can be made by exploring practical, everyday objects, such as water tanks or fuel canisters. Here are some useful formulas:

The volume of a cylinder is: $\pi r^2 h$ (in which r = radius and h = height)

The volume of a sphere is: $\frac{4}{3} \pi r^3$

Calculating the capacity of a boat's hull is much more complicated! But you can work on other boating examples, such as: If I had only a certain length of canvas, how big a bag could I make out of it?

Cross-Curricular Links

Science: This unit provides the basic vocabulary for any chemistry project involving capacity or volume, such as Unit 3.

Resources

One website that lists formulas for finding the area and capacity / volume of various shapes is http://math.about.com/od/formulas/ss/surfaceareavol.htm.

Broken and broken
again on the sea, the moon
so easily mends

Chosu

Unit 6 - Writing

Materials:
- Journal
- Writing notebook and/or computer
- One small "ideas" notebook
- Folders in which to collect drafts, clippings, etc.

Guiding Questions:
What makes good writing?
What techniques can I use to communicate my ideas to an audience?

Learning Outcomes:
Students will be able to follow the steps of planning, drafting, revising, editing, and publishing written works.
Students will be able to use their own voice to write with purpose, focusing on a particular audience and topic.

Introduction

Writing is a huge topic that can (and does) fill volumes. The purpose of this unit is to get parents and children started with interesting exercises that develop young writers' literary skills. It is not an exhaustive study of a vast subject but rather a concrete and compact guide from which parent-teachers can forge their own path forward.

The process of writing will reinforce children's memories of unique sailing experiences and stimulate their creativity while developing an essential skill. Even children in the earliest stages of literacy can benefit from "writing" by using the help of a scribe.

Overview

This unit is divided into four sections. *Part 1: Journal Writing* focuses on journal writing as a way of recording and reflecting upon events, thoughts, and emotions. *Part 2: Non-Fiction Writing* guides parent-teachers and students through the process of writing a book report with tips on other forms of non-fiction writing. *Part 3: Creative Writing* suggests how students can use their experiences to inspire works of fiction. Finally, *Part 4: Publishing* provides ideas for polishing student work into a neat package, giving them the satisfaction of being a "real" writer.

In all cases, the main body of this unit describes critical points of each genre in general terms. Detailed instruction on how each age level should approach writing is listed in the following section, *Age-Appropriate Adaptations.* That means that the parent-teacher should first read a section on a given type of writing, and then refer to *Age-Appropriate Adaptations* for further guidance.

Writing Basics

It is important to write regularly and in a disciplined way. Once the habit is established, children will be able to write freely and enjoy the process as well as the satisfying results of that process. Invest some time into establishing a writing routine and you will soon see your child progress. Just as with music or sports, it helps to devote regular practice at a predictable time of day to tune in to writing.

GENERATING AND COLLECTING IDEAS

Writing, especially creative writing, requires a student to have ideas. An author who sits down to write and only then attempts to generate ideas will likely be frustrated. Having children think like writers means collecting ideas throughout the day; that is why a small **"ideas" notebook** is helpful. A funny incident, an unusual sight, a memorable feeling: all these should be noted briefly as they happen. It may take students a few weeks to compile a good ideas notebook that they can draw from. Sailing children take in countless impressions every day that they can draw inspiration from. Pictures or postcards also make excellent stimuli for reluctant writers.

Beginners can use writing time to simply play with words: they can list rhymes, phrases, or idioms, or string together a series of thoughts related to a favorite topic, like sea shells or painting. Students who have done very little independent writing can begin with wide-ranging **reading** as a way of collecting ideas and information about how writing differs for different purposes: a newspaper informs, a picture book entertains, an informative brochure educates. The parent-teacher can point out the differences and specific writing techniques along the way. In doing so, the budding author will collect tools for her writing repertoire. It is critical that parents familiarize themselves with their children's reading material so they can effectively discuss it, as well as to ensure that the material is appropriate to achieving their goals.

THE STEPS OF WRITING

Writing projects can be broken down into five important steps. First comes **planning** in which the author outlines where his work is headed and how to get there. This includes sketching out details like main idea, plot, and characters. The next step is **drafting**: getting a first version of the written piece on paper, and moving on to successive drafts with improved and expanded ideas. When the student is satisfied with the work, he can move on to **revising**. At this point it is useful to get a second opinion: have another person (a parent, sibling, or friend) read the work and explain what they interpret to be the main idea. This is a good test of whether the author's intention is expressed in his or her writing. If not, it will be necessary to strive for a more effective version through further revisions.

During revision, students should critically examine their own work and make improvements. They should check for vague or uninteresting verbs and adjectives like *went* and *good*: older students can learn to refer to a **thesaurus** for alternatives. Students should find ways to link separate sentences or ideas with connecting words such as *like*, *similarly*, *therefore*, or *on the other hand*. Students also should seek to vary their sentence structure. The *Age-Appropriate Adaptations* section lists specific tips for revision.

Then students can **edit** their work – look for errors in spelling, format, and so on to be sure the final copy is perfect. Finally, they can **publish** their work in the format of their choice. Part 4 of this unit deals specifically with this step in the writing process.

CHOOSING A SUBJECT

Writing is most interesting for both writer and reader when the subject is **meaningful** to the author. Therefore, it is important to allow children to choose their own topics. This doesn't mean that students can't be given assignments, only that the topic of the assignment should be left to the writer. For example, a student could be asked to write a book report that adheres to certain writing conventions; however, the student can choose which book to report on. Similarly, an assignment may be to write a fiction story, even of a specific genre (science fiction or mystery, for instance), but again, the choice of subject remains with the child. This allows children to view themselves as writers creating important and interesting work. Writing should have a purpose: to tell a story or entertain, or to teach, inform, or persuade. Writers should be clear about their **goals** and keep the purpose in mind as they go through steps in the writing process, from planning through publishing.

In the beginning, your goal should be to inspire children to write freely about topics they are enthusiastic about. Only once a routine has been established should students be encouraged to evaluate and improve their own work. Editing and drafting should take place after the initial process of creating, rather than interrupting it. It is useful to have several **folders** to collect successive drafts of each project, as well as pictures or clippings about the topic that serve as inspiration.

Part 1: Journal Writing

Journal writing is a way of capturing emotions and events. Simply choosing which events or emotions are significant enough to write about reinforces those memories and encourages students to **reflect** upon them. Furthermore, keeping a journal provides a form of authentic writing practice. Practice *does* make perfect – even with writing! Once students make writing part of their daily routine, they will find it easier and easier, and the quality of their writing will improve – moving from the nuts and bolts of grammar and punctuation to a focus on thoughtful content and deeper reflections.

GETTING STARTED

Students will need some form of **notebook** in which to record their experiences. This can be anything from a spiral-bound notebook to a fancy, covered diary or even the blank pages of an artist's sketchbook. Ideally, a journal should allow space for artwork and mementos.

Start your child off by establishing the notebook as a place to write and begin with dated, simple entries such as *Today we anchored by a small island, or Today we went snorkeling,* and have her describe the activities of the day in sequential fashion. It is easy to keep a journal during a trip or special experience, but on routine days, it takes a little more imagination and planning.

PLANNING

You can start the day with some prompts that will help students recognize points to record in their "ideas" notebooks. Remember to carry the notebook and a pencil during excursions! Use a variety of open-ended questions beforehand and when sitting down later to write:

- *What did you especially enjoy doing today? Why?*
- *What did you learn today?*
- *Who said an interesting or funny thing today and what was it?*
- *How did you manage to ... (figure out the puzzle / find your way / swim to shore)?*
- *How is the lifestyle here different to ours at home? (Think about transportation, environment, resources, work, or leisure activities.)*
- *When did you realize that ... (you could really do it / it was a bad decision)?*
- *Why did ... (you fall down / the boy share his toy with you)?*

These are all very factual topics, however. A journal can and should be much more than a minute-by-minute recounting of the day. Explore and link separate ideas like a puzzle:

- *What didn't go very well today? What did you learn from that?*
- *What memories came to you today? What's the connection?*
- *How does it make you feel when ... (you see the giant waterfall / you take over the wheel / you hear dolphins squeak)?*
- *How would you compare X (the food / the lifestyle / the means of transportation) here to home or another place recently visited?*
- *If you could share one experience from today with anyone you wanted, what would it be and who would you like to share it with?*

DRAFTING, REVISING, AND EDITING

Journal writing is a very personal form of writing and a forum for free expression. Therefore, it is not really appropriate to revise a journal. However, it is useful for students to look back on journal entries and strive to improve writing quality in the future. (If your child prefers to keep her journal private, ask her to write an entry that she is willing to share.) Do certain **themes** occur most often? Why is that? Is the journal largely **factual** or more **emotional**? Are any details left out that might be important in the future (such as mentioning place names or companions)? Does the writing typically focus on "big" things like scenery but leave out details, or vice versa?

Evaluate the quality of the writing, both in terms of content and writing conventions. Photocopy one entry and help students mark every **verb** with a highlighter. Are certain verbs like *went* or *got* repeated often? What action verbs could replace those repetitive words? What about *walked*, *bought*, or *discovered*? Then highlight the **adjectives** with a different color. What are the repeat offenders? Can you substitute *colorful* for *nice* or *spectacular* for *great*? Advanced students could make sure they use words that **signal changes** in time, place, or thought (*later*, *therefore*, *however*).

Students can also check for **consistency**: usually, the past tense is appropriate. Are thoughts and events recorded in chronological order, or with references to relative order? Finally, analyze the writing in terms of what **senses** students are drawing from. Typically, we humans rely heavily on sight, and as a result, journal entries are often based on visual stimuli: color, size, aesthetics. What about the smells, textures, tastes, or sounds of the day? Lying in his bunk at night, what did the child hear? On the beach, how did it smell? Often we lack a rich vocabulary for these senses and therefore a writer must be creative in capturing them in words – an excellent exercise.

Based on these observations, children can develop a "**hit list**" of things to include in future entries, making the cycle complete by returning to the planning stage. Students can tackle this list gradually rather than all at once. For the next entry, they can try to include more interesting verbs, even if it means some cross-outs. Later, students should remember to notice sounds and report those. Children can also record experiences in creative ways: for example, by writing about the day from the **perspective** of the boat, a dog, or a cloud.

A journal doesn't have to be an immaculate work of art; it should be a genuine, workaday tool. At the same time, children should be encouraged to spice up their journals with sketches or mementos. Although a journal will not be published in the same way that a book report or story will be, it can be enhanced with small additions. Glue in an island map, a postcard, or a colorful stamp. Jot down jokes and memorable quotes, or sketch a scene from the day. Over time, children will not only gain new writing skills by keeping a journal, but also create a special reminder of their experiences.

Part 2: Non-Fiction Writing

Non-fiction is any factual account that doesn't include invented components. There are countless forms of non-fiction writing, including **biographies** (*Christopher Columbus*), **travel guides** (*The Bahamas by and for Kids*), **explanatory / instructional** writing (*How to Filet a Fish*), **persuasive** writing (*Why Homework Should be Banned*), and **comparative** writing (*Star Wars and Madagascar: Two Heroic Tales*). This section will focus on writing a **book report**, an example that transfers well to other genres.

The advantage of the **book report** is that it reinforces literacy skills in two ways: first reading, then writing. The subject of the report can be any book, fiction or non-fiction. A child may choose to report on anything from a favorite dinosaur fact book to most-loved *Harry Potter* fiction. The child can also choose how to go about his report: will it be a basic summary of the work with some connections made to the author's own life, or a review, or even a comparative piece?

PLANNING AND DRAFTING

A book report is not something students should complete in one sitting, but rather work on over an **extended period** of time. Break the task into sub-steps and consider each carefully. Even the youngest children should structure a book report properly. A good book report will include the following points:

- Full title, author, and genre.
- Summary of the story with key ideas or events.
- Description of characters (as applicable). Who are they? What are they like? What problem does the main character face? How did he or she solve the problem? How would the story change if one of the characters were omitted?
- Other interesting points: Does the book have good illustrations? Is the story realistic? Is it part of a series?
- Recommendations: What did the reader enjoy or dislike about the book? Support comments with specific examples. Who would the student recommend the book to?

When the plan is complete, students can flesh it out in successive drafts. Remind students to write **in their own words** rather than parrot lines from the original work. A good essay will have a clear **introduction** and **conclusion**, and be organized into **paragraphs** that begin with a topic sentence. Each paragraph should be each devoted to a certain point and linked to the next. Proceed from the general to the specific. Always keep in mind the **audience** and write appropriately: is this report for a parent-teacher to read or is it aimed at a young audience?

REVISING AND EDITING

When the first draft is done, let students take a break! The next steps are to revise and edit the report, and ultimately, to come up with a finished product with illustrations as appropriate. These steps are often easier after the student has a chance to clear her mind and approach the task with a fresh perspective.

First, check that the report includes every point from the format above. Then students can **revise**. They can replace vague or uninteresting words with more precise and interesting language, using a **thesaurus** for new ideas. Vary sentence structure and paint a rich background through words.

Students should create an interesting **title** for the report. A good title conveys the content without being a boring give-away. An example is *Chaos in the House: A Report on The Cat in the Hat.* Older students should devote some time to working on the **opening sentence**. A good hook will engage the audience and set the stage for an enticing report: *Flying Broomsticks for PE? Potions in Chemistry? Imagine going to a school for wizards! That's just what happened to Harry Potter, the hero of the fiction book by J.K. Rowling.* This is infinitely better than an opening line like *In this book report, I will write about my favorite Harry Potter book.*

Next, have children check that the ideas and paragraphs are **linked** together. If paragraph one discusses everything that makes Harry Potter unique, paragraph two might begin with *Although Harry has magical powers, he is still just like kids my age. For example…* All statements should be **supported** by evidence, either by using direct quotes or by referencing an incident in the book (*Even though Harry Potter has magical powers, he is sometimes scared like any normal kid. For example, he was scared when starting at his new school*). More sophisticated writers will not only summarize points of the story, but also draw their own conclusions and relate it to themselves (*The story of Harry Potter is inspirational because even with magic powers, Harry still had to try hard and rely on his friends to succeed*). All this may seem like a tall order, but it can be achieved with successive drafts.

Editing is the last stage in the process. Students should first self-edit their work, and then ask for a second opinion. Editing concentrates on the nuts and bolts of writing, such as spelling, punctuation, formatting, etc. When the report is complete, it should be published in some form (see *Part 4: Publishing*). Finally, students should revisit the report one more time for a self-assessment, setting goals for improvement in the next non-fiction writing attempt, be it a book report, subject report, or other non-fiction piece (see *Age-Appropriate Adaptations*).

MORE NON-FICTION WRITING

Book reports are a good starting point from which to branch out into other non-fiction projects. A student can create a **subject report** after reading several books on a related topic or from research collected during a field trip. In either case, planning carefully is critical. It is best to choose a **narrow topic**. A report on *Characters in Doctor Seuss stories* is easier to cope with than *Doctor Seuss* stories overall; likewise, a report on food in Panama is more manageable than a report on Panama in general.

A subject report should follow the same outline as a book report, summarizing the main idea, describing interesting examples, and drawing a clear conclusion. A catchy title is a plus; naming a report *Dinosaurs* is a little stale. What about *Dinosaurs: Jurassic Giants*? Finally, it is important to emphasize the importance of recognizing sources in a **bibliography**. For an informative piece, the author is likely to cite several sources.

You can also take a playful approach to non-fiction writing. Children can write a **newsletter** based on travel experiences or personal events (invent headlines like "Birthday Celebrations in Smallville: Town Still Recovering" or "Ten-Year-Old Claims Innocence on Accusations of Messiness"). The newsletter can be silly or serious, fictitious or factual – anything to encourage creativity and writing! Students can link into other subject areas by publishing a newspaper based on a period in history ("The Athenian Times Reports on Triangles; Olympic News Page Two"). These are all fun ways to promote writing and understanding of new content.

Part 3: Creative Writing

Young imaginations can run free with many different forms of creative writing: science fiction, fantasy, historical fiction, mystery, poetry, short stories, myths, or tall tales. Some students are very creative and will find it easy to develop their own fictional storyline. Others may have a harder time getting started. One way to approach fiction writing is to take a real story and adapt it to a fantasy setting. If a student has a strong memory of the first day of school, why not write about a dog's first day at doggie school? The *Harry Potter* and *Percy Jackson* series are good examples of this approach: their success lies partly in the fact that they takes a familiar school or camp setting and give it a twist. Beginning with the **familiar** and progressing to fiction is a tried and true method for inspiring writing.

A visit to an interesting new place can fuel your child's imagination. An ordinary beach can provide the setting for a pirate adventure; children can then embellish it with new characters and wild details. *We were innocently digging in the sand when suddenly a pirate flag appeared over the horizon…* Just overhearing part of someone's conversation can inspire a story!

PLANNING AND DRAFTING

Even the most imaginative mind must work out details. The elements of a story are **characters**, **setting**, and **plot**. What is the main story? What **problem** must the character overcome? Many teachers use a **graphic organizer** to guide students through planning a story. One example is shown here:

Sample Graphic Organizer for Creative Writing

Title				
Main character	Other characters	Setting (time & place)	Problem	Solution

After working out an idea, the student can write the story in a first draft and fill in the details. Not all details will remain in the final, written tale, but they will give the author a clear picture of the background, characters, and setting, which will then translate into better writing.

When drafting, the story must be organized with a distinct, catchy beginning and a middle that builds on the first section. The middle can be expanded as appropriate for the age group. A very young author might write a two sentence "middle," while an older student will write several paragraphs or even short chapters. Young, inexperienced authors sometimes slip into writing a series of episodes that don't really develop into a full story. A graphic organizer will help in such cases. The story should not just fade out; rather, it should end with a clear conclusion in which the character solves the problem.

Students should think of a good **title** for the story. A good title suggests something of the content while retaining some mystery. Usually, a title is relatively short, though there are some notable exceptions. Think of favorite books and their titles: what do they state directly and what is suggested? For a mystery story about the Sphinx losing her nose, a great title would be *The Sneeze that Shook Egypt!* Funny and suggestive, this title immediately sets up the story. Sometimes, a good title is something very short and simple, yet evocative. *Summer Days* might be one, or *The Waterfall*. Encourage your child to think of someone browsing in a library: how would that person choose from the hundreds of titles on the shelves?

REVISING AND EDITING

In revising, writers review their latest draft and seek to make it more clear, interesting, and detailed. They should use good **vocabulary** throughout, replacing weak words like *saw, said,* or *went,* or vague words like *nice* and *good.* Instead of simply stating something, a writer should **demonstrate** it. For example, instead of *She was tired,* the author could evoke the character's tiredness: *The runner was breathing hard and sweat poured down her face.*

Revisions should aim to liven up the work. Students can work on the **opening sentence** and find a hook to attract readers. Next, writers should check that the ideas and paragraphs are **linked** together. They should examine sentence structure: are many of the sentences roughly the same? If so, they should try turning some sentences around, or linking two sentences. A good test is to share the story with someone else. That person should read and repeat the story back. If this reader has understood the main points the author hoped to make, then the story is on track. If not, it will need further revision.

In the **editing** stage, students "clean up" their work: checking spelling, format, punctuation, and so on. Make sure they go over the final draft very carefully. Very young writers should devote significant effort to editing their work with the help of a parent, sibling, or friend.

Part 4: Publishing

While this unit has mostly focused on the process of writing itself, there are many things children can do with the products of their writing. One exciting and affirming project is to **publish** student work. This can be done in a relatively simple fashion using folded paper and artwork. If available, a child can use a software program like *Pages* to create a professional-looking book on a computer.

Whether working by hand or with technology, this will take several tries to get right. Start with a simple, scribbled mock-up with folded sheets of paper. Where will each section start and end? Which **illustrations** will accompany the text? Using illustrations is a good way for very young students to complete a book report without getting bogged down in words. Illustrations must go through a draft process, too; think about adding detailed backgrounds and **speech bubbles** to the illustrations. Encourage students to pay attention to details such as page numbers, the cover and back page, a table of contents, an "about the author" section, an index, a glossary, and even a dedication and date / place of publication. They can even name their own publishing house!

There is something very special and empowering for young writers to see their work bound and published, just like a "real" book. But don't stop there! Give the published work a worthy forum. If your family keeps a sailing blog, feature your children's work prominently. Students could share their work with other children, adults, or even submit stories for publication in magazines or newspapers. Students can post their own book reviews on *Amazon.com,* for example. Written work by young authors is sometimes accepted by community newsletters or children's publications (see *Resources*). Who knows what success your young writer might enjoy?

Age-Appropriate Adaptations

In this section, you will find guidance on how to differentiate, or adapt, this unit for your child. Start with the correct age group, but also glance through the notes for one level younger or older, then mix and match as appropriate.

Self-assessment and reflection are valuable learning tools. They encourage students to think back upon their work and store their new body of knowledge in a meaningful and memorable manner. To that end, a number of self-assessment and reflection questions are listed for each age group. It is not necessary to address all the questions; substitute others as you see fit. Completed assignments and written reflection are useful records to later document student work for a school administration.

Ages 4-6

This is not a book about early literacy; to teach basic reading and writing, you should consult specialized resources. However, even youngsters can become writers with help. In the beginning, reading (or being read to) is as important as writing. It generates ideas and introduces young minds to writing conventions. While reading aloud, pause for the child to read high frequency words. Then encourage the child to generate her own ideas and stories, using a scribe to put these on paper. The student can write or trace high-frequency words for starters and later take over the writing herself. There is no need to bring up all the different possible genres with students of this age although they can begin to identify fiction (made-up) versus non-fiction (true) works.

Young students who are beginning to write should use broadly lined paper or paper that is lined on the bottom half but blank on the top half to allow space for an illustration (make your own with photocopies). Although trends in education come and go, it seems to be common today to allow emerging writers to use creative spellings. There is nothing worse than squashing a creative moment by harping on spelling and punctuation! Those elements can be added later, outside of core writing time and once the student has developed confidence as a writer.

Part 1: *Journal Writing.* Keeping a diary is easy and a good exercise in awareness of the world all around. A journal written through the eyes of a child can be a precious reminder of a special time. One way for very young children to keep a journal is to collect and write on postcards. These provide a nice visual reference, and a brief entry can be written on the back, either by a scribe or the child herself. Allow your child to choose postcards often, and establish a special place to keep them, such as a decorated cookie tin. Gradually, your child will learn conventions like writing the date and place on the card. Use the prompts in Part 1 to get ideas rolling, but don't overwhelm the child. Simply making regular entries is a good exercise for children in this age group.

Part 2: *Non-Fiction Writing / Book Report.* Students ages four to six can begin with oral book reports and then move on to illustrating a version written down by a scribe. Older children who can write will be able to take on sections or an entire report. Start with a favorite book or story and later move on to new books. Book reports authored by young children will likely consist of a simple summary of the book in question. Encourage them to retell it in their own words. Once their confidence is high, begin with some basic revising and editing but make sure to keep new versions in their own voice - don't push overwhelming vocabulary or extensive revisions on your child.

Part 3: *Creative Writing.* Often, very young children can be highly creative - so creative that they make great leaps in logic! In the beginning, parents should simply write down the stories as they come. Then read them back to the child and ask him to elaborate on certain sections, or give reasons for characters' actions. If a child struggles to find ideas, prompt him to use personal experience as a starting point and embellish that into a fictional work.

Young writers often tend toward one of two extremes: they either use very short, basic sentences, or go crazy with an elaborate story told in one endless sentence! If your child tends toward the former, encourage additions in the draft phase of writing. Repetitive stories can be improved with signal words or adjectives for more variety. Move from *The princess went to the beach. The princess went to the castle. The princess went to the tower...* to a more reader-friendly version like *Next, the princess went to the tower,* or *The beautiful princess ran to the deserted beach.* For the other extreme, encourage students to find natural breaks in long, run-on stories. Consider where a reader might take a breath and end one sentence there. Even if the child is not yet reading, she will gradually learn how punctuation fits in with writing.

Encourage students to include illustrations, but don't have them stop at a simple figure standing against an otherwise blank page. Show them how to fill in the background and use speech bubbles that either echo the main text or supplement it. Verbally go through parts of a story (characters, setting, plot) to help the author review his work for clarity.

Part 4: *Publishing.* Young children will enjoy concluding the writing process by making a "real" book out of their creation. Concentrate on creating a simple yet carefully designed book of folded papers, spending time on cover art and illustrations. Share the work with family members and friends to further encourage the young author.

Self-Assessment and Reflection: Students should look back at their own writing and discuss what they observe. Talk through the points below:
- *Where did you get your idea? Why did you choose that topic?*
- *What were the steps in writing your non-fiction essay / fictional story?*
- *How did your writing change from first to final draft? What worked well?*
- *Would you change anything about how you write in the future?*
- *Who or what was helpful to you while you were writing?*

Ages 6-8

Most children in this age group will be writing at some basic level. When their ideas are really flowing, it may still help to use a scribe. Children will need encouragement and prompting but can eventually produce more sophisticated products by using successive drafts. They will probably enjoy illustrating their work, and therefore paper that is half-lined, half-blank can be useful. While it is still important to read to these children regularly, it is time to encourage independent reading, as well. When revising a first or second draft, gradually devote time to conventions such as punctuation, spelling, capitalization, subject-verb agreement, and essay structure. For this age group, it is enough to know the difference between fiction and non-fiction without going into more specific genres – unless the child already recognizes a clear favorite and can learn this by name.

Part 1: *Journal Writing.* Keeping a diary is fun and a good exercise in self-awareness and attentiveness to the world all around. A journal will be a precious reminder of a special time. Collecting postcards is one way for children to keep a journal; they provide a nice visual reference and a brief entry can be written on the back. Children can select their own postcards and keep them in a special place like a cookie tin. On the other hand, some children prefer the grown-up version of writing in a fancy, bound diary. Use the prompts in the journal section of this unit to get ideas rolling. Once your child gets very comfortable with writing in a journal, use the prompts in Part 1 to encourage introspection as well as pure "reporting."

Part 2: *Non-Fiction Writing / Book Report.* Students in this age group are capable of writing a simple book report in their own words and by their own hand. They should have some sense of their intended audience. The first draft will likely be a simple summary; encourage students to include personal insights in successive drafts, such as *Why I like this book* or *Why I like the illustrations.* Young writers can follow the format described in Part 2 using one sentence per section. In a second draft, draw the student's attention to details such as linking ideas together (*another reason, that is why*). Advanced students should make sure they end with a clear conclusion.

Part 3: *Creative Writing.* Even emerging writers can write their own stories, and have fun doing so. Rather than biting off too much at once, young writers often write short, repetitive sentence sections even when they can dictate long sentences. *The princess went to the castle to look for her jewels. Then the princess went to the tower to look for her jewels. Then the princess went to the beach ...* Encourage more variety in the second draft. Students should introduce another action, use stronger verbs, or vary sentence structure. *The princess ran to the beach and she jumped in the salt water.* Or *At the top of the tower, she looked over the lands.* Soon, young writers will get the hang of this and will be pleased with their wonderful, interesting stories.

Pay attention to spelling and punctuation only in the revision and editing stages. It will be natural to include illustrations, but make them good ones with detail true to the storyline. Speech bubbles are essentially a form of dialogue so encourage their use in artwork. Guide students through a graphic organizer to find any gaps in their stories and to instill the idea of structure.

Part 4: *Publishing.* Young children will enjoy putting their creation together as a "real" book. The experience will conclude the writing process nicely and give their work extra value. Concentrate on creating a simple yet carefully designed book of folded papers, spending time on layout, cover art, and inside illustrations. Children can share the work with family members and friends – or even join together with other young writers and throw a publishing party, celebrating their work and giving it a wider audience. Guests at the party can make brief, written comments on the works they read.

Self-Assessment and Reflection: Students should take a critical look at their writing and discuss what they find. They might even select representative samples to put in a portfolio that shows their development as a writer: not just the best pieces, but pieces that show growth over time. Talk through the points below:

- *Trace an idea from original idea to publication. Why did you choose that topic? How did your writing change from first to last draft? What worked well and what was difficult?*
- *What are the things that make your writing interesting or special?*
- *Who or what was helpful to you while you were writing?*
- *What are the characteristics of your favorite stories or books?*

Ages 8-10

Children in this age group can write simple paragraphs and follow the suggested tips for structuring their work. Many will start with simple sentences and can expand on these in successive drafts to add detail, vary sentence structure, enhance the setting or mood of a story, etc. Students should be able to write their first draft independently and revise their own work with some prompts. Don't give your child the impression that more is always better! Learning to write concisely is also an important skill. Writers at this level should start to develop a more sophisticated sense of audience. Ideas should be interconnected with signal words for time (*later, next*) or idea shifts (*but, however).* Students may also study and practice devices such as **similes** *(The wind was like a whisper…)* and metaphors *(In the dead of the night…).*

Part 1: *Journal Writing.* Students should keep a bound diary. Artistic children may like an unlined journal that they can sketch in while others will need lined paper to keep their entries relatively neat. Once the routine of journal writing is established, look back on entries regularly and begin to develop a "hit list" of new strategies to gradually incorporate in future entries, focusing on recording details, writing from different perspectives, and using all the senses. Use the prompts in Part 1 to make sure the journal includes some introspection rather than being a simple list of chronological events.

Part 2: *Non-Fiction Writing / Book Report.* Students should be able to produce a basic book report with little effort. Encourage them to work toward higher quality, however, by moving beyond simple summary to connections with personal experience or judgments. Successive drafts should not only improve the complexity of writing with more varied vocabulary and sentence structure, but also add details such as a table of contents, glossary, and/or index. Begin with a report on a book of one genre and then move on to another to observe differences between them. This may be done in a follow-up discussion or through a comparative report.

Part 3: *Creative Writing.* At this age, students should be able to move beyond basic princess and monster stories to somewhat more original or sophisticated works. The intended audience should be clearly stated: is it a younger audience, or a peer group? Children should use a graphic organizer to develop all elements of the story. Those comfortable with writing can include more than one episode in their story and show the beginnings of character development. Students who really enjoy a certain character could be encouraged to write further stories about the same hero, or introduce interaction with new characters. Drafts should be extensive and show clear changes from early through finished stages. Budding authors can be encouraged to delve into a different genre: why not try a mystery, or historical fiction?

Part 4: *Publishing.* Older children often have higher standards of what a "real" book is and therefore their final product should be something good enough to satisfy them that their work really is valuable. It will help to include "official" details like a dedication, table of contents, and "about the author" section. The finished product can be done by hand or by using a computer program. It's no longer enough for a parent to say "good job"; a wider audience will help affirm the writer's efforts. When possible, seek out other young authors and invite them to share and celebrate their work in a joint publishing party. Exemplary pieces of work might even be submitted to an appropriate publication.

Self-Assessment and Reflection: Students should look back through their journals regularly and judge their own fiction and non-fiction writing once they have a finished product. They can do so orally or in written form, using the following questions as a guide. They might even select representative samples to put in a portfolio that shows their development as a writer, collecting pieces that show growth over time.

- *Are your journal entries varied? How can you bring new ideas into your journal?*
- *How did you go from first idea to final product? What stages were easiest for you? What stages were more difficult?*
- *Which specific strategies did you use in revising your work?*
- *Looking back at your writing samples, can you find change over time? What are some developments you can find? What could you try next?*
- *Who is your favorite author and why?*

Ages 10-12

Older students should aim to reach a high level of writing competency as well as to work independently. Students ages ten and above can closely follow the structures described for each type of writing, and create paragraph-long sections. Writers at this level should start to develop a more sophisticated sense of audience and their own voice in both fiction and non-fiction writing. Ideas should be interconnected throughout the essay with signal words for time (*later, next, in conclusion*) or idea shifts (*but, however, consequently*). They should attempt to plan, draft, revise, and edit their own work before bringing it to a parent for further input at each stage.

Part 1: *Journal Writing.* Students should have a bound diary. Artistic children may like an unlined journal that they can sketch in. Once the routine of journal writing is established, look back on entries regularly and create a "hit list" of techniques to incorporate in future entries. Use the prompts in Part 1 to make sure the journal includes introspection and analysis rather than a mundane listing of chronological events.

Part 2: *Non-Fiction Writing / Book Report.* For older students, writing a simple book report is likely to be boring. Challenge them to write a comparative essay or go into one book in great depth, making personal connections with the literary work. Comparisons should be deeper than *Both books tell the story of a boy with a dog.* A better comparison would be *Both stories center on a figure who struggles with relationships but eventually learns the meaning of a true friend.* Older students can undertake an in-depth book study, which examines literary devices used by the author to keep readers engaged. "Dissect" the writing and quote effective examples. In all cases, the work should be consistently aimed at a specific audience.

Students should make personal connections and judgments based on examples quoted from the text. Successive drafts should not only improve the complexity of writing with more varied vocabulary and sentence structure, but also add details such as a table of contents, glossary, and/or index. Begin with a report on one genre and then move on to others, actively observing differences in their characteristics. Ideally, students will take on a more complex report as a second assignment. In it, they can analyze the similarities and differences between genres, drawing from a number of different works.

Part 3: *Creative Writing.* Authors should write for a specific audience, be it a younger sibling or their own age group. They should use a graphic organizer to carefully plan their stories. Even hesitant writers can develop their skills and create successively more sophisticated drafts. Those comfortable with writing can develop more complex storylines and characters. Revision should be extensive and show clear changes from early through final stages.

Budding authors can be encouraged to explore a variety of genres: try a mystery, a tall tale, or historical fiction. An author can even take a favorite character on a literary journey through several different genres. Stories can also include properly punctuated dialogue. Artwork is not only for young children; allow older children to have fun illustrating their own work.

Part 4: *Publishing.* Older students should aim for a polished product. They can develop technology skills by using computer programs such as *Pages*. On the other hand, there's nothing wrong with a handmade book, especially one that clearly shows care and attention to detail. It is especially important for older students to have a good audience for their works, so seek opportunities to share with other young authors or to submit material to community or literary publications. A student who enjoys adding new episodes to their stories might also create an online blog / story site to reach a wider audience.

Self-Assessment and Reflection: Students can look back through their journals regularly and judge their fiction and non-fiction writing critically once they have a finished product. They can do so orally or in written form, using the following questions as a guide. They might even select representative samples to put in a portfolio that shows their development as a writer, being sure to include pieces that show growth over time.

- *Are your journal entries varied? How can you bring new ideas into your journal?*
- *What process did you follow from first idea to final product?*
- *When you state your opinion, do you provide supporting examples?*
- *Which specific strategies did you use in revising your work?*
- *Who is your favorite author and why? What characterizes her writing?*
- *Do you think your writing "worked" well with your audience? Why?*
- *Looking back at your writing samples, can you see change over time? What are they? What could you try next?*

Enrichment

Don't just tick off the three types of writing suggested in this unit and call it a day. Encourage further writing: another work in the same genre, or a similarly themed work in a different genre. If your child's favorite writing project was a book report about dinosaurs, consider having her write a fictional piece about dinosaurs next. If her favorite project was a story about elves, ask her to write a non-fiction work on elves, exploring the origin of elf stories or a region's folklore. Alternatively, allow your child to choose a genre and follow an **immersion** approach: read several works of that genre, analyze the techniques used, and then write a new work in that genre. This is a good way to explore different types of writing.

The product of writing must not be limited to written media; students can write and act out plays or screenplays if that tickles their fancy. Any story or report can be turned into an **oral report** to parents or other children; this develops presentation skills and reinforces the lessons learned in a unit.

Have students **interview** a local person (a child in a playground, a market vendor) and write a piece about what they have learned. This need not be overly formal: they should simply prepare a few questions, ask for permission to interview, and jot down the answers. Usually people are very willing to share their perspective and love the idea of being interviewed, even by a child! Possible interview questions are *What do you like most about your work? What is the hardest part of your work? What changes have you witnessed in recent years?*

Poetry is another writing medium that can entice young writers. A poem may be fiction or non-fiction. Not all poetry rhymes in a regular pattern, but it is easy to start with rhymes. The opening quote for this unit is an example of **Haiku** poetry. Look up different types of poetry and encourage children to give them a try. Like all writing efforts, poetry gets easier with practice.

Cross-Curricular Links

Writing is an incredibly versatile tool that can easily be applied to any academic area. If children are studying a particular theme in **history**, they can put non-fiction writing skills to work by writing an informative report on the subject or take a creative approach by inserting a fictional character into a historic backdrop. Students can write about any subject in many ways: poetry about **mathematics**, a **scientific** non-fiction report, or a journal entry that muses about **foreign language**. Illustrations will enhance a piece of writing and develop **art** skills at the same time.

Resources

Write on Reader (http://library.thinkquest.org/J001156/) is a website created by students for students. This has some helpful ideas about writing (the writing process, punctuation guide, forms of writing) and even links to **publications** that accept student work. Perhaps the best thing about this site is that it shows young writers that they are not alone; there are many other young, enthusiastic authors out there! Another website that lists publishing opportunities is http://www.noodletools.com/debbie/literacies/basic/yngwrite.html. The *Young Authors' Workshop* (http://www.planet.eon.net/~bplaroch/Write.html) is another useful website.

Families who wish to devote a significant amount of time to writing should look for *Knowing How: Researching and Writing Non-Fiction 3-8* by Mary C. McMackin and Barbara S. Siegel (Portland, Maine: Stenhouse Publishers, 2002). This book will be helpful for families with children ages eight and older. It includes sample essays, a good section on assessment, and many detailed examples of effective writing strategies.

Unit 7 - History:
The Voyages of Christopher Columbus

The sea was like a river, the air soft and mild.

Christopher Columbus

Perhaps, after all, America never has been discovered.
I myself would say that it had merely been detected.

Oscar Wilde

Unit 7 - History: The Voyages of Christopher Columbus

Materials:
Art supplies for assignments

Guiding Questions:
What do we sailors have in common with explorers like Columbus?
What are our differences?
What consequences did Columbus' voyages and discoveries have?

Learning Outcomes:
Students will be able to compare their own trip to Columbus' in 1492.
Student will be able to identify the factors driving Columbus' voyages and the consequences of his "discovery."

Introduction

One could write hundreds of pages on Columbus and the Age of Discovery. Why did Columbus sail west? How did he plan his voyage? What was his voyage like? What did he do after his 1492 trans-Atlantic voyage? This unit summarizes key points about the explorer and the era he lived in. This is a comprehensive unit that can easily fill several weeks. On the other hand, one can condense it or focus on a particular section. The text is written so that young students can read most passages alone. Parents can read aloud and adapt the text and corresponding activities for younger children. At the end of this unit, you will find a number of suggestions for enrichment. It may help to illustrate this unit through one of the recommended books listed in the *Resources* section.

Unit Overview

This unit is divided into four sections. Students will gain a deeper understanding of the subject when they study not only the 1492 journey, but also its historic context and its consequences. However, parents may choose to emphasize certain sections more than others depending on age and time considerations.

Parts 1 and 2 contain the basic information on Columbus' background and his 1492 journey. Parts 3 and 4 follow up with the fascinating second, third, and fourth voyages and the consequences of his discoveries. Only very advanced students will read an entire section in one sitting; most likely, they will divide the work over a number of days and take time between for the recommended activities and assignments. Students may choose just one assignment or work through all of them as a series. While reading the sections below, it is helpful to refer to maps frequently (several are included).

Following the main body of this unit, you will find detailed instructions for *Age-Appropriate Adaptations* of all the materials. This will guide parents in tailoring the unit to fit each child's level.

Part 1: Columbus: The Man and his Times

In 1492, Columbus crossed the ocean blue. This simple rhyme hides many fascinating facts about the man and his times. How did he cross the ocean blue? How did he even get the idea? What made him attempt a feat that many people thought was impossibly dangerous? What were the consequences of his crossing? We shall soon see that there is much more to his story than simply "crossing the ocean blue."

The man whom we call Christopher Columbus was born in **Genoa** (today's Italy) in 1451. His real (Italian) name was Cristoforo Colombo. Since the first English book about him used the Latin version of his name, he is usually called Christopher Columbus by English speakers.

Genoa was at that time a city-state: something like a tiny country of its own, because Italy was not yet united into one country as it is today. Genoa was a lively trading city with many sailing ships coming and going. Although his father was a weaver, Columbus went to sea at about age ten and sailed on many trips around the Mediterranean. In 1476, he joined a trading ship that was headed out of the Mediterranean and into the Atlantic. However, the ship was attacked by the French and the crew was shipwrecked. Columbus survived by swimming and resting on a floating piece of wood until he came to the shore in **Portugal**. This near-disaster had an important influence on Columbus' career. Columbus went to join his brother Bartholomeo, who was working as a chart maker in **Lisbon**, the capital city. In Portuguese, the name Christopher appears as Cristovão or Cristoforo, and Columbus as Colon, Colom, or Colomo.

It is interesting and important to realize what the European world was like at that time. Columbus lived in an era of transition between the end of the **Medieval Ages** and the beginning of **Renaissance** times in Europe (neither era has exact start or end dates). Portugal was at one edge of the known world. More than one hundred years before Columbus' time, **Marco Polo's** adventurous tales of overland travel to Asia were published, and Columbus the boy was fascinated by these stories.

People in Europe were willing to pay large amounts of money for spices, silk, and tea brought from what they called **the Orient**: India, China, and Japan. But in 1453, the **Ottoman Turks** captured Constantinople (today's Istanbul, in Turkey), which until then was the capital of the Byzantine Empire. Turkish control of this important city made products from the East even more expensive and harder to obtain. Therefore, European countries like Spain and Portugal wanted to find their own routes to the riches of the Orient, and to do this they looked across the sea. One important man in this effort was **Prince Henry the Navigator** (*Infante Dom Henrique*, a son of the Portuguese king) who established a navigation center and sent many explorers south along the coast of Africa.

Columbus married a Portuguese woman (Dona Felipa Perestrello é Moniz) and moved to **Porto Santo**, a small island near Portuguese-owned **Madeira**. There, they were on the edge of the **Ocean Sea**. This was what people called what they thought was one, great, connected ocean touching Europe, India, and Asia. In a way, they were right, because the Atlantic, Indian, and Pacific Oceans are all connected in the south. Europeans didn't imagine there was another great continent – the Americas – in between Europe and Asia.

Columbus' father-in-law had a strong interest in the Ocean Sea. He even had a collection of unusual plants and wood that had washed ashore, presumably from unknown lands across the sea. Columbus also had heard some strange stories of islands and people who came from across the Ocean Sea. All this inspired Columbus' curiosity and formed part of the proof he eventually gathered to plan a voyage west.

Columbus thought it should be possible to reach the Orient by traveling west across the Ocean Sea, and calculated the distance to be about 5,000 kilometers. During his many sailing trips – maybe even as far north as Ireland and Iceland – Columbus observed that the prevailing winds came from the west at high latitudes, while in Madeira and the Canaries, the wind was usually from the east. Therefore, he reasoned, he should be able to catch favorable winds both across and back over the Ocean Sea. He called his idea of sailing west to establish trading posts "**the Enterprise of the Indies**."

At that time, few educated people thought the earth was a flat disc that ships could sail off the edge of. This is a misperception we often read in books. Scholars understood that Earth is round. Some even developed a way of estimating its size, though the results varied greatly. Several mathematicians calculated the distance west to the Orient to be about 15,000 kilometers. No ship of the day could carry enough supplies and sail so far. Columbus disagreed with their estimate and said the distance was only 5,000 kilometers. The mathematicians were right about the distance, but in a way, Columbus was right, too. There was indeed land 5,000 kilometers west of Europe, but nobody suspected that it was a new continent later named America!

In 1484, Columbus managed to gain an audience with Portugal's **King Juan II** and tried to convince him to pay for the Enterprise of the Indies. Columbus failed to convince the king and the royal advisors; they disagreed with his estimate of the distance and found Columbus too boastful and demanding. When Columbus tried to convince the king again in 1488, he was too late: explorer **Bartolomeu Dias** had just returned from a passage around the southern tip of Africa, rounding the Cape of Good Hope and entering the Indian Ocean. That meant that Portugal had no need of a dangerous route to the west now that they found – and controlled – a route around Africa.

So Columbus had to try elsewhere, and, after his wife died, he traveled to **Spain** with his young son Diego. In Spain, his name was again changed; there, he was known as Cristoval or Cristobal Colón. He and his son were taken in by monks with an interest in navigation who encouraged his idea. Columbus was eventually granted an audience with the rulers of a newly united Spain, **King Ferdinand** and **Queen Isabella**. They took interest in his idea, especially since their Portuguese rivals were ahead of Spain in finding a way to the Orient. However, their advisors disagreed with Columbus' distance calculations. At the same time, Spain was involved in a long, costly war with the **Moors** (Muslims from North Africa) who occupied the southern part of Spain. The monarchs could not pay for an expedition to the Orient before this war ended. Columbus waited six long years to be able to "sell" his idea. Finally, in 1492, the war was won, and Columbus was granted another audience, but again failed to convince the queen's advisors.

Discouraged, Columbus prepared to leave Spain and try his luck in France when Queen Isabella had him called back. One of Columbus' supporters had convinced Isabella that for a small investment of only three ships, Spain could possibly gain great riches if Columbus succeeded. Even if he was very demanding (Columbus wanted a huge percentage of all profits and hereditary rights that would pass to his children), it was a still a good deal for the Queen. She agreed. At last, he had a sponsor!

Now Columbus was finally ready to cross the ocean blue. For Europe, it would be an exciting new era of exploration, expansion, and conquest; for America (and later, Africa), it was to be a tragic era of exploitation.

PART 1 ASSIGNMENT

Students can try to rewrite history by writing a persuasive letter from Columbus to Portugal's King Juan II dated 1484. That is the monarch who rejected the Enterprise of the Indies because Columbus was not convincing enough, too demanding in his terms, and too boastful in his presentation. List all the reasons why Portugal would benefit from Columbus' voyage. Students should also detail what Columbus expects to receive as a reward. This serves as a good review of Part 1 and a means to practice persuasive writing.

Part 2: Christopher Columbus and the 1492 Voyage

The ocean was a large, unknown blank space on the map and few believed that it could be crossed safely. For sailors in the fifteenth century, it was as much a New World as the Americas would soon prove to be.

Luckily, the Spanish coastal city of **Palos** owed the monarchs a debt and was therefore required to supply two ships for Columbus: these were the *Niña* and *Pinta*. Columbus chartered a third ship, the *Santa Maria*; she was the biggest of the three at about twenty meters. Within a few months, Columbus had his crew and ships ready and set off on his voyage at last. The monarchs promised Columbus ten percent of any profits gained, rule of any new lands he discovered, and the title "**Admiral of the Ocean Sea**."

It probably isn't true that Columbus could hardly convince sailors to join his daring voyage. He was able to get a full crew of mostly experienced sailors from Palos, about ninety men in all. Even though he was making a trip into unknown territory and expected to find some new places on the way to the Orient, Columbus didn't bring any soldiers or many weapons on his first trip. He was very religious and wanted to bring his Christian religion to other people, but he did not bring any priests on the first trip, either. This suggests that **exploration** was his main purpose.

On August 3, 1492, Columbus led his ships out of Palos and set a course first for the **Canary Islands**, a passage of about a week. Most trans-Atlantic sailors today follow the same route. In the Canaries, he completed work on his ships and took on food and water. He had the *Niña's* rig changed to make her a square-rigger instead of a lateen rig (a triangular sail more like modern boats) because he predicted downwind sailing. Then, on September 6, 1492, the three ships departed the island of Gomera for the ocean crossing.

COLUMBUS THE SAILOR & NAVIGATOR

As we have seen, Columbus was already a well-traveled sailor who had made many observations about the Ocean Sea. He had worked as a mapmaker with his brother in Lisbon and spoke several languages, skills that helped on this trip. It is interesting to remember that he was Genoese, even though he worked for Spain and with a Spanish crew. This would bring him problems in stressful times when the Spanish crew looked for any excuse they could to disagree with their captain.

For navigation, Columbus mostly used **dead reckoning,** rough estimates of currents, and magnetic courses (not a corrected, or true, course). Dead reckoning means that he charted his day's course and the distance covered to find where he was. For example, if he sailed west all day and calculated that the ship covered one hundred miles, then he would draw a line west one hundred miles.[1]

Columbus also had two instruments for **celestial navigation** (using measurements of the sun, moon, and stars): a simple quadrant and an astrolabe. Both of these instruments are similar to a sextant and measure the height of the sun, moon, or North Star above the horizon. Columbus tried making a few celestial observations during his voyages across the Ocean Sea but was not successful in reliably establishing his location in this way.

From his experience, Columbus developed a good sense for currents, wind, and weather. He had a rough map showing Japan (called "Cipango") west of Europe, with a few imaginary islands drawn in between.[2] Columbus proved to be an excellent navigator who safely brought his ships through reef-filled waters, as we shall see. Today, sailors would hardly imagine leaving land without modern navigational tools. What tools do we have today that Columbus did not?

Columbus was one of the first ship's captains to keep a **log**, or written record of his voyage, including estimated positions and notes about events. This

---

[1] Strictly speaking, dead reckoning does not allow for leeway (the sideways push of the wind on a boat). Dead reckoning also leaves out any effect of currents that push the boat. However, Columbus was able to work surprisingly well using just dead reckoning because he was consistent in his calculations and good at judging currents. Later he would be able to find the same places using his own records.

[2] The circa 1481 Toscanelli chart. This Italian chart maker was one of the first to use a grid of latitude and longitude over the known world, with Europe on the right side of the sheet, the Ocean Sea in the middle, and Asia on the left.

document has not survived but a partial copy made after Columbus' death did, providing many important and interesting details about his first journey.

THE 1492 VOYAGE

Three ships sailed into unknown waters on the Enterprise of the Indies. Try to imagine what it would be like to sail while keeping in sight of two other ships at all times. The ships needed each other for safety; if they became separated, the crews would have no way to find each other again. It must have been very tiring to watch out for each other for weeks at a time. The *Niña* and *Pinta* were faster than the *Santa Maria*, which meant they often had to slow down and let Columbus catch up. By day, the ships would spread out as far as the horizon, but by night, they made sure to come together again.

The ships had a lower deck that was mostly used for storage. The crew would sleep on the open deck. There were no bunks; sailors just lay down wherever they could find a spot. Only Columbus had a tiny private cabin, something like a hut on the deck. Food was simple, mostly preserved goods like hardtack (a type of biscuit) and salted meat. Catching fresh fish was a welcome change to a sailor's **diet**! The crew cooked on a special sand-lined firebox kept on the deck.

The journey began slowly with weak wind. Eventually, they found more wind and moved more quickly. Columbus and his men went through a number of mood swings throughout their voyage (much like modern sailors). There were times when everything seemed to go well and other times when the crew was close to mutiny. There were several false clues and sightings of land that turned out to be nothing; this wore down the crew's patience and trust in Columbus.

Columbus kept two records of their progress: his secret version, in which he estimated their position as exactly as possible, and a second version for the benefit of the crew. This version made their distance from Spain seem less, because Columbus thought that the men would be afraid to know exactly how far they really were from home.

The crew eagerly watched for signs of land. They saw a tropical bird just a week after departure and thought land could not be far. Patches of Sargasso weed again tricked them into thinking that land was near. They made the same mistake with weather observations: "It started to rain without wind, which is a sure sign of land," Columbus wrote (Fuson, Pg. 64). On Sept. 21, still twenty days from landfall, they "saw a whale, which is another sign of land, for whales always stay near the coast" (Fuson, Pg. 66). On October 7, they saw large flocks of birds and thought they must be close to land. Alas, they were witnessing birds on migration, flying south for the winter. Can you imagine how the crew's faith in the Enterprise of the Indies was tested by this ongoing guessing game of "Are we there yet?"

Even the captains of the *Niña* and *Pinta* were beginning to have their doubts. Columbus convinced them to sail on for three more days, and just in time, on October 12, the fleet finally sighted land. After thirty-three days at sea, they had arrived in the **Bahamas** and in a new world. Columbus went ashore on the small island he named **San Salvador**. He planted a flag to claim it for Spain. Now Columbus could really call himself "Admiral of the Ocean Sea, Viceroy and Governor of lands that he may discover."

Soon the Spaniards made contact with the native **Lucayo** people, a subgroup of the **Arawak** natives spread across the Caribbean. Columbus, thinking he had reached the far edge of the Indies, called them **Indians**, a term that was then widely – if incorrectly – applied to indigenous people throughout the Americas.

Columbus thought this island (called Guanahani by its inhabitants) must lie at the end of an archipelago leading to **Cipango** (Japan). It is perhaps strange that Columbus should think he was at the edge of lands belonging to a great Asian Emperor and, at the same time, claim them for Spain. However, the land seemed nearly empty, settled only by "primitive" people, and was therefore fair game as far as the fifteenth century European mind was concerned.

Experts disagree about exactly where Columbus made his first **landfall**. Based on Columbus' description, his route across the Atlantic, and backwards calculations from his later discoveries, many believe it to be Watlings Island (which was actually renamed San Salvador in 1925). However, other historians argue that Cat Island, Samana Cay, and Grand Turk (of the Turks & Caicos) are other possibilities.

Route of Columbus' First Voyage

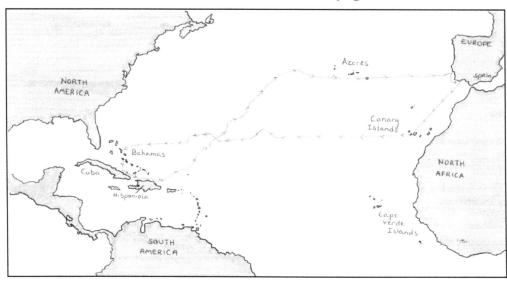

Columbus was excited to see that some of the "Indians" wore **gold** jewelry. Through sign language, they showed that gold could be found on larger islands nearby, and soon Columbus set off again. The indigenous people made important contributions to Columbus' explorations. They had dugout canoes and knew their waters very well. Their instructions led Columbus from island to island and eventually, just as they had said, to very large islands farther south and west. They also described islands of the Lesser Antilles farther south through sign language and "sketched" charts with beans as islands. These proved extremely useful to Columbus on this and later voyages.

At sea, the men thought only of land; once on land, they seemed to mainly think about finding gold. After navigating the shallows of the Bahamas – an admirable feat for a captain without detailed charts and ships that drew two meters of water – the fleet sailed on to **Cuba**, and then to an island Columbus named *La Isla Española* (today's Hispaniola, shared by Haiti and the Dominican Republic). Along the way, they made repeated, mostly peaceful, contact with indigenous people. Columbus was furious when the captain of the *Pinta*, **Martin Alonso Pinzon**, disobeyed orders and sailed away to Great Inagua

Island, following up on rumors of gold. He soon was to cause Columbus more headaches.

Columbus thought he was in Asia and interpreted everything accordingly. Place names, like Cibao (the central part of Hispaniola), sounded close enough to Cipango (Japan) to him, and he assumed that many plants were Oriental spices such as cinnamon even when they were oddly different. At the same time, he did notice certain unique local goods, such as **tobacco** (unknown at that time outside the Americas) and **hammocks**, which soon became an important piece of sailor's kit throughout the world.

Ironically, after sailing safely across an unknown ocean and countless shoals, the *Santa Maria* ran onto a reef off Hispaniola on Christmas night. In calm conditions, the tired helmsman let a ship's boy take the wheel, and in the darkness, they went aground. The ship could not be saved. Local **Taino** people (another branch of the Arawak language group) helped the crew save everything they could. Columbus, an extremely religious man, took this as a sign that God wanted him to establish a settlement at this location. Thirty volunteers, tempted by the promise of gold around every corner, stayed to man the new fort called ***La Navidad***. The *Niña*, now with Columbus and extra crew aboard, headed back to Spain with news of their incredible feat. By chance, they encountered renegade Captain Pinzon aboard the *Pinta* and continued on together.

Their return journey, starting at the height of winter on January 16, was to be much more difficult than the outgoing trip. Columbus turned his ships north until they reached westerly winds to bring them back to Spain. However, a series of terrible **storms** separated the ships and had the crew praying for their lives. Columbus even wrote a summary of his discovery and threw it overboard in a cask; in the event of sinking, he was desperate that someone find out about his great achievement.

The *Niña* and her crew survived the storms and eventually stopped on the island of Santa Maria in the **Azores** in mid-February. As if he had not already been tested enough, Columbus now had the problem that half of his company were jailed when they went ashore the Portuguese-owned island to go to church! He did manage to clear this up and sail on, but encountered yet another violent storm that nearly pushed the Niña against a dangerous section of the Portuguese coast. Columbus made another emergency stop in Lisbon, and eventually sailed on to Palos in Spain.

Martin Pinzon and the *Pinta* had arrived in Spain just before Columbus. As first to arrive, he had the chance to upstage Columbus. Pinzon tried to see the King and Queen first, but they refused him an audience and waited for Columbus. Pinzon, disappointed and ill from the difficult journey, died within a month. Columbus made quite a splash with his parade of tropical birds, Taino natives,[3] and samples of gold. He had earned his title of Admiral of the Ocean Sea and proven his many critics wrong. He was sure he had opened the door to Oriental riches for the Queen and King of Spain. In fact, he had discovered a **New World**, though no one yet suspected it. This is evident in the fact that the monarchs were willing to give him power over all new lands he discovered – if they had suspected a huge new continent rich in natural resources, they never would have been so generous!

Columbus' discovery was to bring many riches to Spain but many changes to the known world as well, many of them tragic for the people and creatures of the Americas. It was not long before Columbus was planning his next ocean crossing.

PART 2 ACTIVITY & ASSIGNMENT

Activity: Dead reckoning. Columbus' primary means of navigation was dead reckoning (DR). He plotted the course steered (using magnetic headings, not corrected true headings) over the distance he estimated his ship traveled. Do this with your own positions over a period of time and see how your DR position and actual position compare. Then list other factors that influence a boat's movement over the sea that DR does not consider.

---

[3] Accounts differ, but it seems that about ten Taino went to Spain with Columbus. Few, if any, went voluntarily, and not all survived the journey. Others returned to the Caribbean on Columbus' second journey.

Assignment: Make a collage, comic strip, or other artwork depicting Columbus' first journey, or another series of significant events relating to the Age of Discovery.

Part 3: Columbus' Subsequent Voyages

With his 1492 voyage, Columbus discovered much about the Ocean Sea. It is true that **Vikings** had already crossed the ocean five hundred years before Columbus; however, they did not spread news of their discoveries or maintain contact with the new world. The Viking settlement in **Vinland** (today's Newfoundland) was eventually abandoned and forgotten. In contrast, news of Columbus' route west spread quickly. A summary of his trip was published and sold widely, so that people throughout western Europe could read his amazing story. It is in one of these publications that his name was written as Columbus instead of Colombo or Colon.

Let us return to the simple rhyme: *In 1492, Columbus sailed the ocean blue.* Popular history seems to leave his travels at that. In fact, Columbus sailed on three more voyages. These journeys are equally interesting and had a great impact on the New World, which was to be explored, colonized, and exploited at an incredible pace.

THE SECOND VOYAGE, 1493-1496

The Spanish King and Queen wasted no time in financing a second voyage, of totally different character and size. This time Columbus commanded seventeen ships filled with soldiers, priests, settlers – over 1,000 men – in addition to livestock, ready to open the new land for their own use. Europeans were coming to the Americas for good.

After departing Hierro in the **Canary Islands** in October 1493, Columbus took a more southerly course than he did before – exactly the route followed by modern sailors. Remarkably, he took only twenty-one days to cross the Atlantic, comparable to the speed of many modern sailing vessels. More amazing still, he arrived just where he had wanted: in sight of **Dominica** and **Guadeloupe** in the Leeward Islands. The Lucayo had informed him well about which Caribbean islands lay farthest east!

Route of Columbus' Second Voyage

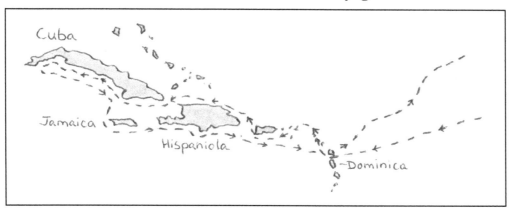

Columbus followed the chain of islands north, naming them as he went. Guadeloupe was named for the church in which he had prayed before his departure in Spain, Antigua for a portrait of the Virgin Mary, and another island for his patron, Saint Christopher (the name of this island is now shortened to St. Kitts). This was probably the zenith of Columbus' happy days as a sailor, leader, and explorer, because a long series of setbacks and failures was soon to set in.

Arriving on Hispaniola in late November, Columbus and his men were shocked to find the small settlement of La Navidad burned, with none of the settlers in sight. Soon dead bodies were found and the local chief, who had been friendly to Columbus in 1492, filled in the details. The Spanish settlers had quickly fallen to fighting among themselves, lost the trust of the locals with their demands, and fought with another group of inland natives who killed them all. Columbus abandoned the site and built a new settlement, **La Isabela**, farther east. The idea was not so much to establish a new colony for Spaniards to move to, but rather a **trading post** where they could get gold and other valuable Oriental goods.

Columbus left most of the men and supplies to set up La Isabela while he continued his explorations with three ships. They explored the south coast of Cuba and **Jamaica**, chasing rumors of gold but mostly finding dangerous shoals and sometimes, hostile natives. Eventually, Columbus returned to La Isabela, where he had the difficult job of governing an unruly group of settlers. Many of the Spanish men were unwilling to work hard to make their venture a success and resented Columbus' position as Viceroy (a position with local powers of a king). Conflicts with the locals intensified, gold was slow to flow, and supplies were running low. After a difficult year at La Isabela, Columbus returned to Spain in 1496 to seek more help.

THE THIRD VOYAGE, 1498-1500

Columbus was to experience new lows during and after his third voyage. Three ships sailed directly to La Isabela with supplies, while three others, led by Columbus, set off on further explorations. After all, they had still not found the Orient itself.

Columbus sailed farther south than ever before, calling first at the well known **Cape Verde Islands** (off the African coast) before turning west for the Caribbean. The fleet made a fast passage and landfall in **Trinidad**. While exploring the Gulf of Paria, Columbus thought that the coast in sight was another large island. In fact, it was the continent of South America. Suffering from poor health, Columbus eventually turned north for Hispaniola. He sailed directly across the Caribbean Sea and arrived in Hispaniola almost exactly as intended. Consider what a navigational feat this was! Using only dead reckoning, Columbus connected two separate ends of a chart that he was essentially drawing as he sailed, again covering completely unknown waters and drawing on his faith in himself to reach his chosen destination.

Few celebrated his return. The poor location of La Isabela had been abandoned and a new trading post, Santo Domingo, had been established under the leadership of Columbus' brother, Bartholomeo. However, life there proved no easier than at La Isabela. Soon, Columbus was dealing with a **revolt** of Spanish settlers who resented his leadership. A new governor (Francisco de Bobadilla) arrived from Spain to take over. Bobadilla immediately exercised his new powers by **arresting** Columbus and sending him back to Spain, humiliated.

Route of Columbus' Third Voyage

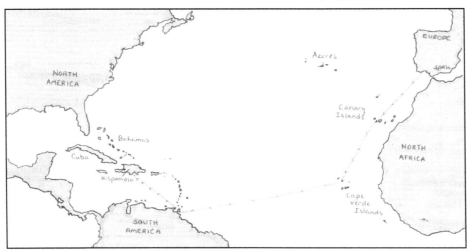

Luckily, Queen Isabella proved a faithful supporter of Columbus and immediately freed him. She even allowed him to keep his grand titles, but, recognizing his weaknesses as a colonial leader, these were now empty of any power. Other people would govern the lands he found; other sailors would explore the new coasts he had discovered. However, Columbus was not ready to give up, and managed to convince the crown to finance his fourth, and final, voyage.

THE FOURTH VOYAGE, 1502-1504

Columbus, aging and humiliated, was determined to finally find a way through his "Indies" to the Indian Ocean. It was to be an incredible voyage of misadventure and survival. Setting out with four ships from Cadiz in 1502, Columbus made a quick twenty-one day crossing to Martinique and retraced the steps of his second voyage along the Lesser Antilles to the colony at Santo Domingo.

Columbus' vast experience and keen powers of observation told him that a **hurricane** was approaching. However, the new governor of Santo Domingo ignored his warnings and even refused Columbus entry to the port! In spite of Columbus' forecast, a fleet of thirty ships left port at the end of June, loaded with gold and goods for Spain. Columbus' ships weathered the hurricane well in a nearby river, but more than twenty ships of the treasure fleet were sunk with the loss of all their gold and hundreds of lives (among them, Columbus' old enemy, Bobadilla).

Route of Columbus' Fourth Voyage

Soon, Columbus set off again to look for his route to the west. His ships sailed first along Hispaniola, Jamaica, and Cuba, before moving farther west and making the first European sighting of **Central America** in today's Honduras and then **Panama**, fighting headwinds most of the way. Again, Columbus learned a valuable piece of information from natives. They told him that another ocean lay just over the mountains at this narrow isthmus. Still, Columbus imagined himself to be somewhere on the edge of Asia and did not understand the importance of this information. He sailed on and missed the chance to "discover" the Pacific Ocean and establish the Americas as continents.[4]

As always, the Spanish fleet was guided by its lust for gold, and in a region of Panama they named Veragua, they saw plenty of it. Eager to find its source, Columbus established a base in the Rio Belen, another poor location. Repeating the same cycle of earlier voyages, relations with the locals again turned bad

---

[4] Perhaps Columbus also missed his chance to have this new continent named after him. Instead, it took the name of Amerigo Vespucci, an Italian mapmaker who sailed to the Gulf of Paria with another expedition. After his work was published, many Europeans attached the name "Amerigo" and eventually "America" to the continents.

and after several months of trouble, a large number of natives made a coordinated attack on the Spaniards. One ship was abandoned, along with the doomed fort, and Columbus retreated back to Santo Domingo, once again short of achieving his goal.

The remaining three ships were in terrible condition and leaking badly from the attack of their other enemy: **teredo shipworms** which bored into the wooden ships like termites. One of the ships sank at sea and her men were taken aboard the remaining two. After another storm and desperate pumping, Columbus was forced to beach his sorry fleet in St. Anne's Bay, Jamaica. They were **marooned**.

One of his men set off in a native canoe and made the dangerous open water passage to Santo Domingo, a brave and incredible feat. However, he was jailed by the unfriendly governor and delayed for over a year! On Jamaica, Columbus again struggled with an unruly crew and clashes with locals. One can only imagine what a humbling, desperate time this must have been for the Admiral of the Ocean Sea. Eventually rescued, Columbus returned to Spain in 1504. He died two years later, never recognizing that his explorations had paved the way to a new continent.

PART 3 ACTIVITY & ASSIGNMENT

Activity: Students should plot Columbus' trips on a chart along with their own route. Do the trails ever intersect? Student can also study the geography of the area around them. What continents, seas, and islands are important? Can the student imagine sailing without a chart?

Assignment: Which of Columbus' voyages do you find most interesting? Students should write an essay or create an artwork that covers the major points of that voyage and the reasons why it is interesting to them.

Part 4: Consequences of Columbus' Voyages

We often say that Columbus discovered America, but of course he only discovered it for Europe. The original discoverers were people who made their way across the Bering Strait from Asia thousands of years earlier. With the arrival of Columbus and mass European colonialism, their continent was changed forever.

Within a few years of Columbus' voyages, explorers forced their way across the Americas, recognizing they were on a new continent and taking its resources for themselves and their kings. Giovanni Caboto (John Cabot) opened North America to his English sponsors in 1497. In 1500, explorer Pedro Cabral "discovered" Brazil and claimed it for Portugal. Vasco Nuñez de Balboa crossed Panama in 1513 to become the first European to sight the Pacific Ocean from the Americas. Hernan Cortez conquered the Aztecs of Mexico in 1521; in 1533, Francisco Pizarro killed the Incan Emperor, bringing that South American civilization to a sudden end.

Columbus said that the natives he encountered were mostly peaceful people living in a simple state as if in the Garden of Eden. However, Spanish efforts to take over the land and convert the indigenous people to Christianity quickly made their world into something more like hell. Together with the fierce **Carib** people, the Taino lost their land, were forced into slavery, and even actively hunted. (Lucayo, Taino, and Carib are all different groups of native people, together part of the broader Arawak group, inhabiting the Caribbean and the Bahamas at the time of Columbus' journeys.) Those who escaped direct violence – even natives who never saw a European – suffered from **diseases** like measles and smallpox brought by the Spaniards. Within fifty years, the native population of Hispaniola went from an estimated 250,000 to only five hundred. One priest, **Bartolomé de Las Casas**, chronicled the tragic decline of native populations and fought for human rights reforms, but it was too late (see *Resources*). The Taino / Arawak natives were nearly "extinct."

Land not taken by the Spanish was soon claimed by the Portuguese, English, and French. They looked beyond gold to **plantation agriculture** and eventually turned the Caribbean into a massive sugar factory. Because the declining populations of native people were unsuited for such work, the Europeans brought in a new labor force: **African slaves**. We sailors who explore the Caribbean today see a completely different population from the one originally occupying the area. An entire race was replaced by another, who developed a new, unique culture of their own, with African roots and Caribbean adaptations.

On most islands, the only reminders of native peoples are rock carvings. One exception can be found on the island of Dominica, where hardy Caribs (properly known as **Kalinago**) took refuge in the mountains and survived. Today, the Kalinago Cultural Center allows visitors a rare view into this culture. Another surviving group, the "**Black Caribs**" of St. Vincent (so named after the population mixed with escaped slaves) were forcibly relocated to the Honduran island of Roatan in 1797.

Columbus' second and subsequent voyages introduced European livestock and seeds to the New World: these began their own attacks on native populations. Countless species went extinct or became endangered as a result of the intruders. Huge areas of native forest were lost to farmland. **Environmental issues** we discuss today (extinction, introduced species running out of control, overuse of natural resources) are nothing new. Interestingly, one European import – the horse – was quickly embraced on the mainland by North American tribes.

The New World had its imports to Europe as well. Corn and potatoes were brought back, and the latter became an important part of the European diet. Other imports from the New World were unwelcome, such as the disease syphilis. The unhealthy habit of smoking tobacco quickly spread in the Old World, as well.

Another consequence of Columbus' voyage was its importance for sailors like us. Columbus pioneered a new, optimal route across the open sea, which many of us follow and enjoy today, sailing in the wake of history.

COLUMBUS: HERO OR VILLAIN?

For many years, Columbus' story was told in heroic terms. Since 1889, the United States has celebrated Columbus Day as a national holiday. More recently, different points of view have created a more mixed portrait of Columbus and the impact of his voyages. 1492 was an exciting starting point for Europeans, but it was the beginning of the end from the indigenous point of view.

Columbus was an enterprising and adventurous man whose vision allowed him to accomplish what no one dared try before. Many of his decisions and conclusions were based on his **religious beliefs**. Columbus wanted to convert natives to Christianity while promoting their exploitation as a work force. Although this may seem contradictory to us today, it is consistent with the era in which he lived.

Columbus set into motion an unstoppable series of events with terrible, tragic consequences not only for the native people of the Americas, but also for the African slave force eventually brought in to support colonization. He did not set out to purposely steal or kill, but those were some consequences of his actions. It is known that Columbus personally dealt in **slavery** in 1496, when he sent three hundred natives to be sold in Spain. However, Queen Isabella objected to slavery and returned those people to the Caribbean. Spain did support a system of ***encomiendas***, in which a Spaniard would be given rights over certain natives, from whom he could demand labor or goods, while teaching them Spanish and converting them to Christianity.

Was Columbus a hero or a villain? You will have to decide for yourself.

PART 4 ACTIVITY & ASSIGNMENT

Activity: Students should create a list, diagram, or artwork that depicts the different groups of people, creatures, and lands affected by Columbus' discoveries. They should think about people and the environment on both sides of the Atlantic. Alternatively, students can search maps to find as many places named for Columbus (or versions of his name) as possible.

Assignment: Go back to the simple rhyme we started with: *In 1492, Columbus sailed the ocean blue*. Students have learned that there is much more to his story than that. Now they should write more lines to complete the rhyme and make it more correctly reflect Columbus' impact on world history, positive and negative.

Age-Appropriate Adaptations

In this section, you will find guidance on how to differentiate, or adapt, this unit for your child. Start with the correct age group, but also glance through the notes for one level younger or older, then mix and match as appropriate.

The text of this unit can be simplified for young children. Parents can first read through it themselves and mark with a highlighter those passages they will read aloud or the passages that their children can read.

Self-assessment and reflection are valuable learning tools. They encourage students to think back upon their work and store their new body of knowledge in a meaningful and memorable manner. To that end, a number of self-assessment and reflection questions are listed for each age group. It is not necessary to address all the questions; substitute others as you see fit. Completed assignments and written reflection are useful records to later document student work for a school administration.

Ages 4-6

Young students can do much of the suggested work in some form, but be selective in what you undertake. At this age, the most important concepts to reinforce are the basics of Columbus' explorations, and the fact that history has more than one side. Suggestions for adapting the activities and assignments are listed here. All written assignments should be converted to verbal or role-playing activities.

Part 1 Assignment: *Write a persuasive letter from Columbus to Portugal's King Juan II.* Obviously there is no need for any written work at this level. However, young students could have fun and reinforce what they have learned by role-playing Columbus' meeting with King Juan II in 1484. They might try one polite and one demanding version of the same exchange.
Part 2 Activity: *Practice dead reckoning.* If preschool students are to attempt this activity at all, it should be in extremely simplified form. Using a sheet of graph paper and a sketch of the cardinal directions, dictate a series of moves to your child. For example, what if our boat sailed south three boxes, then west ten boxes, etc. Where would we be then? Parents can draw a rough sketch of

the boat's geographic area on the paper and have their children advance the boat toward the destination, keeping to the simplest directions possible (whole numbers and basic north/south/west/east steps only).

Part 2 Assignment: *Make a collage or comic strip depicting Columbus' first journey.* Parents can help students select one episode to represent through the art form of their choice.

Part 3 Activity: *Plot Columbus' trips on a chart along with your own.* Young children can simply trace and color the map provided and add their own route, perhaps connecting dots provided by parents. This exercise will reinforce the geography of your own trip in the child's mind.

Part 3 Assignment: *Which of Columbus' voyages do you find most interesting?* One might add, which voyage would the student most like to be a part of and why? This assignment could be carried out verbally or in the form of an art project.

Part 4 Activity: *Create a list, diagram, or artwork that depicts the different groups of people, creatures, and lands affected by Columbus' discoveries* or *Search maps to find Columbus-related place names.* This age group can omit this activity or do the Columbus name search with parental guidance.

Part 4 Assignment: *Extend the rhyme: In 1492, Columbus sailed the ocean blue.* Young children develop their language skills through rhymes, so challenge them to find words that rhyme with *blue* and see if you can come up with any more lines, no matter how silly or off topic they may be!

Self-Assessment and Reflection: Students should review any artwork produced. Ask students what the art represents about this chapter in history, and then pose questions such as:
- *Are you pleased with the results of your work? Be specific.*
- *How did you achieve what you did?*
- *What did you do especially well? What could you have done better?*
- *What do you have in common with sailors like Columbus? What are your differences?*

Ages 6-8

Young students can do most of the activities and assignments in this unit in modified form. The most important concepts to reinforce are the basics of Columbus' explorations, and the fact that every story has more than one side. Written assignments can be converted to verbal or role-playing activities, or they could be attempted in list or bullet-point form completed with guidance.

You can work through the text through a combination of an adult reading passages aloud, together with the child reading selected sections. The reading will go smoothly if you highlight which sections each reader should speak, the parent's part in one color and the student's in another. You may find it necessary to simplify the text or omit some passages.

Part 1 Assignment: *Write a persuasive letter from Columbus to Portugal's King Juan II.* Students in this age group could prepare a list of important points and role-play the encounter between Columbus and King Juan II. More advanced students might use letter format. They could try one polite and one demanding version of the same message.

Part 2 Activity: *Practice dead reckoning.* Students ages six to eight should be ready to work with basic or combined cardinal directions (northwest, SSE, etc). The most advanced children of this age bracket might be ready to work with 360° courses. It is unlikely that they will have much appreciation for the concept of true versus magnetic courses or other factors that affect the movement of a boat over the sea.

Part 2 Assignment: *Make a collage or comic strip depicting Columbus' first journey.* Students should create a series of images to represent Columbus' first journey.

Part 3 Activity: *Plot Columbus' trips on a chart along with your own.* Point out and define geographic features such as continents, islands, peninsulas, etc. Discuss the idea of the Ocean Sea and look at a modern world map. Roughly sketch the route of Columbus' trips onto relevant sections of your chart. Imagine his thoughts as he explored new lands. Do you ever intersect his course?

This exercise will help reinforce your own trip in your child's mind as well as support the history lesson.

Part 3 Assignment: *Which of Columbus' voyages do you find most interesting and why?* This assignment could be carried out verbally or in the form of an art project after reading Part 3. One might add: If you had a time machine, which voyage would you most like to be a part of? Why?

Part 4 Activity: *Create a list, diagram, or artwork that depicts the different groups of people, creatures, and lands affected by Columbus' discoveries* or *Search maps to find Columbus-related place names.* The latter activity is well suited to this age group and will build their understanding of geography. However, they can also choose the first option. With parental guidance, students can create a basic list, diagram, or artwork that depicts the different groups of people, creatures, and lands affected by Columbus' discoveries. Whether the list is thorough or not, the important point to consider is how different cultures met and how they influenced each other and the landscape. This age group will probably focus most on changes in the New World.

Part 4 Assignment: *Extend the rhyme: In 1492, Columbus sailed the ocean blue.* Young children develop their language skills through rhymes, so challenge them to find words that rhyme with *blue* and see if you can come up with any more lines. Allow silly or off topic rhymes but also work together to try to add a line or two that is appropriate to the subject.

Self-Assessment and Reflection: Conduct a short discussion in which the student looks back on the various activities and assignments. Think about:
- *Which assignments were difficult (or easy)? Why?*
- *Was there something that was difficult at first that you can now do more easily?*
- *How did you overcome any difficulties?*
- *How is your voyage like Columbus'? How is it different?*

Ages 8-10

A summary of tasks for this age group is listed in bold below. This age group can do most of the activities and assignments without major modifications.

Assignments should take a range of forms, from written work to role-playing and artwork. Children in this age group should be able to read much of the text with minimal aid. Still, it is good practice to provide different deliveries of the text: some sections could be read independently, while others can be read aloud by the student to the parent, or vice versa. It may be necessary to simplify the text or omit more elaborate passages.

Part 1 Assignment: *Write a persuasive letter from Columbus to Portugal's King Juan II.* Students could prepare a list of important points and then draft a formal letter. They could try one polite and one demanding version of the same exchange.

Part 2 Activity: *Practice dead reckoning.* This age group should work with plotting 360° courses. They can be introduced to the concept of true versus magnetic compass course and sketch examples to compare how the difference diverges over long distances (depending on one's position on the globe). Discuss other factors that affect the movement of a boat over the sea.

Part 2 Assignment: *Make a collage or comic strip depicting Columbus' first journey.* Students should create a series of images to represent Columbus' first journey, from finding a royal sponsor to his return with news of his discoveries.

Part 3 Activity: *Plot Columbus' trips on a chart along with your own.* Define geographic features such as continents, islands, peninsulas, etc. Discuss the idea of the Ocean Sea and look at a modern world chart. Sketch the route of Columbus' trips onto relevant sections of your chart. Do you ever intersect his course? Using our modern knowledge of prevailing wind and currents, examine Columbus' routing. Should he have chosen a different course if he had this knowledge? This exercise will reinforce your own trip in your child's mind as well as reinforce important aspects of history and geography.

Part 3 Assignment: *Which of Columbus' voyages do you find most interesting and why?* Students should write an essay or create artwork that covers the major points of that voyage and the reasons why it is interesting. They can change "most interesting" to "most adventurous" or "most difficult." If the student had a time machine, which voyage would she most like to be a part of? Why?

Part 4 Activity: *Create a list, diagram, or artwork that depicts the different groups of people, creatures, and lands affected by Columbus' discoveries* or *Search maps to find Columbus-related place names.* Students should create a diagram or artwork and refer back to the text, an important study skill. Encourage students to complete a second draft that is neat and clear. Students should consider people and the environment on both sides of the Atlantic.

Part 4 Assignment: *Extend the rhyme: In 1492, Columbus sailed the ocean blue.* Challenge students to find words that rhyme with *blue* and see if they can come up with any more lines. Even if they can't make a rhyme, try adding lyrical lines. Try to pinpoint or summarize an important aspect of Columbus' explorations and then apply this to the rhyme.

Self-Assessment and Reflection: Written reflection is appropriate for this age group although students will need prompting to elaborate. Pose questions such as:

- *Which assignment did you enjoy the most (or least)? Why?*
- *Was there something you did incorrectly at first and later did better?*
- *What advice would you give another student doing the same exercise?*
- *What resources did you have available to you? Which was the most useful? Why?*
- *How is your voyage like Columbus'? How is it different?*

Ages 10-12

These "oldest" students can work through the challenges in the above assignment in full. Assignments should take a range of forms, from written work to role-playing and artwork. If the student expresses a particular interest or proposes a different activity, follow it by all means! Students ages ten to twelve will be able to read the text independently. Still, it is good practice to provide different deliveries of the text: some sections could be read independently, while others can be read aloud by the student to the parent, or vice versa.

Part 1 Assignment: *Write a persuasive letter from Columbus to Portugal's King Juan II.* Students in this age group should prepare a list of important points and then draft a formal letter. They should be very thorough in their reasoning and include evidence (in as far as Columbus believed he had evidence) to support their proposals. When listing what Columbus seeks as a reward, be careful lest King Juan II again turn down the proposal!

Part 2 Activity: *Practice dead reckoning.* Students can learn about true and magnetic compass courses and sketch examples to compare how the difference can diverge over long distances. They can plot exact courses on a chart and consider other factors that affect the movement of a boat over the sea. Very advanced students might enjoy the challenge of factoring leeway, tides, or currents into their chart work.

Part 2 Assignment: *Make a collage or comic strip depicting Columbus' first journey.* Students should create an extended series of images to represent Columbus' first journey, from finding a royal sponsor to his return with news of his discoveries.

Part 3 Activity: *Plot Columbus' trips on a chart along with your own.* Help students define geographic features such as continent, island, peninsula, gulf, bay, etc. Discuss the idea of the Ocean Sea and look at a modern world chart. Sketch the route of Columbus' trips onto relevant sections of your chart. Do you ever intersect his course? Using our modern knowledge of prevailing wind and currents, examine Columbus' routing. Should he have chosen a different course? Which sections of his voyages can be considered perfectly routed, according to modern knowledge? This exercise will reinforce your own trip in your child's mind as well as reinforce important aspects of history and geography.

Part 3 Assignment: *Which of Columbus' voyages do you find most interesting and why?* Students should write a thorough essay or create a well-developed piece of artwork that covers the major points of that voyage and the reasons why it is interesting. Students can change "most interesting" to "most adventurous" or "most difficult." Essay writing should be approached very seriously by this age group. Challenge students to produce a thorough and detailed response, always supporting statements with reasons. Guide them through good essay format, from an introductory statement ("There are many different sides to a historical story…") to supporting statements, and finally a conclusion.

Part 4 Activity: *Create a list, diagram, or artwork that depicts the different groups of people, creatures, and lands affected by Columbus' discoveries* or *Search maps to find Columbus-related place names.* Students should create a diagram or artwork and refer back to the text for information, an important study skill. The assignment should consider people and the environment on both sides of the Atlantic. Students should sketch a first draft of their intended format and then complete a more polished second draft. The second activity is simplistic for this age group but is still fun and useful in building a sense of geography.

Part 4 Assignment: *Extend the rhyme: In 1492, Columbus sailed the ocean blue.* Challenge students to find words that rhyme with *blue* and try to add more lines. Even if they can't make a rhyme, try adding lyrical lines. Try to pinpoint or summarize an important aspect of Columbus' explorations and then apply this to the rhyme.

Self-Assessment and Reflection: Students should make a written statement analyzing their own work.
  - *Which assignment did you enjoy the most, and why? The least?*
  - *Was there something you did incorrectly at first and later did better?*
  - *Which assignment did you complete best? Why?*
  - *What advice would you give another student?*
  - *What resources did you have available to you? Which was the most useful, and why?*
  - *What do you have in common with explorers like Columbus? What are your differences?*

Enrichment

If the many activities and assignments above are not enough for you, consider extending the learning experience in one of the following ways:

  - Visit a place related to Columbus and create a **photo essay** about it. How does the site fit in to what you have learned?

- Research **native people** of the Caribbean and Americas, or another area of your choice. What were the similarities or differences between the Lucayo, Taino, and Carib groups?
- Follow up on other **explorers** who sailed in Columbus' wake.
- Study the life of **Bartolomé de Las Casas**.
- Research the **Atlantic Slave Trade**.
- Do a research project focusing on the early European **settlers** of the Caribbean or another area. What brought them to the New World? What was life like for them?

Cross-Curricular Links

This unit connects well with *Unit 9*: *Navigation with Map and Compass*. The handcraft projects (Part 2 assignment, Part 4 Activity) suggested could be expanded for a greater emphasis on **art** and several of the assignments tie in to **writing** skills. One interesting way to link this subject to *Unit 1: Science* (the lunar cycle and model eclipses) is to study an episode of Columbus' fourth journey in February 1504. When marooned in Jamaica, Columbus managed to extort an ongoing food supply from the unwilling natives, thanks to a lunar eclipse. Knowing a total eclipse of the moon was to occur, Columbus told the natives that it was a sign from God, ordering them to feed their Spanish visitors, or else!

Resources

Samuel Eliot Morison is one of the leading authorities on Columbus and has written several biographies. The most practical for advanced students is *Christopher Columbus: Mariner* which is concise yet thorough. Morison re-created parts of Columbus' voyages in sailboats; he examines the historical evidence from the point of view of a sailor. His book was first published in 1942 and has gone through several printings.

Another Columbus enthusiast is Keith Pickering whose easy-to-use website provides a good introduction to the explorer, his voyages, and his means of navigation (www.columbusnavigtion.com). A translation of sections of

Columbus' 1492 log can be found at: http://www.franciscan-archive.org/columbus/opera/excerpts.html.

To research later explorers such as Balboa, start at www.win.tue.nl/cs/fm/engels/discovery, which contains a database of basic facts alphabetized by explorer. Those interested in furthering their studies of native Caribbean people can look at: www.centrelink.org/Cultures.html. This site is sympathetic to the perspective of indigenous people and will guide you to many further links on indigenous people and issues.

Bartolomé de Las Casas, a priest who argued for better conditions and treatment of native people in the 1500s, could be called the first human rights activist in the New World. A study of his life and work would broaden a student's understanding of the Spanish colonial era: http://www.lascasas.org.

Unit 8 - History: The Voyages of Captain Cook

According to the old proverb a miss is as good as a mile, but our situation requires more misses than we can expect...

Captain James Cook

Dedicated to the children of the world who sail in uncharted waters, explore new horizons, and in the joy of these moments improve the lot of all mankind. Such a man was Captain Cook.

Walter J. Hickel
Cook Monument inscription
Anchorage, Alaska

Unit 8 - History: The Voyages of Captain Cook

Materials:
- Writing and art materials
- Planet finder (see *Resources*)

Guiding Questions:
What makes Captain Cook stand out among many distinguished explorers?
What was the historical backdrop to Cook's explorations in the Pacific?

Learning Outcomes:
Students will be able to describe the historical context of Captain Cook's voyages, as well as the contributions he made to navigation and science.

Introduction

Soon after Christopher Columbus opened an Age of Discovery on land and at sea, Europeans were exploring the Americas and boldly edging out into the vast Pacific. Even 250 years after landmark voyages like Magellan's circumnavigation, however, the Pacific was still a great unknown. This all changed thanks to Captain Cook. He was the first to accurately chart huge areas of the Pacific in three epic voyages. An outstanding sailor, navigator, and surveyor, he might be the only sailor to have ever used the expression "a gentle gale." Unlike many other early explorers, Cook generally showed curiosity and respect for the native people he met, in addition to genuine concern for his crew. He left an important legacy through new methods to prevent scurvy, an illness that regularly killed as many as half the crew members of ocean-going ships at that time. From humble beginnings to hero of a nation, Cook truly is a fascinating figure.

Unit Overview

This unit is divided into five parts, each with a corresponding activity or assignment. The *Introduction* follows Cook's transition from country boy to accomplished naval officer and establishes the historical context of the era. Parts 1, 2, and 3 describe his expeditions throughout the Pacific, material that could fill a trilogy of Hollywood action films with near misses and exotic locations. Part 4 summarizes Cook's lasting legacies in many fields. This unit is written with fairly advanced vocabulary. For very young children, parents can summarize and retell each section in a series of exciting adventure stories while the student follows along on a map or picture book. Older students can read part or all of the text themselves over the course of several sessions. This unit may be summarized for a more compact approach, or take as much as a month of in-depth study.

Introduction: James Cook - The Man and his Times

James Cook was born in the Yorkshire countryside of England in 1728, not in a seaside town as one might expect. Thanks to diligence and hard work – plus a bit of luck – he rose from humble apprentice to naval captain and went on to leave his mark not only in England but far, far beyond. Cook had the fortune to be born during an exciting, if dangerous, era: a time of exploration, territorial conflicts, and war, as well as an era of scientific inquiry known as the Enlightenment.

FROM THE COUNTRYSIDE TO THE SEA

In a time when naval officers usually came from aristocratic families, it is amazing to consider that James Cook was born to a family of simple laborers who worked the land of a local estate owner. This generous lord recognized young Cook's potential and paid for his schooling. At age sixteen, James Cook moved to a seaside village to apprentice to a shopkeeper. However, he found more interest in the sea, and at eighteen went on to a new apprenticeship under a ship owner in the coastal town of Whitby. Cook quickly learned seamanship and navigation on coal-carrying ships called *cats*. Eventually, Cook was offered the command of a ship, but he turned it down. Instead, he took the unusual step of joining the navy at the advanced age of twenty-seven to satisfy his ambition of sailing the world.

A WORLD OF OPPORTUNITY: COOK'S RISE THROUGH THE RANKS

The European nations of the mid-1700's were in a power struggle for **resource-rich territories** like North America, where England and France vied for control. Other regions, such as the far reaches of the Pacific, were still largely unclaimed, and Spain, Portugal, Holland, and Russia also had aspirations there. This historical setting offered incredible opportunities for a skilled and ambitious sailor like James Cook.

Although he had to start at the bottom of the ranks in the navy, Cook advanced to the position of master (chief navigator capable of taking command) in only two years. Cook learned the mathematics needed for accurate map-making and navigation, putting this to use when assigned to Canada's east coast. Cook immediately established a reputation as an excellent map maker. The charts he drew, as well as his observations of a **solar eclipse** in Newfoundland in 1766, made a great impression among both naval and scientific leaders in England.

Cook also experienced first-hand the terrible effects of **scurvy**. This malady is caused by lack of vitamin C (found in fresh fruit) and sets in after about six weeks at sea. It was common for as many as half a ship's crew to die of scurvy on long ocean voyages. One ship Cook sailed on lost twenty-six men on a single passage. At that time, scurvy was as great an obstacle to ocean exploration as violent storms, dangerous coastlines, and tropical diseases.

As Cook was rising through the ranks, England's naval ambitions faced three challenges: there were navigation methods to be improved, lands to be claimed ahead of rivals, and problems like scurvy to be overcome. At the same time, the **Age of Enlightenment** set in motion a desire to understand the natural world through science. The stage was set for a grand undertaking, and James Cook was the right man in the right place and the right time.

The **Royal Society**, England's scholarly elite, proposed a naval expedition to observe the **transit of Venus** across the face of the sun in June 1769. Measurements of the event would help determine distances in our solar system, so astronomers were dispatched to various points of the globe to observe the once-in-a-century event. Cook was promoted to the rank of Lieutenant, given command of the ninety-seven foot ***Endeavour***, and entrusted with the mission to observe the transit of Venus from Tahiti, as well as to map new lands. It was an audacious voyage that was to extend over three years. Tahiti was known from Captain Samuel Wallis' 1767 journey in the *Dolphin* just a few years earlier, and New Zealand had been spotted briefly by Dutchman Abel Tasman a century before – but little else was known of the world's largest ocean.

INTRODUCTION ASSIGNMENT: WRITE A PERSUASIVE LETTER

Students should imagine that they are the young James Cook and write a persuasive letter to his parents explaining the reasons for giving up his good position commanding coal ships to start all over again in the navy. The letter should list the skills Cook had learned to that point as well as the exciting opportunities the navy opened to an able sailor like himself.

Part 1: Cook's First Voyage, 1768-1771

The *Endeavour* departed England in August 1768, crowded with ninety-four sailors and "gentlemen" like wealthy scientist **Joseph Banks** (who brought four servants and two dogs), Swedish scientist Doctor Daniel Carl Solander, and young artists **Sydney Parkinson** and Alexander Buchan. The latter were along to record the landscapes, people, plants, and animals of the exotic lands ahead of them. After a layover in Brazil, Cook continued his westabout circumnavigation via **Cape Horn**, entering the Pacific in January 1769.

At every stop, Banks, Solander, and the artists would hike the countryside looking for new species while Cook and Charles Green, an astronomer, unloaded their measuring equipment to take celestial sights, establish accurate positions, and carefully chart every coast. They had telescopes, a sextant, an astronomical quadrant, a barometer, and two clocks to be used in timing the transit of Venus (not, however, for practical use in navigation).

To supplement the usual **diet** of biscuits and salted beef, Cook had his men eat sauerkraut, salted cabbage, or broth cakes to prevent scurvy. Sauerkraut was so despised by the crew that some had to be forced to eat it – sometimes by being whipped! Cook also ran a very clean ship, insisting that the men wash their clothes and scrub and air the lower decks regularly. In 1768 these measures were unheard of – and extremely effective. Cook had a healthy crew to man his ship in the Pacific, a state of affairs no previous voyager had ever enjoyed. On the way to Cape Horn, two men died in accidents but none from scurvy, thanks to Cook's revolutionary methods.

Cook's First Voyage: Exploring the South Pacific

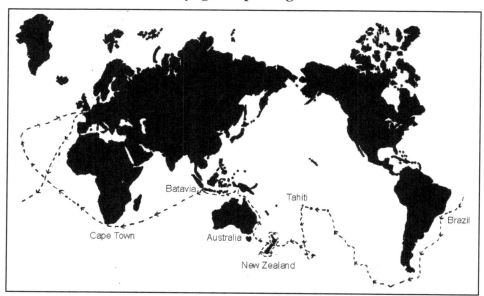

At that time in history, sailors knew how to establish their **latitude** by using a quadrant or sextant to measure the height of the sun at its zenith. However, few could reliably calculate their **longitude**. In England, a great effort was underway to find a practical solution to the longitude problem, with a huge cash prize offered. Cook was one of the rare sailors who could use the **lunar distances method** to establish his longitude. However, it was incredibly complicated, requiring perfect measurements and extensive calculations that compared changes in the moon's position in relation to key stars. Using this method, Cook was able to pinpoint the exact position of landmasses, assuming he had a clear sky, a visible moon, and a stable platform from which to take measurements – not exactly a formula that could be transferred to everyday conditions on a ship!

TAHITI & THE TRANSIT OF VENUS

Heading north into the tropics, the crew could shed their layers of clothing as the *Endeavour* approached **Tahiti**. Sailors today look forward to such landfalls with excitement; we can only imagine what it must have been like for Cook and his men in a time without radio, GPS, or colorful magazine images of what lay ahead. Anchoring in Matavai Bay, Cook was very strict with his men about the need to maintain good relations with the islanders. One of the rules Cook read to his men upon arriving in Tahiti was "To endeavour by every fair means to cultivate a friendship with the natives and to treat them with all imaginable humanity" (Edwards, 40). The main problem Cook experienced with the friendly islanders was petty theft, a problem throughout all of his Pacific voyages.

Cook quickly set his men to building a fort and observatory, and on June 3, 1769, he and Green observed the transit of Venus. They had accomplished one of the major aims of this voyage. (Unfortunately, the edge of the planet was not clear and the readings did not reveal as much as had been hoped when later analyzed in England.) Soon the ship was readied for departure, a sad occasion for most of the crew who had thoroughly enjoyed beautiful Tahiti and the **Society Islands**, making friends and girlfriends among the locals. They took with them Banks' Tahitian acquaintance, **Tupia**, along with his servant boy, Tiata, who proved helpful as translators at the next landfall.

The *Endeavour's* second goal was to explore New Zealand, which had been sighted briefly in 1642 by **Abel Tasman**. Popular belief held that there must be a giant southern continent on Earth to balance out the landmasses of the northern hemisphere; this imagined place was known as ***Terra Australis Incognita***. Cook's next mission was to chart New Zealand and find out whether it was part of this mysterious continent.

NEW ZEALAND

Two months after leaving Tahiti, with stops at neighboring Society Islands and a detour south that revealed no land, the *Endeavour* turned west and sighted the east coast of New Zealand. The crew found a rich green landscape and fierce, tattooed **Maori**. Cook was often frustrated in attempts at friendly trade with them. On a few occasions, his efforts went wrong and violence broke out. For an explorer of his day and in his situation, Cook showed remarkable restraint in the use of firearms. Still, several Maori were killed in these altercations.

Today we can see the faulty logic of Cook and his men. Yes, the men of the *Endeavour* wanted to establish good trading relationships, but they did so on their own terms and in full confidence that firearms gave them the upper hand. Cook went so far as to kidnap locals: "I embarked with an intent ... to surprise some of the natives and to take them on board and by good treatment and presents endeavour to gain their friendship" (Edwards, 71). Even after killing a Maori, Cook immediately presented more gifts to show his "friendliness." History has generally looked favorably upon Cook, who regretted the death of any native and generally demonstrated more respect for locals than other Europeans did. But every story has two sides, and the indigenous perspective does not cast Cook in a favorable light.

What no one can dispute are Cook's amazing seamanship and the quality of the charts he produced. He took the *Endeavour* counterclockwise around the **North Island** of New Zealand. As the ship sailed along the coast, he and his men charted what they saw. Eventually, the *Endeavour* circled all the way around to its starting point, then set off on a clockwise loop of the **South Island**, eventually completing a figure eight around both. Few of today's pleasure cruisers would ever dream of such an undertaking, even though they are armed with weather forecasts, radar, and charts! Having established that New Zealand was not part of a great southern continent, the crew rested and provisioned for some weeks near **Queen Charlotte Sound** in the **Cook Strait** (between the two islands) before heading west to further discoveries.

DISASTER IN AUSTRALIA AND BATAVIA

While the west and north coasts of **New Holland** (Australia) were relatively well known since the time of Abel Tasman's century-old expedition, little was known of the east coast, where Cook made landfall in April 1770. Following the coast north, he made the famous discovery of **Botany Bay**. Cook commented of the **Aborigines**, "all they seemed to want was for us to be gone" (Edwards, 125); unfortunately, this was not to be, as the site was later chosen for settlement through a penal colony. His men also noted a mouse-colored animal with a long tail that hopped "upon its hind legs only" (Edwards, 153), their first sight of a kangaroo. Next, the *Endeavour* sailed north past Port Jackson, where **Sydney** was eventually established.

Today, sailing without a chart is considered foolhardy and irresponsible. We benefit from the work of daring explorers like Cook who sailed blindly into the unknown. Soon all his skill and wits would be needed, because the **Great Barrier Reef** lay ahead. It was the beginning of miserable months and scrapes with disaster for the crew of the *Endeavour*.

Usually a keen lookout kept the ship from danger. When in doubt, a small oared boat could be lowered to determine whether it was safe to proceed. The ship's boats could even tow the *Endeavour* in calm conditions if necessary. But now the ship sailed into a maze of shoals. She went hard aground on a reef and was only saved by the combined efforts of the entire crew, all fighting for their lives. The pumps could barely keep up with the water flooding in until midshipman **Jonathan Monkhouse** suggested "**fothering**" the hole. This consisted of running a sail covered with tar, wool, and hemp fibers under the hull to temporarily plug the hole. The crew then towed the *Endeavour* to a bay on the site of today's **Cooktown** in Queensland and beached her for improvised repairs.

After a few weeks, Cook gingerly coaxed the patched *Endeavour* out of the bay. "After having well viewed our situation from the mast head I saw that we were surrounded on every side by shoals… dangerous to the highest degree in so much that I was quite at a loss which way to steer," wrote Cook (Edwards, 159). Somehow, he managed to weave his way out and proceed to **Batavia** (Jakarta), a Dutch port where further repairs would be possible.

Although Cook did obtain friendly assistance in Batavia, the port was a death-trap of **diseases** like dysentery and malaria. After working so hard to keep his crew healthy, Cook looked on helplessly while one after another of his men died – including sailors like Monkhouse, artist Sydney Parkinson, and the Tahitians, Tupia and Tiata. The *Endeavour* could barely limp away with a partial crew, many still sick but desperate to leave swampy Batavia. By the time he reached **Cape Town**, South Africa, Cook had lost a total of thirty-four men.

After stops at Saint Helena and the Azores, the survivors sailed into history with their return to England in July 1771.

In England, Cook submitted a report of his voyage and was widely acclaimed. By claiming important discoveries like New Zealand and eastern Australia, he had strengthened his country's position in the South Pacific at a time when its North American colonies were slowly slipping away. Unlike previous explorers, Cook had also **accurately mapped** these discoveries, opening them up to future exploitation. Along the way, he proved that a crew could spend months at sea without succumbing to scurvy. Soon Cook was promoted to the rank of Captain (although he had commanded the *Endeavour*, his rank at that time remained Lieutenant). Meanwhile, Joseph Banks made a huge splash in London with his own discoveries and stole popular attention from the humbler Cook. Their tremendous successes sparked ideas for a second journey. After only one busy year at home, Captain Cook prepared to set sail once again.

PART 1 ACTIVITY: OBSERVE THE NIGHT SKY

One goal of Captain Cook's first voyage was to observe the transit of Venus. The activity for this section is for students to observe the night sky and identify planets. Most planets can be seen by the naked eye; they look like slightly bigger, brighter stars. However, only certain planets are visible at any given time, so you should use a planet finder to help locate and identify them (see *Resources*). As a different activity, serve a lunch made only of biscuits, beef jerky, and sauerkraut to give your children an appreciation of the eighteenth century sailor's bland diet!

Part 2: Cook's Second Voyage, 1772-1775

Cook had reported a huge body of information about the Pacific, but the legend of *Terra Australis Incognita* lived on. Cook himself was skeptical that a great southern continent really existed, and he was willing to prove it. To do so, he would conduct an exhaustive search that would take him into even more hazardous waters for the next three years.

Cook's new plan called for two ships for safety. These were the 110 foot ***Resolution*** and the sturdy ***Adventure*** under Captain Tobias Furneaux. Determined to avoid the dangers of Batavia, Cook decided to base his explorations out of reliable places like Cape Town, Queen Charlotte Sound in New Zealand, and Tahiti. In addition to many veterans of the first voyage like Cook's young nephew, **Isaac Smith**, the crew included new faces, such as scientist Johann Förster and fifteen-year-old sailor **George Vancouver**, who would go on to become a great explorer in his own right.

NAVIGATION

James Cook lived in a time of extraordinary developments. He used and improved what can be considered cutting-edge advancements of the day. One example was his innovative solution to the problem of scurvy. Another related to navigation. On this eastabout circumnavigation, Cook had the benefit of the very latest technology: a reliable **clock**. Tempted by the prize offered for a solution to the longitude problem, carpenter **John Harrison** had succeeded in building a model suited for the rough conditions of ocean travel. Harrison's "H4" was incredibly dependable and whittled his closet-sized original to a five inch "watch-machine." Cook carried a copy of this clock (a "Kendall" clock) and therefore had a second – and much easier – method of calculating longitude (comparing time of local noon to Greenwich Mean Time in England, kept by this clock). Compared to the lunar method, this improvement might have seemed as easy for him as modern sailors find using a GPS today!

INTO ANTARCTIC WATERS

Cook left England in July 1772, made a short stop in Cape Town, and began the first of several determined forays into frigid **Antarctic** waters. French explorers had reported sighting land far south, but these claims were difficult to support: was there really land there, or had they been deceived by icebergs and fog? Cook was determined to leave no doubt. The ships headed ever farther south and found "ice islands" but no land. Cook pushed beyond the Antarctic Circle to **67° South**, farther than any human before him had gone. Eventually, he turned east along latitude 60° to New Zealand's South Island, stopping at **Dusky Sound** and then Queen Charlotte Sound in May 1773. After four months of extreme sailing conditions in the gale-blown, iceberg-filled Southern Ocean, the crews earned a well-deserved rest.

Cook's Second Voyage: In Search of a Southern Continent

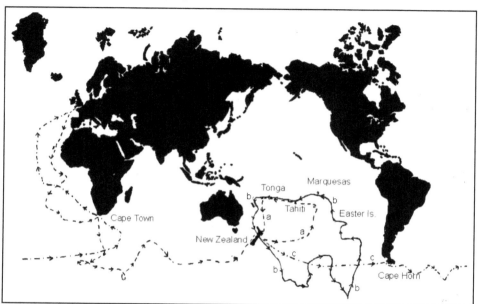

THE SOUTH PACIFIC

After rainy but pleasant weeks in New Zealand marked by peaceful interactions with local Maoris, the ships pressed on, arcing north to Tahiti through an unknown stretch of the Pacific (course marked *a* on the above map). Cook kept the fringing reefs of the **Tuamotus** in sight but at arm's length, faithfully recording what he saw. By August 1773, the ships were in the **Society Islands**, where they spent four weeks and took aboard a young islander. **Omai** would travel as far as England and eventually return home during Cook's third voyage. He was to prove very helpful at the next stop, **Tonga**, translating what turned out to be a universal Polynesian language.

On the way back to New Zealand, where the expedition planned to prepare for a second season's push to the south, brutal gales separated the ships. Cook was probably not too sad about this since Captain Furneaux had proven to be neither as daring nor as disciplined as Cook. Hoping the *Adventure* had survived the storm, Cook waited in Queen Charlotte Sound for some weeks before leaving a message and heading off on another South Pacific loop in late November

1773 (summer in the southern hemisphere). As it turns out, the *Adventure* had sought shelter elsewhere and arrived only a week after Cook's departure. Theirs was to be a less benign visit than the crew of the *Resolution* had enjoyed. When eleven men sent to collect supplies did not return, a search party was horrified to find body parts of their comrades roasting in baskets of the Maori, who were known to eat the flesh of conquered enemies. The *Adventure* made straight for England via Cape Horn.

Meanwhile, Cook headed even farther to the south than before (course marked *b* on the accompanying map). He took the *Resolution* as far as the Antarctic Circle, came back north like a diver coming up for a breath of air, then plunged down again. Cook's journal describes the stark scene: "The cold so intense as hardly to be endured, the whole sea in a manner covered with ice" (Edwards, 325). Taking advantage of summertime's constant daylight, the *Resolution* pushed as far south as the unthinkable **71°10'**. With nothing but icebergs in sight, Cook was "now well satisfied no continent was to be found in this ocean but what must lie so far to the south as to be wholly inaccessible for ice" (Hough, 288). As usual, his instincts were right.

By February 1774, it was too late in the season to head home around Cape Horn, so Cook instead continued exploring the Pacific. Spanish, French, and English sailors had already seen and named islands like Pitcairn, Easter Island, and the Marquesas, but finding them again was entirely a matter of chance since their "situations are not well determined," as Cook put it (Edwards, 344). The *Resolution* now located and charted **Easter Island** and the islands of Tonga, with a stop in Tahiti in between. Today's sailors approach these islands with an image of what to expect: colossal stone statues, magnificent mountain peaks, and so on. Imagine the suspense and wonder Cook and his men must have experienced! Throughout his explorations, Cook worked hard to maintain good relations with native people. In the **New Hebrides**, the English made contact with a noticeably different **Melanesian** population. Most were friendly, but one was killed by gunfire in a scuffle when Cook's men went ashore to collect water. Cook consequently punished the offending gunman – this captain was not the trigger-happy bandit that some other explorers proved to be.

Continuing onward, the *Resolution* charted **New Caledonia** and **Norfolk Island** before arriving back in Queen Charlotte Sound. There, the crew was puzzled by the local Maori's nervous behavior. Soon they learned of the ambush on Furneaux's men. It is a testament to Cook's restraint that he refused to embark on a revenge mission: "Notwithstanding they are Cannibals, they are naturally of a good disposition and have not a little share of humanity," he commented levelly (Hough, 297). Cook remained focused on repairs and charting local waters until leaving in mid November for Cape Horn (course marked *c* on the accompanying map).

THE SOUTH ATLANTIC AND HOME

The *Resolution* enjoyed mild weather and spent a pleasant Christmas ashore at **Tierra del Fuego** before rounding Cape Horn into the Atlantic. Cook even made a final dash south to disprove the existence of any landmass greater than South Georgia or the South Sandwich Islands. In Cape Town, he heard news of the *Adventure's* safe return to England a year earlier. The *Resolution* left South Africa at the end of April, but Cook was not satisfied with a short stop at Saint Helena; instead, he pressed far to the west to establish the position of **Fernando de Noronha**, a small island off Brazil! He then turned north for the Azores and Plymouth, reaching England in July 1775.

The magnitude of Cook's accomplishment would be hard to believe if the records didn't prove it: the *Resolution* had sailed 70,000 miles in three years, suffered only four deaths from scurvy, and last but not least, definitively disproven the existence of a southern continent suitable for any kind of practical endeavor. Cook was promoted to the high rank of Post-Captain and also named a member of the elite, academic Royal Society – another notable feat for a man of common birth and largely informal education.

PART 2 ASSIGNMENT: TIMELINE

The assignment for Part 2 is to make a timeline capturing major events related to Captain Cook's life or voyages. The timeline should be measured carefully so that distance on the line accurately represents relative time. The timeline can focus on one of Cook's voyages or his entire life. It may be expanded later to include his third voyage. See *Age-Appropriate Adaptations* to match this activity to each student's level.

Part 3: Cook's Third Voyage, 1776-1779

Cook returned to a world of change. North America was on the brink of a revolution and threatened to slip away from England. Since South America was divided between Spain and Portugal, England was pitted against Russia, France, and Spain in a race to claim any land still available – such as the resource-rich territories of **northwest North America** (today's western Canada and Alaska). Never mind that native people already inhabited these lands – Europeans were determined to claim their treasures for themselves.

In the east, the **Ottoman Turks** controlled overland routes to Asia, forcing Europeans to take alternate routes to the Pacific. Passages around the Cape of Good Hope and Cape Horn were long and dangerous. A newly proposed route was the **Northwest Passage** over North America. Like the great southern continent, this was something of a legend at the time; no one was sure it really existed. Now that Cook had thoroughly charted the South Pacific, he would take on the task of exploring the far north. If he found no Northwest Passage, his instructions were to attempt a passage over Asia. At first, Cook took part in talks to determine his successor as explorer extraordinaire, but eventually accepted the challenge himself rather than retiring to a quiet shore-side position at the side of his ever-patient wife, **Elizabeth**.

Cook would again sail the *Resolution* to the known ends of the earth and beyond. Trusted veteran **Charles Clerke** commanded the ***Discovery***, a smaller second ship. George Vancouver would complete his second circumnavigation on this voyage, and American-born **John Gore**, his fourth. Also aboard was twenty-two year old **William Bligh**, who, like the young Cook, had already proved himself an excellent surveyor. Unlike Cook, he was a volatile man who would go on to suffer two mutinies to his command – once as captain of the infamous *Bounty*, and later as governor of the new colony in Australia. Rounding out the ship's complement was **Omai**, who had been the exotic hit of London. Cook was also instructed to transport European **livestock** to the Pacific so that future sailors would have a supply of meat; this brainchild of **King George**

III not only crowded the ships, but was also to have terrible consequences for native species of the Pacific.

After extensive delays, Cook bid his wife and children goodbye and left England for the last time in July 1776. By this point in her long career, the *Resolution* could have almost sailed herself down the Atlantic to Cape Town. But all was not business as usual. The *Resolution* suffered a close call off the **Cape Verde Islands** when lax navigation almost let her wreck upon rocks. Then extensive leaks were discovered in the decks and hull, the result of poor preparation in England. Such errors were not typical of Cook. Was something amiss? Incidents such as these and later outbursts of anger suggest that Cook was in some way a changed man.

EXPLORATIONS IN THE FAR SOUTH

Even though the focus of this voyage was the Northwest Passage, Cook could not resist a detour south from Cape Town to an island group reported by the French, the **Kerguelen Islands**. He found little of use there but meticulously charted the islands together with Bligh. Heading east toward New Zealand, the ships stopped in southern **Tasmania** first. In one of the few "misses" of his many voyages, Cook failed to recognize that Tasmania was an island. He then sailed on to **Queen Charlotte Sound**, his familiar layover point.

Other than provisioning and keeping a wary eye on the Maori, the crew let loose rabbits and pigs; they and their numerous offspring quickly invaded the countryside. Having experienced long delays in England, Cook missed his season and was too late to sail far north. Instead, Cook remained in the South Pacific, exploring what we now call the **Cook Islands** and more of **Tonga**. Bligh kept busy surveying, while the artists recorded natural and cultural points of interest. Petty theft continued as usual, but Cook's **overreaction** was out of character. He had thieves flogged and, more alarmingly, ordered their ears to be cut off "in a manner rather unbecoming a European," as one of his crew judged (Hough, 360) – another clue that something was wrong.

Cook's Third Voyage: In Search of the Northwest Passage

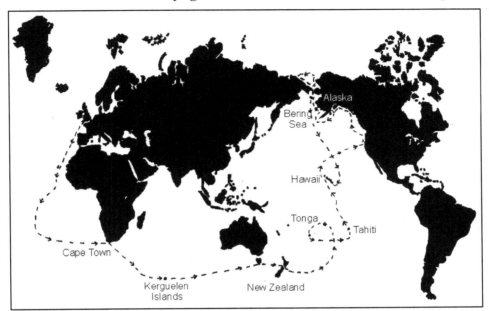

NORTH OF THE EQUATOR

Eventually the ships moved on to **Tahiti** and the Society Islands, where they stayed for four turbulent months. The theft of a goat led Cook to have houses and canoes burned; more ears were lopped off. Having resettled a tearful Omai back on his home island, the *Resolution* and *Discovery* finally headed north of the equator. In January 1778, they stumbled upon a major discovery: the **Hawaiian Islands**. Thieving again led to violence and the death of one Hawaiian. After a month, Cook continued north on his principal mission, the search for a Northwest Passage.

The ships first closed with the North American coast at a point near today's Eugene, **Oregon**. Spain had laid claim to California but had not established a solid footing this far north, an opportunity that Cook immediately seized. His surveying work along the coast was thorough as usual – except for missing the **Strait of Juan de Fuca**, first reported by the Spanish explorer in 1592 (this oversight was later corrected by George Vancouver, who charted Puget Sound during his own expedition in 1792). The region was rich in **timber** and valuable **furs**, and the coastal natives proved willing to trade.

The crews were eager to find a passage north and therefore claim their share of the £20,000 **prize** offered by the crown, but were continually deceived by dead ends like **Prince William Sound** and the **Cook Inlet**. They were to suffer foul weather all the way around the Alaskan peninsula, and a near disaster when they sailed too quickly in fog near submerged rocks. Cook was acting without his usual caution. At **Unalaska**, they found an open route north to the **Bering Strait**, named for the Dane who first briefly passed through it in 1728. Cook managed to penetrate much farther into Arctic ice than Bering ever attempted, but finally admitted defeat at **70° 44' North** – nearly matching his previous "record" in the southern hemisphere. "The season was now so very advanced and the time when the frost is expected to set in so near at hand," he wrote, "that I did not think it consistent with prudence to make any further attempts to find a passage this year in any direction so little was the prospect of succeeding" (Edwards, 577).

DEATH IN HAWAII

The *Resolution* was showing the wear of thousands of miles at sea, as were her men; it was mid September and time to sail south. With the intention of returning to the Arctic the following summer, Cook turned back to the **Sandwich Islands**, as he had named Hawaii. The *Resolution* arrived in Maui in November 1778, and moved on to the island of Hawaii in December. Her captain suddenly imposed strict rules on board and even threatened to take away the crew's grog (watered-down rum). Cook's inconsistent behavior has led to speculation that he was suffering from a long-term illness caused by an intestinal parasite, with severe side effects that would account for such a transformation in personality. Historians will never know for sure.

At the same time, the Hawaiians also behaved strangely. Cook was greeted in an elaborate ceremony by the high priest **Koa**. On shore, people knelt before Cook and called the name ***Orono*** (or *Lono*), a god whose legend said he would one day appear in a great canoe and cruise the islands much in the way the *Resolution* now did. It is not clear whether the Hawaiians actually took Cook to be a god or simply an important mortal visitor. Cook and his men didn't know the local legends, but they could see the implications and did nothing to persuade the Hawaiians not to associate this English captain with their god. And why should they?

This coincidence was to have a bitter end for Cook. After a great reception and weeks of gifts, it became clear that the islanders were ready for their visitor to leave, god or no god. Still the expedition remained, consuming valuable local supplies. The Hawaiian chiefs, wrote officer **James King**, "became inquisitive as to the time of our departing and seemed well pleased that it was to be soon" (Edwards, 608). In February, the two ships finally left, but were turned around by a storm that split the *Resolution's* foremast.

Their reception was noticeably cooler than before. A shore party collecting water was stoned by aggressive locals, but got away. Soon after, the theft of a cutter (a small boat) from the *Resolution* set off the final escalation of events. Cook went ashore, planning to kidnap the local king as collateral for the cutter. At first, the friendly king went willingly with Cook toward the shore, but an angry mob intervened and violence erupted. Even European weapons could not hold back the huge crowd; Cook was stabbed and set upon by the Hawaiians. Four marines were also killed, while the rest retreated to the ships in shock. Their leader, the veteran of so many adventures on land and at sea, was dead. Whether Cook's death was the result of being revealed as a false god (after all, gods don't get turned back by a storm) or simply the act of an angry mob will never be known.

The crews launched a revenge attack, bombarding the nearest village and sending a party ashore to recover Cook's body. This took several days; eventually, the dismembered body parts were delivered along with peace offerings. Cook was buried at sea and the expedition headed for home. Clerke, the captain of the *Discovery*, died from a long illness a few months after Cook, leaving Lieutenants John Gore and James King to guide the ships back to England, returning after more than four years away.

PART 3 ASSIGNMENT: PLAN A NEW MISSION OR PERSPECTIVE WRITING

Students should imagine they are in the Royal Navy or the Royal Society and that Captain Cook returned safely from his third voyage. The task is to plan a new mission for Cook, specifying the place and objective – another attempt at the Northwest Passage, perhaps, or a new mission to South America? Students should summarize Cook's qualifications for the job as well as the reasons for this new voyage in the context of the historical period.

Alternatively, students can choose to write an account of Cook's visits to New Zealand or Tahiti from the perspective of a native islander. They can imagine what it might be like when strange men in large ships suddenly appear, roam the island, and then depart; later, other ships begin to arrive more and more regularly, with each successive crew leaving a more permanent mark on the islands.

Part 4: The Legacy of Captain Cook

It is amazing to consider that Cook's three voyages all took place in less than eleven years, when the danger and beauty of the Pacific went from vague tales to documented realities. We read about his adventures by turning a few pages, but consider what it means to sail – without charts – for years at a time! Cook put to rest the myth of a southern continent and the possibility of finding a navigable Northwest Passage, while indirectly fueling new legends about the Pacific and its people. Cook is an important historical figure not only for his feats of navigation, but also for his curiosity and respect for the native people he was to meet. This sets him apart from other explorers, who sometimes looked upon locals as an inferior race and killed without remorse.

Cook helped expand not only the British Empire but scientific understanding that reached beyond borders. Even when England was at war with the newly formed United States, **Benjamin Franklin** urged American ships to let Cook and his crew pass, treating them as "common friends to mankind" (PBS, 2002), so important were Cook's discoveries. His voyages inspired further scientific work continued by the likes of **Charles Darwin**, who sailed with Captain Fitzroy in the *Beagle* from 1831-1836.

In addition to charting the Pacific, Cook also left a legacy in his ground-breaking measures to prevent scurvy on long voyages; this permitted long-range voyages without desperate losses. The crew and officers he trained and set an example for went on to historic deeds themselves, charting other dangerous shores and opening the way for safe travel by successive sailors. The charts we sailors use today stem from such efforts.

From another perspective, Cook, like **Columbus**, heralded the beginning of the end as far as some indigenous groups were concerned. Although Pacific islanders did not undergo the same outrages that the doomed Caribbean population suffered at the hand of conquering Spaniards, their story is still one of exploitation, the torment of introduced diseases, and loss of independence and cultural traditions. Some groups, such as the Polynesians or Maori, were able to maintain a measure of autonomy, while others, like Australia's aboriginal population, suffered terrible deprivations. Although Cook himself was generally respectful of native people, he has become the target of resentment by those who consider him the one to launch an era of invasion. Still, Cook was not alone in opening the Pacific, nor was it exclusively his crew who unleashed foreign species upon fragile island environments with decimating effects on endemic species.

PART 4 ACTIVITY: REMINDERS OF COOK TODAY

What remains of Cook today? Students should search for reminders of Cook that carry over to modern times. This might take the form of finding a monument to the explorer and writing a report about it (sites can be found, among other places, in England, Australia, Alaska, and Hawaii; see *Resources*). Students can also find places named for Cook, his ships, or crewmembers, and identify the corresponding voyage and its goal. This serves as a type of final quiz to review the story of Captain Cook.

Age-Appropriate Adaptations

In this section, you will find guidance on how to differentiate, or adapt, this unit for your child. Start with the correct age group, but also glance through the notes for one level younger or older, then mix and match as appropriate.

Self-assessment and reflection are valuable learning tools. They encourage students to think back upon their work and store their new body of knowledge in a meaningful and memorable manner. To that end, a number of self-assessment and reflection questions are listed for each age group. Remember that completed assignments and written reflection are useful records to later document student work for a school administration.

Ages 4-6

Students ages four to six will enjoy the adventure of Cook's voyages and can trace them on a world map, locating major oceans and continents. Dates and names are not as important as the main idea that Cook was special in being more than just another explorer who passed through. They can learn about scurvy and use Cook's reputation as a surveyor as a link into Unit 9, *Navigating with Map and Compass.*

Introduction Assignment: *Write a persuasive letter from Cook to his parents explaining his reasons for joining the navy.* Very young students might skip this assignment or do it orally to review the early part of Cook's life.

Part 1 Activity: *Observe the night sky.* Young students will enjoy looking at the night sky. Make a special event out of staying up late and treat the activity like a scavenger hunt: can your child find an unusually bright "star" that is actually a planet?

Part 2 Assignment: *Make a timeline of Cook's life or voyages.* Sequencing events in time is an important exercise for this age group. Begin with a personal timeline that runs from the child's year of birth to the present. Have your child think of memorable landmarks in her life and mark them on the line. Then move on to a timeline of James Cook. It is not important that the timeline breaks years into equal intervals, and just a few key dates will suffice. Students can mark events in words or in pictures.

Part 3 Assignment: *Plan a new mission* or *perspective writing.* The first assignment can be done in oral form, written as basic bullet points, or noted down by a scribe. The second option may be most appropriate since taking perspectives is an important skill to introduce at a young age.

Part 4 Activity: *Find traces of Cook in today's world.* This activity can be turned into a fun scavenger hunt for young children using maps. Better yet, visit a site or exhibit related to Cook if possible (see *Enrichment*).

Self-Assessment and Reflection: Young students should review their work orally. Challenge students to critique their work honestly; the idea is to judge outcomes while developing this important learning strategy.

- *Which activity or assignment did you learn the most from? Why?*
- *Which activity or assignment did you find especially hard? How did you manage to do it? What should you remember for next time?*
- *What do you have in common with Captain Cook? What is different? Would you have liked to sail with him? Why or why not?*
- *What are you curious to learn more about? How could you find more information on that subject?*

Ages 6-8

Students ages six to eight can compare their cruising track to Cook's to get an appreciation of the scale of his endeavors. Young students will only be starting to formulate their own ideas of past history so the concept of the Enlightenment (and Columbus-related eras like Medieval times and the Renaissance) is important to reinforce, even though dates and names are less important. The main idea to reinforce is that Cook's approach was unique and that he made many contributions to various fields.

Introduction Assignment: *Write a persuasive letter from Cook to his parents explaining his reasons for joining the navy.* Students can prepare their basic arguments and first make an oral appeal, acting the part of Cook while a parent plays Cook's father or mother. In this way, parents can ask questions that prompt children to expand their ideas. A written letter is optional.

Part 1 Activity: *Observe the night sky.* Make a special event of your nighttime lesson, perhaps by preparing a thermos of hot chocolate or telling stories of the constellations. Begin by having students look for patterns in an unstructured way and then move on to a more focused search for the brightest points, establishing which are planets.

Part 2 Assignment: *Make a timeline of Cook's life or voyages.* Start with a timeline of the child's life before moving on to Cook. It is not important that the timeline represents time in even intervals; more important is the student's ability to identify key events among less important ones. Students can use illustrations to enhance their work.

Part 3 Assignment: *Plan a new mission* or *perspective writing.* If students choose to assign Cook a new mission, they can generate a list of possibilities rather than settling on one single idea. Be sure the student lists Cook's qualifications for this voyage; this acts as review. The second option is valuable for two reasons: first, it encourages an open mind and empathy for others, and second, because this unit focuses on the European point of view, which generally neglects equally relevant Polynesian, Aboriginal, or Maori cultural histories.

Part 4 Activity: *Find traces of Cook in today's world.* Students may look over maps for places named for Cook, or focus on a particular monument or exhibit and associate it with a specific voyage. Does the monument or exhibit do a good job conveying information about Cook? What aspect of Cook's work does the monument or exhibit focus on?

Self-Assessment and Reflection: Whether in oral or written form, it is important for students to devote time to reviewing their own work. Challenge students to critique themselves; this will help them to become critical thinkers and effective learners.

- *Which activity or assignment did you learn the most from? Why?*
- *Which activity or assignment did you find especially hard? How did you manage to complete it? What should you remember for next time?*
- *What connections can you find between Cook and yourself? Would you have liked to sail with Cook? Why or why not?*
- *What would you like to learn more about? How could you follow up on that interest? (Native cultures, specific regions, life on an eighteenth century ship.)*

Ages 8-10

Without getting caught up in details, students can learn key dates (Cook's lifespan, the Enlightenment, other world events). The main idea is that Cook was unique among explorers and that he made many important contributions to various fields: navigation, geography, health, and anthropology. Discuss how history can be written from a one-sided viewpoint.

Introduction Assignment: *Write a persuasive letter from Cook to his parents explaining his reasons for joining the navy.* Role-playing is a good way to get started. Allow the student to prepare basic arguments and later write an edited and revised letter. If a student's letter is not convincing, give him tips on improvement and have him revise.

Part 1 Activity: *Observe the night sky.* Start your observations in an unstructured way so that your child can find her own points of interest in the night sky. Gradually move on to identifying patterns and looking for planets. Then show your child a planet finder and how to use it.

Part 2 Assignment: *Make a timeline of Cook's life or voyages.* A student who has never made a timeline can start with one of his own life. He should attempt to represent time in corresponding space intervals on the line. Be sure the student is not randomly picking dates from the Cook story but rather considering what makes something significant. The student can devise a way to distinguish major from minor events on his timeline. Advanced students may also include key world events (the American Revolution, other historic voyages, John Harrison's work on a timepiece) to reinforce the idea that events are interconnected.

Part 3 Assignment: *Plan a new mission* or *perspective writing.* If students choose to assign Cook a new mission, they should be specific in both the region to be explored and the underlying purpose. How will England benefit from the proposed voyage? At the same time, the idea is to summarize key aspects of Cook's résumé, so make sure this is done adequately. On the other hand, the second option is also a valuable exercise. Students will have to consider different points of view, counterbalancing the heavily European focus of this unit.

Part 4 Activity: *Find traces of Cook in today's world.* Students can study a particular monument or exhibit, or scan maps for places related to Cook and associate them with specific voyages. Does the monument or exhibit do a good job conveying information about Cook? What aspect of Cook's work does the monument or exhibit focus on? Does it provide a balanced view of the explorer's role in history? This can be followed with a brief oral or written report to develop communication skills.

Self-Assessment and Reflection: Students should review their work in written form. Self-assessment builds critical thinking skills and helps students recognize helpful strategies, as well as become more independent.

- *Why is Captain Cook an important figure to learn about? How can his achievements be captured in a monument or exhibit?*
- *Which activity or assignment did you learn the most from? Why?*
- *Which assignment did you do a good job on? What makes it good? What points will you keep in mind next time?*
- *What connections can you find between Cook and yourself? Would you have liked to sail with Cook? Why or why not?*
- *What would you like to learn more about? How can you find out more about it? (Native cultures, specific regions, life on an eighteenth century ship.)*

Ages 10-12

Students ages ten to twelve can complete all the activities and assignments in this unit at a relatively advanced level. They should know key historical dates and link Cook to major world events. Reinforce the idea of Cook as a multi-faceted contributor to eighteenth century knowledge (navigation, geography, health, anthropology, and botany through his scientists). Students should understand how history can be recorded from different perspectives.

Introduction Assignment: *Write a persuasive letter from Cook to his parents explaining his reasons for joining the navy.* Students should draft their arguments first and write a thoroughly edited and revised letter.

Part 1 Activity: *Observe the night sky.* Students in this age group may be given the task of locating a planet finder on the Internet and setting it to the correct position and date. Students can be introduced to the idea that planets gradually move through the constellations. That is because planets are within our solar system and therefore are closer than stars. Imagine biking along a lane and watching nearby trees move past quickly while the landscape behind you shifts more gradually; it's the same idea. Have students repeat their observations a week later to observe how the planets wander past the stars.

Part 2 Assignment: *Make a timeline of Cook's life or voyages.* Students should make a rough draft and then a carefully measured timeline. They should be able to justify which events are included. To place the Cook story within a larger picture, have students mark key historical events that paralleled Cook's voyages (such as the Longitude Prize offered in 1714, the American Revolution of 1776, or the eighteenth century Enlightenment).

Part 3 Assignment: *Plan a new mission* or *perspective writing*. If students choose the first assignment, they should specify both the region to be explored and the underlying purpose in good detail. How will England benefit from the proposed voyage? Make sure the student spends time summarizing key aspects of Cook's résumé, a way to review his story. The second option is also a valuable assignment that will develop writing skills while reinforcing the idea of varying cultural perspectives.

Part 4 Activity: *Find traces of Cook in today's world.* Students can study maps for place names related to Cook (or his crew) and study a particular monument or exhibit. Does the monument or exhibit do a good job conveying information about Cook? What aspect of Cook's life does it focus on? Does it provide a balanced view of the explorer's role in history? Are indigenous people recognized? This can be followed with a brief written or oral report that critiques the monument or exhibit, listing positive points as well as weaknesses.

Self-Assessment and Reflection: Students should review their work in written form. This habit builds critical thinking and effective learning skills, and encourages students to become independent learners.
- *Which activity or assignment did you learn the most from? Why?*
- *Which assignment are you especially proud of? What makes it good? How could you have improved your final product?*

- *What connections can you find between Cook and yourself? Would you have liked to sail with Cook? Why or why not?*
- *How can you tell if a history book tells a fair and balanced story?*
- *What would you like to learn more about? How can you follow up on that interest? (Native cultures, specific regions, life on an eighteenth century ship.)*

Enrichment

A visit to a historical site or museum associated with Captain Cook would help to either kick off or wrap up this unit. Try to connect the facts related here to the artifacts, portraits, or maps available. If that isn't possible, visit the British Library's outstanding Cook website at http://www.captcook-ne.co.uk/ccne/index.htm. Follow any option on the *Themes* page to see maps made by Cook, landscapes drawn by Parkinson and others, and an entire section on Cook's impressions of native people of the Pacific.

Students who have completed the Columbus unit can draw comparisons between the two explorers. In what way were their methods and personalities similar or different? While Columbus was extremely religious, Cook was notably pragmatic, each man a product of the era in which he lived. However, they shared the same visionary outlook and confidence in approaching the unknown. Another option is to research one of Cook's protégés (like Vancouver or Bligh), or another explorer who followed, such as Robert Fitzroy. Today, students from English-speaking countries typically learn about heroes of the English sailing tradition, but little about the French or Dutch: Crozet, Bougainville, La Perouse, Tasman; all would be interesting subjects. Spain and Russia had temporary holds on Western North America; look up Vitus Bering (a Dane who worked for the Russian Czar) or Spaniard Salvador Fidalgo, who left his mark in Alaska.

Cross-Curricular Links

You can make many authentic connections between this unit and any number of subjects in addition to the obvious links with Unit 7, *The Voyages of Columbus,* and Unit 9, *Navigation with Map and Compass*. There are several opportunities to tie several assignments in this unit in to specific **writing** skills (see Unit 6).

Art: In conjunction with the *Part 4* Activity, students can try their hand at designing a new Cook monument (or perhaps one for Omai, Parkinson, or another associated figure) that is more imaginative than the rather bland obelisks commonly used. What inscription would the monument bear? What scene or symbols might it depict? Where should it stand?

History: Children could study how tools of navigation developed over time. Older students will enjoy reading Dava Sobel's outstanding book, *Longitude* (see Unit 9 *Resources)*. Or they might move on to other historical topics: for example, how did the national rivalries of Cook's time play out in Europe? How do the American (1776), French (1789), and Haitian (1791) revolutions fit in? In what way did the advancements of the Enlightenment herald the Industrial Revolution?

Science: Nutrition is a topic that connects well to a study of Captain Cook (vitamins, balanced diet, etc). Students can also try their hand as junior botanists, sketching and measuring an interesting plant at a new landfall and then researching it. Students could learn more about the transit of Venus (use NASA's webpage devoted to *James Cook and the Transit of Venus:* http://science.nasa.gov/science-news/science-at-nasa/2004/28may_cook/). The next transit of Venus will not be until 2117!

Social Studies: If your cruising route intersects any of Cook's voyages, students can undertake a study of local culture. Children can also research methods Pacific Islanders used to navigate (see Unit 9).

Resources

Captain Cook is the subject of countless books, including a good selection of children's titles. A fun book that children of all ages will enjoy is Mark Bergin's clever *You Wouldn't Want to Travel with Captain Cook!* (Brighton: Salariya Book Company, 2006). Readers learn about life on board the *Endeavour* through cartoon-style illustrations and the eyes of young Isaac Smith. A book appropriate for readers ages ten or above is David Haney's *Captain James Cook and the Explorers of the Pacific* (New York: Chelsea House Publishers, 1992). As the title indicates, the book also covers other expeditions and would therefore be useful for follow-up studies.

An incredibly detailed Internet resource is *South Seas Voyaging and Cross-Cultural Encounters* created by the National Library of Australia (http://southseas.nla.gov.au/index.html). Covering from 1760-1800, this site comes complete with maps, the full journals of Cook, Joseph Banks, and Sydney Parkinson, as well as indigenous histories. The Captain Cook Society has an excellent website (www.captaincooksociety.com/ccsu410.htm#S5) with a subsection on "Modern places associated with Captain Cook."

To locate and identify stars for the Part 2 activity, use a planet finder like http://www.lightandmatter.com/planetfinder/en/ which offers a concise overview, or http://www.nakedeyeplanets.com/index.htm for a more detailed presentation. Both allow you to enter your location and date.

Unit 9 - Navigation with Map and Compass

Skill'd in the globe and sphere, he gravely stands,
And, with his compass, measures seas and lands.

John Dryden

I never had so much trouble with anything in my life as I
did with this map.

Mark Twain, on his map of Paris

Unit 9 - Navigation with Map and Compass

Materials:
- Maps (variety of types)
- Hand-bearing compass
- Graph paper
- Ruler

Guiding Questions:
What information does a map contain about a place and about the map maker? How can I crack the "code" of a map?

Learning outcomes:
Students will be able to describe, read, and create a variety of maps.

Introduction

Map making and reading are exciting activities that stir a child's imagination and enthusiasm. Maps hint at interesting new places, near and far, and ways to get there. On a boat, charts are indispensible! Learning to read and create maps fosters a sense of independence. Often, however, children have simplistic views about the information a map provides. So let's get started!

Overview

This unit begins with a general overview of maps and then moves on to sailing-specific topics such as locating points of latitude and longitude. In *Part 1: What is a Map? What's on a Map?* children will learn that maps are ways of representing real things in a symbolic format. They will study scales, legends, and other features common to maps. In *Part 2: Common Map Types*, children will look at how different maps suit different purposes, and then go on to *Part 3: Tools of Navigation*. This section focuses on compass use but also discusses celestial navigation and modern technology. *Part 4: Coordinate Graphing* takes a practical look at an important map-reading skill for sailors that also transfers to mathematics (most school curricula require students to master age-appropriate coordinate graphing skills). Along the way, students will be challenged with hands-on activities such as making a map, planning and following a route, using a compass, and pinpointing locations on a grid.

Part 1: What is a Map? What's on a Map?

Students can tune in to this unit by examining a number of maps or charts with various scales and purposes: nautical charts, highway maps, hiking maps, town maps, even an airport terminal map. You can go on the Internet and compare different world maps, such as a Japanese map of the world and one from North America. What features are found on these maps? How are they similar? How are they different?

Maps are full of different symbols. These are a type of code. Some of the symbols are very clear, but others are harder to understand at a glance. What clues help us to crack the code? Start with a road map and ask what information it gives – names of places, road numbers, and distances. Now ask your children to think about what's *not* on a road map. Common road maps usually have no indication of anchorages or offshore rocks, and few, if any, hills. Why does a road map tell us about certain things and not others? Brainstorm some ideas. Road maps are made for a particular **purpose**, and contain only information pertinent to that purpose. When is a road map not useful? These are the type of questions that will guide our inquiry into maps. Compare the road map to a nautical chart. What information does each contain? What type of "code" does each use? Take a few minutes to list and compare the features of different maps with your child.

A map is a symbolic way of putting the real world into a compact, two-dimensional format. All maps have some things in common: indications of direction, distance, and important orientation points. Maps usually use the **cardinal directions** for **orientation**: north, south, west, and east. Most people in the western world think of north as up, but actually, on a round planet orbiting through space, "up" is a relative term. Search for maps that do not have north at the top. They usually have some other **reference point** instead (a shopping mall map might use a major road as its reference point, or a "corrected world map" from Australia with Antarctica on top).

Another important part of most maps is **scale**: the way distances are shown on a map. Have students study the maps once again and find scales. A town map will have a good degree of detail compared to a world map. Every map is a compromise: to show details, a map maker has to leave out the bigger picture. To fit a large area in, map makers must use a small scale and therefore lose detail ("small" being a confusing term here; a map of a large area uses small scale, while a map of a detailed area uses a large scale).

Usually, maps indicate the scale with a bar scale or a ratio. This large-scale hiking map provides a bar scale in miles and kilometers.

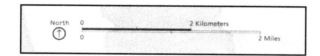

This small-scale road map provides both a ratio and a bar scale.

The metric scale is much easier to work with. In a 1:4,000,000 map, one centimeter represents 40 kilometers (4,000,000 centimeters). Imperial measurements are more complicated: one inch on a 1:250,000 US map represents 250,000 inches in the real world – that's about four miles. If children were to map a small yard, they could use a metric scale of 1:50 (one centimeter on the map representing 50 centimeters of the park) or an imperial scale of 1:12 (one inch on the map representing one foot).

Nautical charts, on the other hand, don't always show a separate scale bar because the latitude lines printed along the sides indicate scale. One degree of latitude is sixty nautical miles, and each degree is subdivided into one, five, or ten mile sections for convenience. Without going into confusing detail about nautical miles being slightly shorter at the extremes of the earth, remind children to use the latitude that corresponds to their location; never use the latitude scale farther north or south of the ship's location!

Interestingly, distance and orientation are not important on every type of map. Think of a subway map, for example. It shows stops in their rough locations relative to each other. Since the subway driver and the tracks take over the navigating, passengers only need to know key points, such as the name of their stop. Can students think of other types of maps in which orientation by cardinal directions or distance is not important?

Most charts have a **legend**, or a box where all the symbols and color codes for **landmarks** are explained. Have students find the legend on each of their maps. For a hiker, a small creek is a good landmark, but that will not work for a driver rushing by in a car. A driver needs landmarks like road intersections, street names, or big rivers. A sailor will look for different landmarks, like lighthouses or buoys. Ask students to list landmarks that would be important for different examples, such as a pilot or a cyclist.

Another important feature of maps is **projection**. The globe is round but a paper map is flat, so there is always some problem converting three dimensions to two. To see the problem, peel an orange and flatten out the peel on a plate. It forms an irregular pattern that wouldn't neatly take up all the space on a sheet of rectangular paper. So what do we do?

First, we can ignore the problem! That works well with a detailed (large- scale) map that looks at something close up. For example, this issue doesn't affect an airport map that shows the locations of gates and terminals. However, a map that covers a huge area must address this problem. One solution for a world map is to simply draw an **"interrupted" world map** laid out like a peeled orange, with gaps between the splits in the peel. This is not very useful, however, because it separates sections of the earth that are connected in reality. Another solution is to **distort** the earth's surface, squeezing some parts and stretching others so that the map fits nicely on a sheet of paper.

One type of map that does this is a **Mercator** projection map (including standard nautical charts). This is a useful representation, but since it is squeezed and stretched, the relative sizes of places, especially near the poles, become distorted. Compare the size of Greenland on a Mercator map to the size of the African continent. Greenland looks nearly as big! However, an **"equal area"**

map[1] reveals that Greenland is in fact about the size of Mali, one small piece of Africa. So why not just use an equal area map? This projection distorts the relative shapes and positions of land while preserving their relative sizes. There is no "right" way to show the round Earth on a flat sheet of paper, but there are different ways that suit different purposes, and that is the main lesson to reinforce.

Navigators traveling long distances usually follow a **great circle route**. This means that they take advantage of the earth's converging shape near the poles to shortcut to their destination. The great circle route will only appear as a straight line on a **gnomonic** projection map.

Mercator Projection   **Gnomonic Projection**

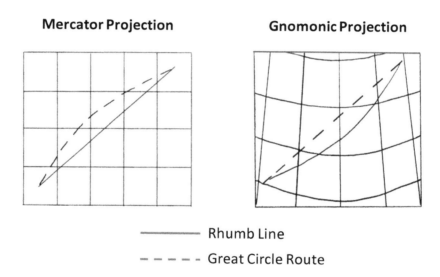

——————— Rhumb Line

– – – – – – Great Circle Route

For example, a plane flying from New York to London doesn't fly on a straight line as seen on a Mercator projection map (this is known as a **rhumb line;** see above left). Instead, it shortcuts north over Labrador in Canada. The same goes for sailors: when sailing from the Canary Islands to the Caribbean, they follow the shorter, great circle route. Navigators must constantly change the compass course they steer on a great circle route, but the distance is less. Near the poles,

---

[1] These can easily be found on the Internet under "Equal Area Map," "Mollweide Projection," or "Gall-Peters Equal Area Map."

the difference between the great circle and rhumb line distance is greatest. Nearer the equator, the difference is less. There is no difference at all on the equator, which is actually a great circle line itself (as are all meridians, the imaginary north-south lines that circle the globe).

Remember that maps are only as good as the person who made, measured, and drew them. Even when using a good chart, sailors should still use common sense and their own observations to get around. What if something changed the day after the chart was printed? I sailed to Gibraltar and was surprised to see a prominent shipwreck where none was marked. This was a good lesson to trust my eyes instead of following a chart! You might be surprised to find that nautical charts are often based on very old soundings (depths); surprisingly, these are often reliable, while other features change.

PART 1 ACTIVITY: CHART YOUR ANCHORAGE / DRAW A TREASURE MAP

Some of the greatest names in the history of exploration – Captain Cook or Lewis and Clark – were not necessarily the first to find new territory, but they were the first to create accurate maps of those places. Now it's time for students to make their own maps. Advanced students can paddle around an anchorage with a hand-held GPS and take soundings with a lead line to make their own detailed chart. Younger students might draw a treasure map instead – one leading to some object they have hidden. In either case, make sure the scale, orientation, and relevant landmarks are all clearly indicated.

Part 2: Common Map Types

Most maps fall into a few basic categories. A road map is a flat representation from a bird's-eye view. This is called a **planimetric map**. The peaks of major hills might be labeled, but otherwise the height of landscape features is not indicated. It may not be important for an engine-powered car to know the exact location of every bump in the landscape, but for a hiker, this is very important information. That is why hikers use another type of map: a **topographic map** on which **contours** (slopes) are shown. To a practiced eye, a topographic map provides a 3D picture of the landscape.

Contour lines only exist on maps. They show height above sea level. They never cross, though they might come close, indicating a steep slope or cliff. The main contour lines are labeled 500, 600, 700 – meaning height above sea level (in meters or feet; check the legend). Between contour lines are **contour intervals**. Wide open spaces show a flatter landscape, and hikers can choose their routes accordingly. To a beginner, a topographic map may be a little confusing. For better understanding, not to mention good fun, go through *Activity 1* (on the following page) with your child.

A Nautical Chart with Topographic Features (NOAA, 1983)

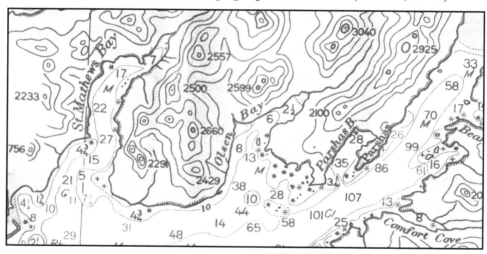

A **nautical chart** is a special type of topographic map in which depth below sea level is marked (instead of height above sea level). Important information for sailors, like water depth or a buoy's location, is marked on a chart, along with hazards like rocks, reefs, and wrecks. Lighthouses are marked on charts with an abbreviation of the pattern and interval of their flashing light so that they can be recognized at night. Most charts also show a few contours and features on land so that sailors can use the landscape to verify their position.

A map can tell us as much about the map maker as the territory. If a child finds a ripped piece of a mysterious, hand drawn map, he could probably deduce something about the map maker from it. A map with individual trees and rocks marked on it shows the map maker found these to be important for some reason; maybe it is a treasure map! The types of maps most commonly found today (planimetric, topographic, and nautical charts) reflect a certain way of thinking. However, at different points in history, different cultures have used very different ways of representing the world.

For example, **Native Americans** had their own way of creating and using maps. Winding rivers might be drawn as relatively straight and distances were not represented to scale. An oral description was an essential part of each map, which usually focused on describing a journey or the symbolic meaning of a landscape. This was not always understood by early explorers who viewed maps with a different set of assumptions. **Inuit driftwood maps** are small, carved pieces of wood that can be "read" by touch. A bumpy, roughly oval piece of wood is used to represent the curves of a coastline; instead of turning a page, the navigator turns a corner of the driftwood to follow the coast as it extends – truly a unique form of map making! **Pacific Islanders** used quite a different means of mapping their ocean-dominated world. Their master mariners made maps by weaving palm strips together to represent ocean currents and star paths, with shells to represent island locations inside a complex web of currents rather than a fixed place on Earth.

This shows us that there are many different ways of perceiving the world and creating maps, and every map has a unique purpose. Students interested in learning more might pursue a project on maps from different cultures and periods of history.

PART 2 / ACTIVITY 1: HANDS-ON TOPOGRAPHIC MAPPING

This activity is fun for all ages but is especially recommended for younger students. You will need a rock, a bowl or bucket, sand or rice, a measuring cup, a see-through plastic sheet, and a thin permanent marker. The rock should be an irregular shape, not rectangular like a brick.

Have your child place the rock in the bowl and pour in one cup of sand or rice to cover the bottom portion of the rock. Lay the plastic sheet across the top of the bucket and tape one side firmly down. Looking straight down, carefully draw an outline of the visible portion of the rock on the plastic sheet. Label it "100"; this is the first contour line. Now the child can pour in another cup of sand to cover more of the rock and draw the next contour line. Eventually, only the very top of the rock will peek out above the sand. This will be represented by a small circle or oval. There you have it – your very own topographic map! Finish it with a directional arrow and a name. Advanced students can play a game by mapping everyday articles (a shoe, a conch shell); whoever can guess the item wins!

Hands-On Topographic Mapping

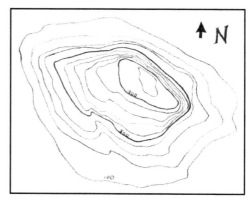

Sailors can also try the activity in reverse to illustrate the idea of nautical charts with depth contours. To do so, fill the bowl with water so that only the top point of the rock is above "sea level." Then students can suck out water with a straw (don't swallow!), stopping regularly to draw contour lines as more and more of the rock is exposed.

PART 2 / ACTIVITY 2: PLAN AND FOLLOW A ROUTE

Using the map of their choice, students should plan and follow a route. They must calculate the distance to the destination by using the map scale and write down a set of directions that includes landmarks along the way. This exercise can be completed on land or on the water. For example, a student can act as navigator for his parents while sailing to a new anchorage. Or, a student can use a topographic map to work out a hiking route. Obviously this exercise requires parental oversight but students should be allowed to take the lead as much as possible.

Remember that a straight line isn't always the most practical route to take. Have children turn the map to line up with the direction they are facing. Young students should choose a nearby destination that can be reached using a map and landmarks alone (this is known as **line of sight** navigation).

Part 3: Tools of Navigation

A map is one important tool of navigation, but is certainly not the only one. Columbus managed to find his way safely across the Atlantic and back without a map (actually, worse than that, he used a rough map that was completely wrong! Read about the Toscanelli map in Unit 7). Columbus did, however, have a **compass**. A small, magnetic pointer in a compass aligns with the earth's magnetic field. Once a traveler finds north, he can find any other direction. With this information, he can theoretically point in the right direction, head off into the unknown, and return to his starting point.

PRACTICE 1: Students who have rarely used a compass should do a little outdoor practice. The first step is to find north. Students should look up to locate a landmark in that direction and take twenty steps toward it. Next, they should turn due east and take twenty steps. Repeat to the south and finally west. They should return to the exact place they started. Not many people do on the first try!

It is important NOT to look down at a compass while moving. A person who stares at his compass is likely to follow a crooked line even though the compass needle faithfully points north the whole time. Instead, find a landmark that lies in the correct direction and use that for orientation. Once there, look for the next landmark. Sailors out of sight of land have an extra challenge but can use the sun or stars as short-term landmarks.

PRACTICE 2: Two people can have a fun time observing the problem of staring down at a compass while moving. Stand together and agree on a direction. One person should find a landmark on the bearing and remain stationary. The second person should take the compass and walk about forty steps along that bearing, keeping her eyes on the compass (in other words, doing what she shouldn't). The person standing still will see how the walker gradually veers off course. When the walker stops, show her how much she "drifted" off the original line. Now change places and repeat so that each person experiences the effect from both points of view. This demonstrates a common and natural human error.

Now have students point their hand-held compasses at different objects: a buoy, lighthouse, or hill. This is called taking a **bearing**. But there's a catch. You'd think that a compass points north to the North Pole (or **true north**), but that is not the case. A compass actually points to **magnetic north**. The greatest magnetic pull from inside the earth is in fact centered at a spot a thousand kilometers away from the North Pole in the Canadian Arctic!

If you happen to be someplace on Earth where magnetic north and true north line up, you are lucky; your compass shows the correct direction. Everywhere else, you will have to add or subtract a few degrees to correct your bearings for this **variation**. The exact variation depends on your exact location on Earth as well as local magnetic anomalies (exceptions to the main pattern). It also gradually shifts over time, and that is why maps list variation in reference to a certain year. Sailors could end up dangerously off course if they do not take variation into account. Most maps indicate variation along with other important information. Try to find maps of different regions and see how the variation changes from place to place.

Advanced students will be able to learn to correct for variation. Look on a map and find the intended course. Variation should be **added** if it is **west** and **subtracted** if it is **east** (think "west is best") when working from a course drawn on a map (a true course). On the other hand, if transferring a bearing from a compass (a magnetic course) to a chart, be sure to adjust for variation, but now, subtract west and add east.

> True ⇨ Magnetic course: add west variation, subtract east
> Magnetic ⇨ True course: subtract west variation, add east

Next, show students a quick experiment with a compass. What happens if you put a piece of metal near a compass? The pointer swings away from north because the magnetic field around it changes. This is called **deviation** and anyone using a compass must be careful to take it into account. Deviation is an inconsistent value; a compass may be more affected when reading north than west, for example. Always avoid bringing metal near a compass!

Using just a compass and a measure of distance traveled, navigators can use **dead reckoning** to chart their course ("dead" comes from the word "deduced"), just as Columbus did across the Atlantic. If he sailed west all day and calculated that his ship covered 100 miles, he would draw a line 100 miles to the west and mark his new position. This is a useful method, but it does have some problems. On the water, currents can push a boat sideways so that it actually moves northwest instead of west. A traveler can also get off course when moving over uneven terrain on land.

Another way to find a position using a map and a compass is called **taking a fix**. If a student takes a bearing on a tower and finds it to be at 180° he can draw a line along this 180° heading. He is somewhere along that line. But where exactly? Then he should take a new bearing on another object, such as a buoy marked on the same chart. If that bearing is 090°, a line drawn along that heading will cross the first line – and X marks the spot! It is good practice to take three or more bearings to confirm a position. Advanced students should remember to correct their bearings for local variation.

Taking a Two-Point Fix (NOAA, 1983)

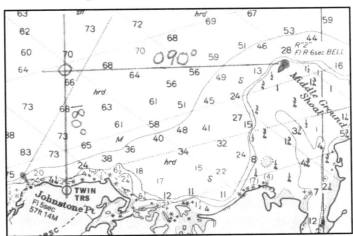

Another way to establish a position using a compass and a chart is taking a **running fix**. This involves taking a bearing on a certain landmark, and then taking another bearing on the same point after moving past it. Based on calculations of speed, course, and angles, sailors can find their position.

For reference, the world is divided into a lined grid. **Latitude** measures position north or south of the **equator**, while **longitude** measures distance west and east from an imaginary line called the **Prime Meridian**[2]. Positions on the globe can be pinpointed with one point of latitude and one point of longitude. This is called **coordinate graphing**, a topic covered in Part 4.

In addition to maps and compasses, early navigators developed other tools to help find their location. The sun, moon, and stars are landmarks in the sky; using them to find a position is called **celestial navigation**. Because these "landmarks" are overhead, a navigator measures their height (that is, the angle between the horizon and the sun, moon, or star in the sky) at a given time. From the difficult to use quadrant, astrolabe, and octant, navigators eventually invented an improved **sextant** to measure these angles. Using celestial observations and tables developed by astronomers, a navigator can calculate latitude (position north or south of the equator).

But this is only part of the picture. Without longitude, a navigator can only guess at her position on an east/west line. For example, Beijing, China and Ankara, Turkey are both at latitude 39°55'N, but their longitudes are very different (116°E and 032°E, respectively). Early astronomers realized that longitude could be determined by comparing local noon (when the sun reaches its highest point) to noon at a known location like the Prime Meridian. This would show how far east or west the new position is from the known position (think of time zones). The problem was building a reliable **clock** that could withstand temperature changes and rough handling. In the late eighteenth century, an English inventor eventually succeeded in building a reliable timepiece. Only then did navigators have a practical means of calculating latitude *and* longitude (see *Resources* for an excellent book on this topic).

---

[2] The Prime Meridian was established along a line that runs north and south through Greenwich, England, where one of the first leading observatories was located.

Today, **GPS** (Global Positioning System) gives travelers their position instantly, determining latitude and longitude from signals sent by satellites in orbit around the earth. Electronic gadgets are extremely helpful, but beware of depending on them exclusively – sailors have discovered the hard way that there can be flaws in interpretation, information, and set-up (such as matching the GPS unit to a map's datum, like WGS 84).

Radar and **sonar** are two more modern navigational tools; both emit signals (sound or electromagnetic) which bounce back from objects, creating a picture of things outside the range of vision. However, it is a bit unfair to call sonar and radar "modern human inventions" since bats and dolphins evolved the ability to use **echolocation** (using sound waves) long before modern man even considered such technology! Some animals navigate the oceans and find their way "home" without compass, navigation tables, or GPS. After thousands of miles of travel, leatherback turtles return to the very beach where they once hatched to lay their own eggs. How they manage this incredible feat hasn't been fully explained, but it seems that sea turtles have an internal compass. As far as mankind has come, it can still be humbling to think that Mother Nature has many remarkable inventions of her own!

PART 3 ACTIVITY: COMPASS CHALLENGE

In this unit, students already tried one compass exercise. Now they can try a more difficult challenge. Starting at the edge of a field, students should mark their initial position with a small rock. Then they should pace out an equilateral triangle that is 100 meters on each side. Remind children not to look down at the compass but to follow a landmark along a bearing.

First, students should pace out 100m in one direction. Then they should add 120° to their bearing and walk 100m in that direction. Finally, add another 120° for the last 100m. By adding 120° at each turn, they will achieve a full 360° rotation. A person who started walking north (000°), for example, will turn to 120° and then to 240° after each 100m leg.

A good navigator will come out exactly in the same spot. The distance and the terrain can be varied to create an easier or more difficult challenge. This exercise demonstrates the importance of taking good bearings and using landmarks for orientation. Advanced students can try this in the woods or over irregular terrain. Parents should supervise children in all cases.

Part 4: Coordinate Graphing / Latitude and Longitude

Now it's time to practice coordinate graphing through a study of latitude and longitude. A coordinate graph is one that uses points along two perpendicular lines (**axes**) to mark a position. The x axis runs horizontally and in sailing it is used to mark longitude. The y axis runs vertically and is used to mark latitude. (Take a moment to think this through: although latitude lines are drawn horizontally, they "rise" along a vertical scale.) In a mathematical context, a coordinate grid will have positive and negative quadrants. In navigation, we use north / south and west / east to distinguish sectors.

In this section, students will use relevant information from their cruise or passage to practice coordinate graphing. For our purposes, it is adequate to use a single latitude/longitude data point for each day. This will help students to understand a fundamental skill of both navigation and mathematics. Many national and state mathematics curricula place coordinate graphing in *Shape* or *Spatial Sense* strands of work.

GAME PRACTICE

Even young students can use coordinate graphs in simplified form. Think of the game *Battleship*, in which players guess the position of their opponent's ships using letter/number coordinates (ten letters along the bottom, or x axis, and ten numbers along the side, or y axis). For younger students, a modified form is appropriate (see *Age-Appropriate Adaptations*). Older students will enjoy this game as a warm up to their latitude/longitude project. They could even be challenged to design a new version of Battleship that incorporates latitude/longitude. An educational computer game called *Hurkle* practices the same plotting skills as children try to find a hidden beast on a grid (http://www.aimsedu.org/aimskids/ipuzzles/hurkle/index.html).

PART 4 ACTIVITY: MARK POSITION ON CHART

Your crew will be logging daily positions on a chart throughout the trip. Students should transfer this information to their own data sheets. One sheet should simply be a table of the date, latitude, and longitude. It will quickly become clear that such a list does not convey information in a useful format – hence the need for a graph or chart. This is an important point to stress.

Each child should use an appropriate level of detail in his or her work (degree only, degree/minute, or degree/minute/second). Students should transfer their position onto a sheet of graph paper daily. This exercise makes them familiar with coordinate graphing. Students who quickly grasp this task can go on to measuring point to point distance made good and calculating average boat speed. On passages, students could create an annotated coordinate graph that serves as a snapshot journal, with brief notes made directly onto the graph (whale or freighter sightings, air temperature). In fact, this could turn into a nice souvenir of the passage for the entire crew!

Age-Appropriate Adaptations

In this section, you will find guidance on how to differentiate, or adapt, this unit for your child. Start with the correct age group, but also glance through the notes for one level younger or older, then mix and match as appropriate.

Self-assessment and reflection are valuable learning tools. They encourage students to think back upon their work and store their new body of knowledge in a meaningful and memorable manner. To that end, a number of self-assessment and reflection questions are listed for each age group. Remember that completed assignments and written reflection are useful records to later document student work for a school administration.

Ages 4-6

Young children can complete the activities described in this chapter with some modifications and assistance. Concentrate on the main cardinal directions and disregard variation/deviation. Parents will have to provide a lot of help in handling a compass. The important thing is to take the mystery out of map reading and demonstrate the logic. Basic experiments with magnets would be an effective way to round out this unit (see *Enrichment*).

Part 1 Activity: *Chart your anchorage* or *Draw a treasure map*. Making a treasure map is a suitable activity for students in this age group. Brainstorm ideas before putting pen to paper. Young children might enjoy creating a map from different materials, not just pencil and paper. The map should have a good degree of detail and include some basic legend or scale information. Students will need help in measuring spaces or labeling features.

Part 2 / Activity 1: *Hands-on topographic mapping.* Very young children will likely be confused by contour lines and therefore this activity is beneficial, not to mention fun. Children can measure and pour in sand while a parent draws the contours.

Part 2 / Activity 2: *Plan and follow a route.* Parents can ease young students into map reading by narrating their own route-planning aloud while the child traces the route with a finger. Then the child can move on to a basic version of this activity, given a fairly simple, predetermined task on land rather than on the water. The parent-teacher should suggest start and end points and may act as scribe to write the plan down.

Part 3 Activity: *Compass Challenge.* Young children should begin by trimming down the simple twenty step square exercise (Practice 1) to ten steps. Then they can try the triangle challenge by using twenty steps instead of 100 meters. Practice taking even paces first! Choose an area where the terrain is fairly level and free of obstacles, like a sports field. Spice up this exercise by encouraging an imaginative setting: you are explorers in a dense jungle! You are climbing over ice floes on the way to the North Pole!

Part 4 Activity: *Coordinate Graphing.* A simplified game of *Battleship* will introduce young minds to the idea of coordinate graphs on a basic level. Set up a simple 4x4 game with sea animals across the side and colors across the top, guessing the location of the explorer submarine by calling out "blue octopus," for example. When students become familiar with this game, show them how latitude/longitude on a chart are similar.

Self-Assessment and Reflection: Children should orally review their experience with questions such as:

- *What did you learn about reading a map?*
- *What was difficult and what was easy for you in drawing a map / planning a route / using a compass?*
- *What are some ways in which maps and navigation are useful to you?*
- *What would you teach another student about maps and compasses?*

Ages 6-8

Students ages six to eight are capable of working through all the activities in this unit with minor modifications or adult guidance. The concepts of variation and deviation might be introduced to the older end of this age group.

Part 1 Activity: *Chart your anchorage* or *Draw a treasure map*. Making a treasure map is a suitable activity for students in this age group. Have your child outline some ideas first. Maps should be as detailed as possible and include a legend, scale, and a point of orientation.

Part 2 / Activity 1: *Hands-on topographic mapping.* Contour lines can be very confusing so this activity is highly recommended for children in this age group. They will need a fair amount of assistance drawing the contour lines but will enjoy the hands-on nature of the job!

Part 2 / Activity 2: *Plan and follow a route.* Parents should provide support for the child's first map-reading attempt with a simple version of this activity on land. The student should make some written notes about distances and landmarks. Proficient map readers can move on to an easily navigated area. Alternatively, the child can partner with an adult to plan and execute one route, and then work more independently on a second, similar route.

Part 3 Activity: *Compass Challenge.* Students should try the triangle challenge by using thirty steps instead of 100 meters. Practice taking even paces first! For starters, choose an area where the terrain is fairly level and free of obstacles. Next, try it with more steps or in an area with more obstacles. Afterwards, discuss the challenges of using a compass over uneven ground. Spice up this exercise by encouraging an imaginative setting: you are an explorer in Borneo! You are scrambling through a deep canyon!

Part 4 Activity: *Coordinate Graphing.* The game *Battleship* is a good lead-in to coordinate graphing, and students in this age group can begin to plot latitude/longitude in whole degrees once they see the link. For this, they need help setting up a sheet of graph paper that is marked with the relevant latitude/longitude range. They might enjoy solving simple challenges such as naming a higher latitude, and pointing to where (off the chart) it would be. Where is home? Where is the other boat we overheard on the radio?

Self-Assessment and Reflection: Students should reflect on the process they went through by answering questions such as:
- *What is the hardest thing about reading a map?*
- *What was difficult and what was easy for you in drawing a map / planning a route / using a compass? How accurate was your work?*
- *What are some ways that maps and navigation are useful to you?*
- *What are the most important things to remember about maps and navigation?*

Ages 8-10

Students in this age group are fully capable of going through all the activities as detailed in the text, working independently after initial guidance. They can be introduced to the concepts of variation and deviation without necessarily making corrections to their own compass bearings. They should learn that one degree is made up of sixty minutes.

Part 1 Activity: *Chart your anchorage* or *Draw a treasure map.* Students must invest significant effort into creating a quality product. It is a good idea to go through a draft process and outline ideas first. The map should include reference to scale, orientation, and a legend. More advanced students with a good understanding of maps can try charting an anchorage.

Part 2 / Activity 1: *Hands-on topographic mapping.* This activity will help students to interpret the picture that contour lines create. Once the activity is set up, they can work fairly independently.

Part 2 / Activity 2: *Plan and follow a route.* Students in this age group can plan a somewhat longer route that follows clear landmarks over a large area. Students should draw up a written plan that includes distances and landmarks, and act as first mate for the day. Parents should allow children to lead the way as much as possible.

Part 3 Activity: *Compass Challenge.* Students should "warm up" by practicing even pacing and calculating the length of their step. Then they can try the triangle challenge with fifty instead of 100 meters. If they come out far off the mark, give them a few pointers and try again. Eventually, students can work their way up to greater distances.

Part 4 Activity: *Coordinate Graphing.* Students ages eight to ten can manipulate lat/long values to the minute and aim to plot positions accurately.

Self-Assessment and Reflection: Students should complete a short written reflection with points such as:
- *Are certain types of maps easier or harder to understand? Why?*
- *What was difficult and what was easy for you in drawing a map / planning a route / using a compass? How accurate was your work?*
- *What are some ways that maps and navigation are useful to you? What are some ways that maps and tools of navigation are useful to other people?*
- *What are the key points to remember about maps and navigation?*
- *What are you able to do now that you couldn't do before?*

Ages 10-12

Students ages ten to twelve will enjoy the opportunity to play the adventurer and expand their independence through mapping activities. They can apply the concepts of variation and deviation to real-life situations.

Part 1 Activity: *Chart your anchorage* or *Draw a treasure map.* Students in this age group should take on the task of charting an anchorage. They should outline ideas and make a plan before getting started. The anchorage chart should be specific, detailed, and neat, and include a legend, scale, and a point of orientation.

Part 2 / Activity 1: *Hands-on topographic mapping.* Students who quickly grasp the idea of contour lines might skip this activity. Still, it is a good way to reinforce the concept and therefore might be included for fun.

Part 2 Activity 2: *Plan and follow a route.* Students can move from a simple route to a more complex challenge in less familiar territory. A plan should be written down with careful attention to detail. Parents should provide as little input as possible within obvious limits of safety.

Part 3 Activity: *Compass Challenge.* Older students can first get the hang of this activity over an easy course and then move on to more challenging terrain. They should travel at least 100 meters on each side of their triangle and work independently, handling the compass and reading bearings alone.

Part 4 Activity: *Coordinate Graphing.* Older children can handle full latitude/longitude positions and should be encouraged to plot them directly onto the ship's chart. If traveling with other yachts, children can plot the positions of multiple boats onto a chart and then calculate the distance between them, as well as the average speed. They can deal with the sixty seconds in a minute, sixty minutes in a degree issue more easily than younger children.

Self-Assessment and Reflection: Students should complete a written reflection with points such as:
- *What are the key points to remember about maps and navigation?*
- *What can a map tell us about the person who made it?*
- *What was difficult and what was easy for you in drawing a map / planning a route / using a compass? How accurate was your work?*
- *What are some ways that maps and navigation can be useful to you? What are some ways that maps and tools of navigation are useful in other situations?*

Enrichment

Any way of exploring the real world using a map will enrich your child's understanding of this topic. The more practice, the better! There are also a number of interesting ways to study the theory behind the practice. For example, get a set of **magnets** and iron filings to demonstrate magnetic fields and forces. Better yet, make a simple compass or even an astrolabe (see *Resources*). This unit details several map/compass activities, but there are many more. For example, try dead reckoning or taking a fix from several bearings.

A visit to a historic lighthouse or maritime museum can show students early tools of navigation and explain the difficulties that early explorers had in using them. If you can locate a Fresnel lighthouse lens, your discussion could even branch into a discussion of optics. Meanwhile, animal lovers can extend this unit by researching animal navigation, such as echolocation in bats or dolphins, or the ability sea turtles have to "feel" the earth's magnetic field.

A study of place names on maps quickly turns into a **geography** / history lesson. If New Zealand is new, where is old Zealand? (It's part of Holland, spelled Zeeland.) Many Caribbean islands have a place named "Soufriere" – why? (It comes from the French word for sulphur, indicating volcanic activity). Can you find places with indigenous names? Explore the meaning behind names such as Massachusetts, Mauna Kea, or even Ulladulla (Australia).

Cross-Curricular Links

This unit absolutely bursts with potential cross-curricular links. One mathematics link (coordinate graphing) is already integrated into this unit.

History: This unit links directly to Unit 7, *The Voyages of Christopher Columbus,* and Unit 8, *The Voyages of Captain Cook*. Children could study how tools of navigation developed over time, or read about how Lucayo islanders used bean maps to show Columbus the layout of the Caribbean. Why was Captain Cook so interested in the transit of Venus? Older students will enjoy reading Dava Sobel's outstanding book, *Longitude* (see *Resources)*.

Mathematics: Maps and scales lend themselves to a review of fractions and conversions. Why does a scale of 1:250,000 come out to roughly four miles? Why does 1:1,000,000 translate to 1 centimeter for 10 kilometers?

Science: Celestial navigation is closely tied to astronomy. Some relevant topics are introduced in *Unit 1: Earth and Space Science*. Others can be pursued through further research. Why is the North Star useful in navigation? What exactly is local noon? How can the sun help us to establish our position?

Social Studies: Students can research non-European map-making traditions. An excellent comparison of European and Native American map-making can be found at www.lewisandclarkexhibit.org/4_0_0/page_4_1_2_1_0.html. To see a driftwood map, check http://spacecollective.org/mslima/3220/Inuit-Wood-Maps. Some Pacific Islanders have a great reputation for "reading" natural signs in the sky and water to help them find their way. Even the best modern-day navigator would be hard pressed to match them! See www.lat34north.com/cities/CitiesNavigation.cfm#PolynesianNavigation.

Resources

A website with a great collection of maps of all types (some animated) is http://subdude-site.com/WebPics/WebPicsMaps/WebPicsMaps_dir.htm. You can find a good, interactive mapping resource in the www.fossweb.com science site: see *Landforms* under (US) Grades 3-6. To make a compass, see http://www.madsci.org/experiments/archive/860218908.Es.html. To make a simple astrolabe, see the University of California at Berkeley's excellent site for Activities 7 (*Making an Astrolabe*) and 8 (*Using an Astrolabe*): http://cse.ssl.berkeley.edu/AtHomeAstronomy/activity_07.html.

Rachel Dickinson's *Tools of Navigation: A Kid's Guide to the History and Science of Finding Your Way* (Nomad Press, 2005) includes many hands-on activities, making this is a useful book for families who wish to delve more deeply into navigation. Dava Sobel's fascinating and highly readable *Longitude* is a history book that reads like a mystery novel. It is highly recommended for parents and advanced young readers. There are several editions available. The book has also been made into a TV and DVD series.

Unit 10 - Physical Education:
Heart Rate and Exercise

True enjoyment comes from activity of the mind and exercise of the body; the two are united.

Alexander von Humboldt

Education is what remains after one has forgotten what one has learned in school.

Albert Einstein

Unit 10 - Physical Education: Heart Rate and Exercise

Materials:
Stopwatch

Guiding Question:
How does my body react to exercise?

Learning Outcomes:
Students will be able to measure their heart rate and understand why it varies.
Students will be able to predict how the body reacts to exercise.

Introduction and Overview

It's hard to imagine going to Physical Education class on a sailboat, isn't it? In fact, students can learn a fundamental lesson even within the confines of a boat: our bodies react to physical activity in predictable ways. After all, P.E. is not only games: it is a study of health, fitness, and the human body.

This unit includes an active component and a reflection section. The heart rate "lab" is a physically active experience in which students study their own bodies' reactions to exercise.

Heart Rate "Lab"

Begin with a discussion of the heart's function in the body. The heart is part of the cardiovascular system. It is a strong muscle that never rests. The heart is a pump that pushes blood through the body, bringing oxygen in and taking away byproducts of exercise.

Each student should practice finding his or her pulse. This is best achieved by putting the index and middle finger over the carotid artery in the neck. This is one place where the pulse is easy to feel. Never take a pulse with your thumb, because blood flow through the thumb can produce a noticeable pulse that will affect the measurement. It is usually easy to find your pulse by squeezing your fingers against the notch in your neck, high up under the chin and slightly to one side. Most students who fail to feel their pulse touch the wrong area or do not press down enough. This takes some practice but even young students can find their pulse with time and guidance.

Next, the student should practice counting his or her pulse. One method is to measure the pulse over ten seconds and multiply by six to find heart rate in beats per minute (BPM). One person times ten seconds while the student counts. To complete this exercise, students must be able to find their pulse quickly and count accurately (for very young children, a parent can take the pulse). A heart rate monitor would instantly provide an exact reading of one's pulse – too bad they are rarely found on sailboats!

Now students can establish resting heart rate. This is best done when the body is in a very relaxed state, preferably lying down or at least sitting quietly for several minutes. Take the pulse for ten seconds (this is a raw score) and multiply by six to get BPM. Some people prefer to count the pulse for six seconds and multiply by ten, but this method leaves more room for error in miscounts. Normally, a resting heart rate is around 60-80 BPM, though some people are even lower. If it is higher, the student probably isn't fully at rest.

Rather than jumping into the activity, parents and children might spend some time simply measuring heart rate at various points of the day for practice. This will also begin to get the student thinking about why the heart rate is different during different activities.

Now prepare an exercise circuit. Students should do each activity for one minute, take their pulse immediately after the activity, and take their pulse again after resting for one minute. Then the student will do a different activity and measure again. The idea is to compare how different activities make different demands on the heart and observe how soon the body begins to recover from exertion. Move quickly from one activity to the next to keep rest times to one minute.

Prepare a table in which students can record their results, or use this table. Feel free to change the activities or add more.

Station	Beats counted after 1 min. activity	BPM (x 6)	Beats counted after 1 min. rest	BPM (x 6)
Winch turn				
Sit-ups				
Toe raises				
Pull-ups				
Step-ups				
Resting	(after 2 minutes)		(after 3 minutes)	

EXERCISE CIRCUIT

This exercise circuit has been designed to work different muscle groups. Ideally, two people would complete the "lab" so that students have more than one set of data to compare later. All activities should be done at a pace and intensity that the student can keep up for longer than one minute. They should not go all out as if it is a one minute race!

Winch turn uses the arm muscles (mostly biceps) to turn a winch (ideally, a winch under some load, even if the load is simply another person putting resistance on the line).

Sit-ups or **abdominal crunches** work the stomach muscles. These exercises start with the student lying on his back with arms behind the head or crossed over the chest. Then lift the upper body up from the floor. For a sit-up, lift all the way up so that the elbows touch the thighs. For a crunch, just lift the upper body a few centimeters off the ground. Crunches are considered the safer exercise since they put less strain on the back. Each works the abdominal muscles.

For **toe raises**, the student must stand upright, lightly holding a table or hand grip for support. Lift onto the toes, then come down to flat feet, then lift again, over and over. This works the calf (soleus) muscles.

Pull-ups work the arms again. Students should hang on a bar and pull their bodies up as far as possible and hold there for as long as possible, or go up and down. Alternatives are to simply **hang** from an overhead handhold, pull the body up a rope, or to do **push-ups**.

Step-ups work the quadriceps (the large muscle group on the front of the thighs). These can be safely performed in the companionway, using handholds for stability. Do not use a step that is higher than knee height as this will stress the joint unnecessarily. If the steps are too big, use a low step if available. Alternatively, students can stay on one step, lower one leg as if to go down, but then step that leg up again, and repeat with the other side. Another alternative would be to run in place or scissor the feet: one foot forward, one back, hop to switch feet quickly, over and over.

Any other activity could be substituted here: bouncing on settees, tossing and catching a ball, etc. Just try to alternate which muscle groups are involved and aim for activities of different intensity or difficulty.

After the last exercise, students will take their heart rate after one minute, then again (two minutes after exercise stopped) and again (three minutes after exercise stopped). This is to see how quickly the heart returns to or near its resting level. A very fit person may reach a high heart rate during exercise but will recover more quickly than a person who is out of shape.

Occasionally, students over-count their heart rate; the best way to deal with this is to discuss any outlying numbers found. For example, an exercise heart rate of 220 is improbable or too high. Ask students to think why this happens. Perhaps the child miscounted, or simply worked harder than necessary; how might he or she approach the exercise next time?

ANALYZE DATA

Students should analyze their recorded heart rates after the exercises. They should answer the following questions:

- *Which exercise put the most or least demand on my heart? Why?*
- *Did my heart rate return to the same level between each exercise? Why or why not?*
- *How quickly did my heart rate return to normal?*
- *What do these results tell me about my fitness?*

Advanced students can consider why different people have different heart rates even while doing the same exercise. Age, body size, fitness level, and intensity of exercise are all factors that affect heart rate. Generally, fit people can sustain exercise more easily (hence at a lower overall heart rate) than less fit people and recover very quickly (heart rate dropping back toward resting rate). Smokers, unfit, or overweight people will usually reach a higher heart rate during exercise because their hearts have to work extra hard to sustain the same exercise, and they will recover more slowly than healthier people.

HOW DOES MY BODY REACT TO EXERCISE?

Once the heart rate "lab" is complete, students should list ways their bodies reacted to exercise. The most obvious is that the heart rate increases. Why? (Because the muscles need more oxygen to maintain activity.) Students will also notice that they sweat, turn red, and feel tired. If the muscles get a burning feeling, it is because the byproducts of exercise (like lactic acid) cannot be taken away quickly enough by the blood.

ADVANCED WORK

Older students can address the differences between aerobic and anaerobic exercise. In brief, **aerobic** activity can be maintained over long periods of time. The heart and lungs can deliver enough oxygen to the muscles to keep up with their exertion. Examples of aerobic activities include jogging, skipping rope, or swimming at a medium pace. **Anaerobic** activity is of much higher intensity, when the body runs off chemicals stored in the muscles for short bursts.

However, these chemicals get used up very quickly so we can only maintain anaerobic exercise for about one minute. After some rest, the body recovers and can perform another round of anaerobic activity. Examples include explosive moves such as sprinting, digging powerfully in the sand, or jumping as high as possible.

Aerobic activity is important in keeping the body fit and healthy. Students can learn about the target training zone for aerobic activity. The target training zone indicates the heart rate at which a person should exercise for maximum aerobic benefit. One way to calculate your target training zone is to use this simplified formula:

$$220 - age = maximum\ heart\ rate$$
$$Target\ heart\ rate\ is\ 60\%\text{-}85\%\ of\ maximum$$

For a twelve-year-old, this means that the maximum heart rate is 208 and the target training zone is between 125 to 177 BPM. Anyone working out with a lower heart rate is not getting much benefit from the exercise. Anyone working out over 180 BPM is working at too high an intensity; this may help train the anaerobic system in short bursts but otherwise risks injury or provides little aerobic benefit.

Students can look at their heart rate lab results to determine if they reached the target zone for aerobic exercise. Although one minute in the target zone is insufficient, this builds awareness of the types of exercise students could do to keep healthy if they maintained their effort over time. On a passage-making boat, it is hard to achieve the recommended aerobic exercise minimum of twenty minutes, three to four times per week! However, students can use their newfound information to plan aerobic activities, either on board or once they have the chance to go ashore.

Age-Appropriate Adaptations

In this section, you will find guidance on how to differentiate, or adapt, this unit for your child. Start with the correct age group, but also glance through the notes for one level younger or older, then mix and match as appropriate.

Self-assessment and reflection are valuable learning tools. They encourage students to think back upon their work and store their new body of knowledge in a meaningful and memorable manner. To that end, a number of self-assessment and reflection questions are listed for each age group. It is not necessary to address all the questions; substitute others as you see fit. Completed assignments and written reflection are useful records to later document student work for a school administration.

Ages 4-6

Activity: *Heart Rate Lab*. The main difficulty preschool students have with this activity is finding and counting their heart rate. They should be able to feel their hearts pounding quickly after intense exercise, even without counting, by simply putting a hand over their chest. However, students will not feel their heart rate when it is slower. Even young students who can find their pulse usually do not count beats accurately.

Therefore, parents can take two approaches in guiding young students through this lesson. First, one could complete the lesson without measuring heart rate at all and only use perceived fatigue as an indicator. Students will certainly notice when their breathing becomes faster or more labored, and can compare different activities. They can then draw a conclusion as to which activity made their bodies work hardest. Alternatively, a parent could measure the student's pulse. Parents will also have to convert the ten second measurement to BPM. Students can keep involved by ticking boxes provided by parents, rating each activity as "easy – medium – tiring."

Self-Assessment and Reflection: This can be a simple matter of reviewing the student's work orally through questions like:
* *What is a pulse? What does it feel like?*
* *How could you get better at finding and measuring your pulse?*
* *How does your body react to exercise?*
* *What exercise do you get in a typical day? Is it enough?*
* *Which activity was the hardest? Why?*

Ages 6-8

Activity: *Heart Rate Lab.* Some students will be able to find and count their pulse, while others will struggle. With help, most students in this age group should be able to find their pulse, if not count it. If this is the case, a parent can measure the student's heart rate. The student should be responsible for recording the values. This lab also provides an opportunity for older students to practice multiplication, converting raw pulse scores to BPM. Beginners with multiplication can use the less accurate six second raw heart rate measurement and multiply by ten to get BPM.

Verbal answers to questions would suffice though it is a good exercise for students to write at least short answers to the questions in the *Analyze Data* section of this unit.

Self-Assessment and Reflection: Children ages six to eight can reflect on the process they went through in a discussion based on these points:
- *What is the heart's job? What is a pulse?*
- *How does the body react to activity?*
- *How quickly did your heart rate return to normal?*
- *Do you feel fit? How can you tell? What activities do you do?*
- *How well could you track changes in our heart rate? How could you improve?*

Ages 8-10

Activity: *Heart Rate Lab.* With practice, students ages eight to ten can find and measure their own pulse and therefore work through the heart rate lab in full. They can convert their ten second pulse to BPM. The upper end of this age group can be introduced to the concepts of aerobic and anaerobic exercise, and analyze their results accordingly. Which activities seem to be aerobic and which anaerobic?

Self-Assessment and Reflection: Students in this age group should begin with a discussion and then summarize key points in a short written reflection. Key points include:
- *What is the heart's job?*

- *What is a pulse? How do we find it? What can it tell you?*
- *How does the body react to activity?*
- *How quickly did your heart rate return to normal?*
- *Do you feel fit? How can you tell? What activities do you do?*
- *How well could you track changes in your heart rate? What errors did you make? How could you do better?*

Ages 10-12

Activity: *Heart Rate Lab.* These students can complete the heart rate lab in full and work quite independently, including calculating BPM and target training zone. They should use the terms *aerobic* and *anaerobic*, as well as learn about the target training zone for aerobic activity, how to calculate it, and what it is used for.

Self-Assessment and Reflection: Students ages ten to twelve can complete a written reflection about their work. The following questions can guide them.
- *What is the heart's job?*
- *What can your pulse tell you? How do you find it?*
- *How does the body react to activity?*
- *Discuss any outlying numbers and identify possible reasons to explain them (overcounting, working at a very high intensity, etc).*
- *Did you reach the target heart rate zone during any of the activities? Why or why not?*
- *Do you feel fit? How can you tell?*
- *What areas can you improve in?*

Enrichment

After completing the lab, students could create their own fitness circuit that can be completed on board or on shore. Those discussing aerobic activity could measure their heart rate at intervals throughout an extended exercise period when the opportunity arises. Exercise can be playful like kicking a ball or playing catch on a beach, though it should work the body continuously for twenty minutes or more.

Another opportunity for enrichment would be to discuss the elements of fitness with students ages eight and above. **Health-related** components of fitness include cardiovascular endurance (the ability of the heart to work at intensity for an extended period of time), muscular strength (the ability to exert a force), muscular endurance (the ability of specific muscle groups to perform over time, like doing sit-ups or playing an entire tennis match), flexibility (how "bendable" the body is), and body composition (the ratio of muscle to fat). All of these areas can be improved through an exercise program.

Sometimes, specialists refer to **skill-related** components of fitness. These include reaction time, speed, agility, balance, coordination, and power (slightly different than strength: this is the ability to apply an intense effort in a short burst). Students can discuss which components are most important in various activities: swimming, basketball, cycling, sailing, etc.

Very motivated students could even test their fitness in the various health-related components. When you have Internet access, look up one of the following sites:

Top End Sports (http://www.topendsports.com/testing/tests.htm) lists practical methods to test each component of fitness.

The (US) "Presidential Fitness Test" (www.presidentschallenge.org) guides students through different tests and allows them to compare their results to national norms. Are their scores below or above average? Which areas are their strengths? What are their weaknesses? How might these be developed? To find a description of tests and standards, follow prompts for *teachers - fitness file - program details – physical fitness test*.

Cross-Curricular Links

Mathematics: Students can create a line graph from the data they collect in the course of this study to link in with Unit 4. This will illustrate how their heart rate rises during exercise and drops after rest periods.

Science: This unit is a good complement to Unit 2, the Fish Dissection, in which students study the organs and body systems of a fish. While fish and humans are clearly different, seeing a heart first hand helps students better appreciate the body's responses to physical activity and the organs involved.

Resources

The Magic School Bus series provides several excellent supporting materials for this unit. The characters are students who take amazing field trips. The series is aimed at elementary school children but is very instructive for older students as well. Learn more about human anatomy through Joanna Cole's *The Magic School Bus Inside the Human Body* (illustrated by Bruce Degen). This book tells an educational and humorous story, surrounded by fact boxes filled with supporting details and illustrations that help bring systems to life. It takes an inside look at the heart and other organs at work (published by Scholastic Books, New York, 1989).

In the three-part DVD *The Magic School Bus Super Sports Fun*, one episode called "The Magic School Bus Works Out" illustrates the processes studied in this unit. The Magic School Bus travels inside the teacher's body while she takes part in a race. The video does an excellent job showing how the body reacts to exercise, as the bus travels through the heart and blood to the muscles (Scholastic, Inc. and Warner Brothers Entertainment, September 2009).

Appendices

Appendix A: Sample Unit Breakdowns

This appendix demonstrates how the units in this book can be divided into manageable daily lessons of forty-five minutes to one hour each. The two examples subdivide Units 1 and 7 into ten or more lessons. Other units in this book are shorter and might be covered in three to five lessons using the same general approach. Most divide naturally at the end of Part 1, 2, and so on. Unit 6: *Writing* can be extended over several months or repeated in cycles to gradually develop a child's skills. To complete your lesson plans, consult the *Age-Appropriate Adaptations* section in each unit to tailor lessons to your child's level.

These examples cover one subject in isolation. Math and literacy lessons would run in parallel to these sample science and history units. Often, you can find authentic links to other subject areas and weave them in, or at least use them as a springboard into another subject area (see Appendix B).

Sample Breakdown of Unit 1 - Earth and Space Science

Lesson 1	Introduction: brainstorm and generate questions. Begin Part 1: formulate questions, plan research and methods, and prepare data collection notebook. Begin data collection.
Lesson 2	Begin Part 2: Set up model. Model day/night/time zones and lunar orbit. Discuss phases of moon and tides.
Lesson 3	Continue Part 2: Model solar and lunar eclipses.
Lesson 4	Research any questions that arose in previous lessons and list new ones. Read fiction stories related to moon (see *Resources*).
Lesson 5	Begin Part 2 assignment.
Lesson 6	Complete Part 2 assignment. Explore a cross-curricular link in a parallel lesson (for example, Columbus).

Lesson 7	Check in with Part 1: Review data collected to date and revise methods as necessary. Which trends seem to emerge? Then move on to explore an Enrichment topic (constellations, moon study) or do *At Home Astronomy* activities (see *Resources*).
Lesson 8	Begin work on Part 1 assignment after the lunar cycle observations are completed.
Lesson 9	Complete work on Part 1 assignment.
Lesson 10	Wrap up questions generated. Complete self-assessment and reflection on unit.

This is just one way that Unit 1 can be subdivided into a series of lessons. Similarly, Unit 7 can be covered in a dozen or more lessons that span two weeks to a month. The final, follow-up lesson should take place a few days after completion of all other lessons. This short break should allow a fresh perspective and facilitate clearer self-assessment and reflection.

Sample Breakdown of Unit 7 - History: The Voyages of Columbus

Lesson 1	Introduce topic, establish connection as sailors and brainstorm questions. Begin Part 1.
Lesson 2	Complete Part 1 including assignment. Literacy link: writing a persuasive letter using a specific voice.
Lesson 3	Begin Part 2, focusing on *Columbus the Sailor and Navigator.* Dead reckoning activity. Math link: measurement.
Lesson 4	Continue Part 2, focusing on the first part of *The 1492 Voyage.* Locate referenced places on map. Generate questions to research later.
Lesson 5	Complete Part 2, focusing on the second part of *The 1492 Voyage.* Begin Part 2 assignment.

Lesson 6	Research questions that have emerged so far and note new questions that arise. Complete Part 2 assignment.
Lesson 7	Begin Part 3, *Second* and *Third Voyages.* Begin activity (plot Columbus' trips on a chart). Math link: coordinate graphing.
Lesson 8	Continue Part 3, *Fourth Voyage.* Complete activity (plot Columbus' trips on a chart). Science link: model an eclipse.
Lesson 9	Do Part 3 assignment: essay or artwork. Work toward age-appropriate writing benchmarks in the essay.
Lesson 10	Begin Part 4: *Consequences.* Work on Part 4 activity.
Lesson 11	Continue Part 4 with Part 4 assignment. Explore an *Enrichment* topic.
Lesson 12	Complete outstanding work and/or Part 4 assignment. Follow up on questions generated along the way or explore *Enrichment* topics.
Lesson 13	Complete self-assessment and reflection.

It makes sense to break the unit into a specific plan, but be flexible. Experienced teachers know that even meticulous plans are bound to change as the unit unfolds.

Appendix B:
Resources, Interdisciplinary Units, and Field Trips

This appendix will help you find ready-made lesson plans that you can adapt for your own purposes, as well as to design interdisciplinary units and effective field trips. As a parent-teacher, you will quickly learn to identify and make the most of teachable moments. A child's natural curiosity can be kindled by only a small hint, and you're off on an interesting lesson!

RESOURCES

There are many resources available to help parents design their own lessons. Public school systems usually post curricular documents on the Internet. You can refer to *Appendix C* to find documents that often include topic overviews, guiding questions, learning outcomes, and in some cases, even detailed lesson plans, worksheets, test samples, and so on.

Entire directories of lesson plans abound on the Internet, organized by grade level and subject area. These often include links to supporting resources and PDF files you can download before setting sail. Some reliable sources include:

- www.eduref.org/Virtual/Lessons/
- www.lessonplans4teachers.com
- www.lessonplanspage.com
- www.lessonplans.com
- www.fossweb.com. This site offers detailed science research units, with math links, developed by UC Berkeley for teachers and parents.
- http://mathforum.org/library/resource_types/lesson_plans/: This site features an extensive library of mathematics lesson plans (linked to U.S. mathematics standards) that include activities, materials, exercises (Internet-based and paper/pencil), and even literature links.
- http://jmathpage.com: Johnnie's Math Page is a comprehensive website created by an experienced math teacher. It includes links to math games, worksheets, puzzles, books, and stories.

There are many sailing families are out there, living aboard and providing a sound education for their children. Their blogs often discuss daily schooling routines and their satisfaction with different home schooling programs. Take a look at www.womenandcruising.com or search sailblogs.com for "Kid Kruisers" (www.sailblogs.com/groups/groupdetail.php?gid=10).

You can also refer to one of the many home schooling websites that exist. On the other hand, too much information can become overwhelming! Don't get bogged down but rather trust in your ability to do a good job. After all, nobody knows your child as well as you.

DESIGNING INTERDISCIPLINARY UNITS

As you gain experience as a teacher, creating your own lesson plans will be easier. However, research and planning are required to transform a general interest lesson into one that also develops critical skills across subject areas.

The *How To's* section of this book went through steps in designing your own educational units and daily lessons. You can follow the same process for creating an interdisciplinary unit that combines a number of different subjects. To do so, start with an interesting theme and look for ways to bring in specific skill sets from a variety of subjects. These skill sets can be culled from learning outcomes, available from school districts or government bodies such as the ones listed in Appendix C.

Let's say the kids are excited about volcanoes. In many prime sailing destinations, you will be among active, inactive, or extinct volcanoes, so conducting a basic lesson in volcanoes and geology will be easy – but you want to ensure progress in important math and literacy skills at the same time. Study your downloaded list of school standards for literacy and mathematics. How can you embed those within the context of volcanoes?

Take Virginia's Grade 2 literacy standards, which include: "The student will write stories, letters, and simple explanations." Bring that into your volcano unit by including a lesson on writing an explanation of how volcanoes work, including self-editing and details like: "Use correct spelling for high-frequency sight words, including compound words and regular plurals." You can pull in math the same way, keying in to standards such as: "The student, given grid paper, will estimate and then count the number of square units needed to cover a given surface in order to determine area" (Virginia Department of Education, 2010). Adapt this by using a map and estimating the area of a local volcano.

Through interdisciplinary units, you can encourage your child's interests and keep learning real while developing subject-specific skills. This doesn't all have to happen in one lesson, nor does every lesson have to be a masterpiece of interdisciplinary planning. But when you can pull different threads together, the resulting learning experience will be all the more powerful.

PLANNING EDUCATIONAL FIELD TRIPS

A field trip is a great way to link formal education with real-life experiences and to make cross-curricular links. The problem with formal schooling is that it is often too abstract to truly captivate children. The problem with a *casual* field trip, however, is that it remains an isolated experience without a view of the big picture. That is why an *effective* field trip should be the second of three steps. First comes preparation. Have your children list what they know – or think they know – about the topic. Read background information to find out more and dispel any misconceptions. Generate a checklist of points to observe and questions to answer during the field trip. A thorough checklist will turn your child into a focused researcher rather than a casual tourist.

During the field trip, have your children take notes that answer their own questions as well as a bigger, guiding question. This question should be an open-ended one that leads to further inquiry and can be pursued in various directions; use the guiding questions in each unit of this book as a guide. Finally, follow up afterward with a small project that reinforces the lesson. This could be a journal entry, a fictional story inspired by the field trip, or a handmade "Kids' Field Guide to Volcanoes." The idea is to reconcile the child's previous knowledge with the new and to build connections with core subjects.

Appendix C: Links to National and State Curricula

This appendix cross-references the science, mathematics, and writing units with national or state curricula from four different countries. The purpose is to help parents identify how *Lesson Plans Ahoy!* units relate to schoolwork "back home." Home schooling families on extended cruises are advised to download full curriculum documents from their region. In order to present a vast body of information within a compact format, I have paraphrased or condensed the wording into references that can be viewed at a glance. The history, navigation, and physical education units are not referenced here since they contain very targeted information; nevertheless, these units can be differentiated and adapted to closely match national and state curricula.

It would be impossible to list the curricula of all US or Australian states and Canadian provinces. Therefore, I have chosen to use the examples of Virginia (US), Ontario (Canada), and Victoria (Australia). You can find the curricula of other regions through a quick Internet search. In the case of the UK I have referenced the national curriculum. Please note that all curricula are constantly being re-worked; use the links listed below to check for the most up-to-date documents.

In most cases, the units in *Lesson Plans Ahoy!* correlate closely to work required in school systems. In a few cases, however, a certain grade or year level does not match exactly. For example, while the Earth and Space Science unit fits very well with Virginia grades 1/3/4/6 and UK years 1/3/4/5/6, the subject matter does not appear in Virginia grade five or UK year two. In such cases, I have listed the closest match in parentheses.

NOTES

Virginia (US): The source document for Virginia's curriculum is dated 2004. The link is: http://www.doe.virginia.gov/instruction/index.shtml. Follow the right side column to *elementary/middle school* and then subject. For a more compact overview, it can be useful to look at one district's home page: http://stafford.schoolfusion.us/modules/cms/pages.phtml?pageid=59627#6-8. For four-year-olds, use Virginia's *Foundation Blocks for Early Learning* from 2007: http://www.doe.virginia.gov/instruction/early_childhood/school_readiness/index.shtml.

Ontario (Canada): The source documents for Ontario's curriculum are dated 2005 (Mathematics) and 2007 (Science and Technology). The link is: http://www.edu.gov.on.ca/eng/curriculum/elementary/subjects.html. You can also find the draft document for Ontario's new (2010) *Full Day Learning – Kindergarten Program* for four- and five-year-olds at: http://www.edu.gov.on.ca/eng/curriculum/elementary/kindergarten.html.

Please note that in science, Ontario uses a "Continuum for Scientific Inquiry/Experimentation Skills." In order to fit the continuum descriptors within this overview, I have assigned levels to specific grades (for example, "Exploring" level under grade three). The Ontario curriculum does not assign any level of the continuum to any specific grade. Parents should scan the science links document to understand the subtle differences between levels in the continuum and aim for the level they think best challenges their children.

Victoria (Australia): The source document for Victoria's curriculum is: http://ausvels.vcaa.vic.edu.au. Look under *Download Curriculum* in the headline banner. Links to all Australian state curricula can be found under: http://www.curriculum.edu.au/ccsite/default.asp?id=20029. The Victoria curriculum aims at levels to be completed over a two year period; the second year extends the challenges of the first. That is why you will see the same descriptor for two different years that fall under the same levels. As this book went to press, Australia was drafting a new National Curriculum for Science. This could bring changes to the information listed here.

United Kingdom: A source document for the UK National Curriculum is http://www.education.gov.uk/schools/teachingandlearning/curriculum. This describes broad, two year "Key Stage" standards. You can also refer to much more detailed, useful lesson plans that break down the very broad Key Stages into manageable units of work. Go to www.schoolsnet.com and click on "Lessons" (at the top), then primary or secondary lessons under "classroom" (on the left), and finally the subject area (such as "Science") to find the precise units referred to in the *Curricular Links* tables that follow.

CURRICULAR LINKS TO UNIT 1 - EARTH AND SPACE SCIENCE

Age	Virginia (US)	Ontario (Canada)	UK (National)	Victoria (Australia)
4-5	Early Childhood. (Create a shadow and describe how it was created.)	Early Learning. (State problems and pose questions.)	Reception. Ask questions about the natural world. Study seasons.	Pre-K (Level 1). (Observe and measure, collect, record, and display data.)
5-6	Kindergarten. (Conduct investigations in which basic properties of objects are identified by direct observations. Objects are described pictorially and verbally.)	Kindergarten. Describe natural occurrences using observations. Describe and represent cycles in the natural world. Pose questions and make predictions.	Year 1 (Key Stage 1) *Unit 1D: Light and Dark, Section 6: The Sun.* Identify changes that occur when the sun goes behind a cloud (different from changes at night).	Kindergarten (Level 1). See above.
6-7	Grade 1. Investigate and understand basic relationships between the sun and Earth (night and day, the rotation of Earth). Conduct observations, make predictions based on patterns of observation.	Grade 1. *Daily and Seasonal Changes:* study how these changes affect living things. Investigate the changes in the amount of light from the sun throughout the day and year.	Year 2 (Key Stage 1). (Collect evidence by making observations and measurements when trying to answer a question. Compare what happened with what they expected would happen and try to explain it.)	Year 1 (Level 2). Observe and describe phenomena; for example, phases of the moon. Repeat observations over time to make predictions.
7-8	Grade 2. (Conduct investigations in which conclusions are based on observations and simple physical models are constructed.)	Grade 2. (Beginning level: ask questions, make "guesses," record data, propose an answer, describe what was done and observed.)	Year 3 (Key Stage 2). *Unit 3F: Light and Shadows, Section 7: Showing How the Earth Spins.*	Year 2 (Level 2). See above.

Age	Virginia (US)	Ontario (Canada)	UK (National)	Victoria (Australia)
8-9	Grade 3. Investigate and understand basic patterns and cycles occurring in nature. Key concepts include patterns of natural events: day and night, seasonal changes, phases of the moon, and tides.	Grade 3. (Exploring level: ask questions, make predictions, select equipment, record and discuss data, draw a conclusion based on observations, make a simple evaluation of the experiment.)	Year 4 (Key Stage 2). Understand how day and night are related to the spin of the earth on its axis. The earth orbits the sun once a year and the moon takes approximately 28 days to orbit the earth.	Year 3 (Level 3). Investigate changes: for example, day becoming night.
9-10	Grade 4. Model, sequence, and describe moon phases. Create a model of the sun-Earth-moon system with approximate scale distances and sizes, and investigate how eclipses occur.	Grade 4. (Emerging level: ask questions, create a plan, make simple predictions, select equipment, record, organize, and discuss data, draw simple conclusions, evaluate.)	Year 5 (Key Stage 2). *Unit 5E: Earth, Sun, and Moon.* Using models, pupils learn how the three bodies move relative to each other.	Year 4 (Level 3). See previous.
10-11	Grade 5. (Plan and conduct investigations in which data are collected, recorded, and reported. Predictions are made and simple graphical data are extrapolated.)	Grade 5. (Competent level: formulate a question, plan, predict, select equipment, record, organize, and discuss data. Draw simple conclusions, evaluate.)	Year 6 (Key Stage 2). Understand how day and night are related to the spin of the earth on its own axis. The earth orbits the sun once a year and the moon takes approx. 28 days to orbit the earth.	Year 5 (Level 4). Consider how models are used to explain structures; for example, the arrangement of planets in the solar system.
11-12	Grade 6. Study gravity, revolution, rotation, mechanics of day and night, and phases of the moon. Study the relationship of the earth's tilt and seasons, and tides.	Grade 6. *Space.* Investigate the relationship between the earth, sun, and moon. Explain phenomena that result from their movements. Model the earth's rotation around the sun.	Year 7 (Key Stage 3). *Unit 7L: The Solar System and Beyond.* Consolidate ideas about the sun and moon and use models to explain phenomena such as eclipses and the seasons.	Year 6 (Level 4). See above.

Age	Virginia (US)	Ontario (Canada)	UK (National)	Victoria (Australia)
12-13	Grade 7. (Data is gathered and organized in tables, line graphs. Extrapolations from graphs used to make predictions.)	Grade 7. (Proficient: formulate a question and create a plan showing variables to be considered. Predict, select equipment, record, organize, and discuss data. Draw simple conclusions, evaluate the procedure, explain changes to improve it.)	Year 8 (Key Stage 3). Understand that astronomy and space science provide insight into the nature and observed motions of the sun, moon, stars, planets and other celestial bodies.	Year 7 (Level 5). (The nature of scientific thinking is not static and relies upon the knowledge and skills that are built up over time, shared and reflected upon, while incorporating new ideas and experimental evidence.)

CURRICULAR LINKS TO UNIT 2 - SCIENCE: BIOLOGY

Age	Virginia (US)	Ontario (Canada)	UK (National)	Victoria (Australia)
4-5	Early Childhood. Describe what living things need to live and grow: food, water, and air.	Early Learning. (Identify similarities and differences between local environments.)	Reception. (Learn to ask questions about the natural world. Study body parts and the five senses.)	Pre-K (Level 1). Explore living and non-living things. Describe using general and science-specific language (hard, soft, big, small).
5-6	Kindergarten. Investigate basic needs and life processes of plants and animals. Key concepts: living things grow and need food, water, and air to survive. Plants and animals live and die.	Kindergarten. (Sort and classify groups of living and non-living things. Awareness of local natural habitats through exploration and observation. Pose questions and make predictions.)	Year 1 (Key Stage 1). Recognize and compare the main external parts of the bodies of humans and other animals. Humans and other animals need food and water to stay alive.	Kindergarten (Level 1). See above.
6-7	Grade 1. Identify and chart simple characteristics to classify animals: body coverings (fur, scales), body shape, appendages (arms, fins), method of movement, and water or land homes.	Grade 1. *Needs and Characteristics of Living Things.* Students will investigate plants and animals, including humans, and their need for air, water, food, warmth, and space.	Year 2 (Key Stage 1). *Unit 2B: Plants and animals in the local environment. Section 7: Animal Reproduction and Growth.*	Year 1 (Level 2). (Observe and describe phenomena such as insect life cycles. Generate questions and suggest forms of observations and measurements.)
7-8	Grade 2. Investigate and understand that plants and animals undergo a series of changes in their life cycles. Describe how animals are dependent on their surroundings (water, space, and shelter).	Grade 2. *Growth and Changes in Animals.* Investigate similarities and differences in the characteristics of animals. Demonstrate an understanding that animals grow, change, and have distinct characteristics; describe adaptations.	Year 3 (Key Stage 2). Learn that the heart acts as a pump to circulate blood around the body. Humans and some other animals have skeletons and muscles to support their bodies and to help them move. Animals are suited to their environment.	Year 2 (Level 2). See above.

Age	Virginia (US)	Ontario (Canada)	UK (National)	Victoria (Australia)
8-9	Grade 3. Investigate behavioral and physical adaptations that allow animals to respond to life needs (gathering food, finding shelter, defense, rearing young, hibernation, migration, camouflage, mimicry, instinct, and learned behavior).	Grade 3. (Exploring level: Ask questions, make simple predictions, select equipment, record and discuss data, draw a simple conclusion, make a simple evaluation of the experiment.)	Year 4 (Key Stage 2). *Unit 4A: Moving and Growing, Section 3: Comparing Skeletons. Unit 4B: Habitats. Section 3: Animals are suited to the environment in which they live.*	Year 3 (Level 3). Identify and describe the structural features of living things and how they operate together to form systems which support living things to survive in their environments.
9-10	Grade 4. Investigate how plants and animals in an ecosystem interact with one another and the environment (behavioral and structural adaptations, food webs, habitats and niches, life cycles).	Grade 4. *Habitats and Communities.* Demonstrate an understanding of habitats, communities, and the relationships within them. Describe structural adaptations that allow animals to survive in habitats.	Year 5 (Key Stage 2). Learn that the heart acts as a pump to circulate blood around the body. Humans and some other animals have skeletons and muscles to support ad help move their bodies. Animals are suited to their environment.	Year 4 (Level 3). See above.
10-11	Grade 5. (Plan and conduct investigations in which organisms are identified using a classification key. Data are collected, recorded, and reported using graphs, charts, and diagrams).	Grade 5. *Human Organ Systems.* Understand the structure and function of human body systems and interactions within and between systems. Describe organs in the respiratory, circulatory, and digestive systems.	Year 6 (Key Stage 2). See above.	Year 5 (Level 4). Contemplate how systems operate: the human body as a large system consisting of smaller separate systems working together.

Age	Virginia (US)	Ontario (Canada)	UK (National)	Victoria (Australia)
11-12	Grade 6. (Plan and conduct investigations, make observations involving fine discrimination between similar organisms. State hypotheses. Collect, record, analyze, and report data using appropriate metric measurements.)	Grade 6. *Biodiversity.* Investigate the characteristics of living things and classify diverse organisms according to specific characteristics.	Year 7 (Key Stage 3). *Unit 7B: Reproduction.* Compare reproductive patterns in animals and humans. *Unit 7C: Environment and Feeding Relationships.* Animals are adapted to a habitat; adaptations for feeding; food chains.	Year 6 (Level 4). See previous.
12-13	Grade 7. Study adaptations of organisms to a particular ecosystem. Animal needs include food, water, gases, shelter and space.	Grade 7. *(Interactions in the Environment.* Identify factors that affect the balance within an ecosystem. Describe the interactions of producers, consumers, and decomposers within an ecosystem.)	Year 8 (Key Stage 3). *Unit 8A: Food and Digestion. Unit 8B: Respiration, Section 11a: Do (non-human) organisms respire in a similar manner?*	Year 7 (Level 5). Students develop an understanding of themselves as organisms composed of different cells and systems working together.

CURRICULAR LINKS TO UNIT 3 - SCIENCE: CHEMISTRY

Age	Virginia (US)	Ontario (Canada)	UK (National)	Victoria (Australia)
5-6	Kindergarten. Conduct investigations in which a question is developed from one or more observations.	Kindergarten. Conduct simple investigations using inquiry skills (questioning, planning, predicting, observing, communicating).	Year 1 (KS 1). Make simple predictions, turn ideas into a form that can be tested, make observations and comparisons.	Kindergarten (Level 1). Participate in very simple investigations involving observation and measurement; collect and record data.
6-7	Grade 1. Conduct simple experiments, answer questions, make inferences and draw conclusions. Study how different common materials interact with water (dissolve, separate).	Grade 1. Investigate, through experimentation, the properties of various materials. Describe materials as substances from which things are made.	Year 2 (KS 1). *Unit 2D: Grouping and Changing Materials.* Make predictions, record observations, decide whether a test is fair. Relate science to domestic contexts (cooking).	Year 1 (Level 2). Expand scientific vocabulary. Pose questions and repeat observations over time to make predictions and draw conclusions from data.
7-8	Grade 2. Investigate and understand basic properties of solids, liquids, and gases. Key concepts include mass and volume.	Grade 2. Investigate properties and interactions among liquids and solids. Experiment with interactions that occur as a result of mixing and/or dissolving liquids and solids. Use appropriate vocabulary.	Year 3 (KS 2). *Unit 3C: Characteristics of Materials.* Plan investigations, decide on variables, decide whether a fair comparison was made, and use results to draw conclusions.	Year 2 (Level 2). See above.
8-9	Grade 3. Investigate objects and describe materials by their physical properties. Materials are composed of parts that are too small to be seen.	Grade 3. Describe the properties of solids and liquids, identify the conditions that cause changes from liquid to solid water and back.	Year 4 (KS 2). *Unit 4D: Solids, Liquids, and how they can be separated.* Identify changes that occur when solids and liquids are mixed.	Year 3 (Level 3). Classify materials using states of matter. Explore reversible and non-reversible changes using water, vinegar, and bicarbonate of soda.

Age	Virginia (US)	Ontario (Canada)	UK (National)	Victoria (Australia)
9-10	Grade 4. Formulate hypotheses based on cause-and-effect relationships, define variables, and make predictions based on data.	Grade 4. (Emerging level: ask questions, create a plan, make simple predictions, select equipment, record, organize, discuss data, draw simple conclusions, and evaluate.)	Year 5 (KS 2). *Unit 5C: Gases Around Us.* Making and repeating observations, explain everyday phenomena. *Unit 5D: Changing State.*	Year 4 (Level 3). See previous.
10-11	Grade 5. Investigate and understand that matter is anything that has mass, takes up space, and occurs as a solid, liquid, or gas. Study atoms, elements, molecules, and compounds.	Grade 5. Demonstrate an understanding of the properties of matter, changes of state, and physical and chemical change. Investigate changes of state and changes of matter.	Year 6 (KS 2). *Unit 6D, Reversible and Irreversible Changes.* Review reversible changes and introduce burning as an irreversible change that produces new materials.	Year 5 (Level 4). Use a variety of instruments (eg. thermometers) and discuss error. Consider the appropriateness of inferences and solutions drawn from the data.
11-12	Grade 6. Atoms of any element are alike but are different from atoms of other elements. Chemical equations can be used to model chemical changes.	Grade 6. (Competent Level: Formulate a specific question to investigate, make predictions, draw simple conclusions, evaluate the procedure, suggest improvements)	Year 7 (Key Stage 3). *Unit 7E: Acids and Alkalis. Unit 7F: Simple Chemical Reactions. Unit 7G. Particle Model of Solids, Liquids, and Gases.*	Year 6 (Level 4). See above.
12-13	Grade 7. Conduct investigations with repeated trials. Define variables. Identify sources of experimental error, control variables to test hypotheses, repeat trials, interpret data.	Grade 7. Demonstrate an understanding of the properties and applications of pure substances and mixtures, and describe these characteristics using the particle theory.	Year 8 (Key Stg. 3). *Unit 8E: Atoms and Elements.* Use the particle model. *Unit 8F: Compounds and Mixtures.* Distinguish between elements and compounds. Use symbols and formulae.	Year 7 (Level 5). Use the particle model of matter to explain the behavior of materials. Test formal understandings in controlled studies using appropriate experimental tools.

CURRICULAR LINKS TO UNIT 4 - MATHEMATICS: DATA COLLECTION

Age	Virginia (US)	Ontario (Canada)	UK (National)	Victoria (Australia)
4-5	Early Childhood. Use descriptive language to compare data in object- and picture graphs.	Early Learning. Collect data, make representations of observations.	Foundation Stage. Count how many objects share a property. Present results using pictures, drawings, or numerals.	Pre-K (Level 1). Investigate situations requiring data collection and presentation (such as a pictogram).
5-6	Kindergarten. Display objects and information using object graphs, pictorial graphs, and tables.	Kindergarten. Collect objects or data and represent observations (simple concrete graphs, bar graphs, pictographs, tally charts).	Year 1 (Key Stage 1). Answer a question by recording data (tables, pictures, block graphs, pictograms).	Kindergarten (Level 1). See above.
6-7	Grade 1. Investigate, identify, and describe various forms of data collection, using tables, picture graphs, and object graphs.	Grade 1. Collect, organize, and display data using concrete graphs and pictographs.	Year 2 (Key Stage 1). Answer a question by collecting and recording data in tables, block graphs, pictograms.	Year 1 (Level 2). Pose and respond to questions leading to data collection. Use pictographs and bar graphs to organize and present data.
7-8	Grade 2. Read, construct, and interpret a simple picture and bar graph.	Grade 2. Collect, organize, and display data (tally charts, concrete graphs, pictographs, line plots, bar graphs).	Year 3 (Key Stage 2). Use tally charts, frequency tables, pictograms, and bar charts.	Year 2 (Level 2). See above.
8-9	Grade 3. Read and interpret data represented in line plots, bar graphs, and picture graphs, and write a sentence analyzing the data.	Grade 3. Collect, organize, and display data using charts and graphs, including vertical and horizontal bar graphs, with labels along axes.	Year 4 (Key Stage 2). Organize, present, analyze and interpret data in tables, diagrams, tally charts, pictograms, and bar graphs.	Year 3 (Level 3). Use a column or bar graph to display the results of an experiment.

Age	Virginia (US)	Ontario (Canada)	UK (National)	Victoria (Australia)
9-10	Grade 4. Collect, organize, and display data in line and bar graphs and use the display to interpret results, draw conclusions, and make predictions.	Grade 4. Collect, describe, and display data using charts and graphs (stem and leaf plots, double bar graphs).	Year 5 (Key Stage 2). Construct frequency tables, pictograms, and bar and line graphs.	Year 4 (Level 3). See previous.
10-11	Grade 5. Collect, organize, and display numerical data using bar graphs, stem-and-leaf plots, and line graphs to draw conclusions and make predictions.	Grade 5. Collect, organize, and display data using charts and graphs (including broken line graphs).	Year 6 (Key Stage 2). Make and interpret frequency tables, bar charts with grouped discrete data, and line graphs; interpret pie charts.	Year 5 (Level 4). Present data (pie chart, histogram). Reflect on ways data can be represented.
11-12	Grade 6. Collect, analyze, display, and interpret data in a variety of graphical methods: line, bar and circle graphs, stem and leaf plots, box and whisker plots.	Grade 6. Collect, organize, and display primary and secondary data using charts and graphs, including continuous line graphs.	Year 7 (Key Stage 3). Make paper and ICT graphs and diagrams (bar-line graphs, frequency diagrams for grouped discrete data, simple pie charts).	Year 6 (Level 4). See above.
12-13	Grade 7. Collect, analyze, display, and interpret data using a variety of graphical methods (frequency distributions, line plots, histograms, stem and leaf plots, box and whisker plots, scattergrams).	Grade 7. Collect, organize, and display data using charts and graphs (relative frequency tables, circle graphs). Make arguments based on data analysis.	Year 8 (Key Stage 3). Construct graphical representations (paper and ICT) and identify which are most useful. Include pie charts, bar charts and frequency diagrams, simple scatter graphs, and stem and leaf diagrams.	Year 7 (Level 5). Use dot plots, stem and leaf plots, column graphs, bar charts, and histograms.

CURRICULAR LINKS TO UNIT 5 - MATHEMATICS: MEASUREMENT

Age	Virginia (US)	Ontario (Canada)	UK (National)	Victoria (Australia)
4-5	Early Childhood. Make direct comparisons between shapes.	Early Learning. Compare and order two or more objects and use measurement terms (small / medium / large).	Foundation Stage. Use language such as "greater," "smaller," "heavier," or "lighter" to compare quantities.	Pre-K (Level 1). Compare length, area, capacity, and mass of objects using terms such as "larger" or "holds more." Use informal units.
5-6	Kindergarten. Compare two objects using direct comparison or nonstandard units (length, height, weight, temperature).	Kindergarten. Compare and order two or more objects (length, mass, area, capacity). Be aware of nonstandard measuring devices.	Year 1 (Key Stage 1). Estimate, measure, weigh and compare objects, choosing suitable uniform nonstandard or standard units.	Kindergarten (Level 1). See above.
6-7	Grade 1. Compare the volume of two containers by using concrete materials. Use nonstandard units to measure length and weight.	Grade 1. Estimate, measure and describe length, area, mass, and capacity using nonstandard units of the same size. Compare, describe, and order objects.	Year 2 (Key Stage 1). Estimate, compare, and measure lengths, weights and capacities, choosing standard units (m, cm, kg, liter).	Year 1 (Level 2). Make, describe, and compare measures of length, area, volume, mass using informal units. Judge relative capacity of objects and containers by eye.
7-8	Grade 2. Given grid paper, estimate and then count the number of square units needed to determine area. Estimate and count the number of cubes in a box to determine volume.	Grade 2. Compare, describe, and order objects using nonstandard and standard units. Estimate, measure, and record length, perimeter, area, mass, and capacity.	Year 3 (Key Stage 2). (Know the relationship between km and meters, litres and ml. Choose appropriate units to estimate, measure, and record measurements.)	Year 2 (Level 2). See above.
8-9	Grade 3. Analyze 2- and 3- dimensional figures and identify relevant properties. Estimate and then measure using metric and US units.	Grade 3. Compare, describe, and order objects using standard units. Estimate and measure length, perimeter, area, mass, and capacity.	Year 4 (Key Stage 2). *Block D: Calculating, measuring, and understanding shape.* Area and perimeter of rectangles.	Year 3 (Level 3). Estimate and measure length, area, volume, capacity, and mass. Study the relationship between size and capacity of a container.

Age	Virginia (US)	Ontario (Canada)	UK (National)	Victoria (Australia)
9-10	Grade 4. Estimate and measure liquid volume, using metric and US customary units. Describe the use of perimeter and area.	Grade 4. Estimate and measure length, perimeter, area, mass, capacity, and volume. Determine relationships among units and attributes, including area and perimeter of rectangles.	Year 5 (Key Stage 2). *Block D: Calculating, measuring, and understanding shape.* Estimating and measuring weight, length, capacity. Area and perimeter of regular/irregular polygons.	Year 4 (Level 3). See previous.
10-11	Grade 5. Differentiate between perimeter, area, and volume. Determine the perimeter of a polygon and the area of a square, rectangle, and right triangle.	Grade 5. Estimate and measure perimeter, area. Determine the relationships among units and attributes, including the area of a rectangle and the volume of a rectangular prism.	Year 6 (Key Stage 2). See above.	Year 5 (Level 4). Estimate and measure perimeter, area, volume, capacity in metric units. Determine perimeter and area of simple shapes (count squares in a grid).
11-12	Grade 6. Solve problems involving the circumference and/or area of a circle.	Grade 6. Estimate, measure, and record using metric units. Determine the relationships among attributes, including the area of a triangle/parallelogram, and the volume of a triangular prism.	Year 7 (Key Stage 3). Know and use the formula for the area of a rectangle. Calculate the perimeter and area of shapes made from rectangles. Calculate the surface area of cubes and cuboids.	Year 6 (Level 4). See above.
12-13	Grade 7. Investigate and solve problems involving the volume and surface area of rectangular prisms and cylinders.	Grade 7. Report on research into real-life applications of area measurements. Determine the relationships among units and attributes, including the area of a trapezoid and the volume of a right prism.	Year 8 (Key Stage 3). Derive and use formulas for area (triangle, trapezium, and parallelogram). Calculate areas of compound shapes. Know and use the formulas for the volume and surface area of a cuboid.	Year 7 (Level 5). Measure perimeter, area, mass, volume, and capacity. Use formulas for area and perimeter of circles, triangles, and parallelograms and simple composite shapes. Calculate surface area and volume of prisms and cylinders.

CURRICULAR LINKS TO UNIT 6 - WRITING

Age	Virginia (US)	Ontario (Canada)	UK (National)	Victoria (Australia)
5-6	Kindergarten. Identify story elements and communicate ideas through pictures and writing. Write about experiences, stories, people, objects, or events.	Kindergarten. Listen to poems, stories, and non-fiction texts for enjoyment and information. Explore texts independently and retell stories.	Year 1 (Key Stage 1). Convey information and ideas in simple non-narrative forms. Find and use new and interesting words and phrases, including story language.	Kindergarten (Level 1). Write simple texts about simple topics to convey ideas or messages. Use conventional letters, groups of letters, and simple punctuation.
6-7	Grade 1. Write to communicate ideas. Use descriptive words when writing about people, places, things, and events. Use complete sentences in final copies.	Grade 1. Draft and revise writing. Use editing, proof reading, and publishing skills and strategies. Write short texts. Begin to establish a personal voice. Write simple but complete sentences.	Year 2 (Key Stage 1). Decide and plan what and how to write; use person and time. Make adventurous word choices appropriate to the style and purpose of the text. Make sections hang together.	Year 1 (Level 2). Write short, sequenced texts that include some related ideas about familiar topics. Organize subject matter, link ideas in a variety of ways, indicate time and place. Re-read, edit, revise, and clarify.
7-8	Grade 2. Write stories, letters, and simple explanations. Organize writing (beginning, middle, end) and edit for correct grammar, punctuation, and spelling.	Grade 2. Identify the topic, purpose, audience, and form for writing. Use graphic organizers. Write short texts. Use editing / proofreading / publishing skills.	Year 3 (Key Stage 2). Make decisions about form and purpose. Use beginning, middle, and end to write narratives using paragraphs. Signal sequence, place and time.	Year 2 (Level 2). See above.

Age	Virginia (US)	Ontario (Canada)	UK (National)	Victoria (Australia)
8-9	Grade 3. Plan, draft, revise, and edit stories, letters, simple explanations, and short reports across all content areas. Write descriptive paragraphs. Include descriptive details that elaborate the central idea.	Grade 3. Identify / order main ideas and supporting details. Write short texts. Use words and phrases that will help convey meaning as specifically as possible. Vary sentence structure. Maintain continuity using joining words.	Year 4 (Key Stage 2). Use settings and characterization to engage readers' interest. Write convincing and informative non-narrative texts. Show imagination through language to create emphasis, humor, or atmosphere.	Year 3 (Level 3). Write texts containing several logically ordered paragraphs. Write narratives which include characters, setting, and plot. Use illustrative evidence, express a point of view, and provide supporting detail.
9-10	Grade 4. Plan, draft, revise, and edit effective narratives, poems, and explanations. Write several related paragraphs. Use elements of style, including word choice and sentence variation.	Grade 4. Write more complex texts. Use specific words and phrases to create an intended impression. Use sentences of different lengths / structures. Make revisions to improve the content, clarity, and interest of written work.	Year 5 (Key Stage 2). Reflect independently and critically on writing. Edit and improve. Experiment with different narrative forms and styles to write stories. Vary the pace and develop the viewpoint.	Year 4 (Level 3). See above.
10-11	Grade 5. Plan, draft, revise, and edit writing to describe, inform, entertain, and explain. Use precise and descriptive vocabulary to create time and voice. Edit for correct grammar, spelling, punctuation, and sentence structure.	Grade 5. Develop several linked paragraphs. Write longer / more complex texts. Use vivid / figurative language. Vary sentence structure. Use conjunctions to connect ideas and pronouns to make links.	Year 6 (Key Stage 2). Use different narrative techniques to engage and entertain the reader. Establish, balance, and maintain viewpoints. Integrate words, images, and sounds imaginatively.	Year 5 (Level 4). Produce a variety of texts for different purposes using features appropriate to the purpose, audience, and context. Use simple figurative language, variety of sentence structure, and different parts of speech. Plan, edit, and proofread.

Age	Virginia (US)	Ontario (Canada)	UK (National)	Victoria (Australia)
11-12	Grade 6. Plan, draft, revise, and edit narratives, descriptions, and explanations. Establish central idea, organization, elaboration, and unity.	Grade 6. Develop a structured, multi-paragraph piece of writing. Create complex sentences by combining phrases, clauses, and simple sentences. Produce revised drafts.	Year 7 (Key Stage 3). Develop ideas, themes, settings, and characters when writing to imagine, explore, and explain. Analyze and evaluate. Support opinions with evidence.	Year 6 (Level 4). See previous.
12-13	Grade 7. Refine skills with special attention to word choice, organization, style, and grammar. Develop narrative, expository, and persuasive writing. Elaborate the central idea in an organized manner.	Grade 7. Identify audience and purpose for more complex writing forms. Write complex texts of different lengths. Regularly use vivid / figurative language and innovative expressions. Vary sentence structure for rhythm and pacing.	Year 8 (Key Stage 3). See above. Use imagination to convey themes, ideas and arguments, solve problems, and create settings, moods, and characters.	Year 7 (Level 5). Produce texts for a variety of purposes: speculating, hypothesizing, persuading, and reflecting. Write extended narratives and arguments that justify a viewpoint and incorporate challenging themes and issues. Reflect on and evaluate texts.

Bibliography

Aaron, George. "The Lucayans." *Five Hundred Magazine*. April 1990: 6-7. *History Department Millersville University*. Web. 23 January 2010.

Buchheim, Jason. *A Quick Course in Ichthyology.* Odyssey Expeditons, n.d. Web. 21 March 2010.

Bueter, Chuck. "Bad Moons Rising." *Paper Plate Education*. n.d. Web. 19 February 2010.

Cascarano, Wayne. "Baking Soda and Vinegar Reaction and Demonstrations." *Apple Cider Vinegar Benefits*. n.d. Web. 31 May 2010.

Curriculum Cards. Stafford County Public Schools, n.d. Web. 28 April 2010.

What's on the Inside. DASH Project, University of Hawaii, n.d. Web. 21 March 2010.

Dickinson, Rachel. *Tools of Navigation: A Kid's Guide to the History and Science of Finding Your Way.* White River Junction, Vermont: Nomad Press, 2005.

Edwards, Philip, ed. *James Cook: the Journals*. London: Penguin Books, 1999.

Espenak, Fred. *Mr. Eclipse*. n.d. Web. 22 January 2011.

Fish Anatomy. About Fish Online, n.d. Web. 21 March 2010.

Fish Biology and Husbandry. Docstoc.com, n.d. Web. 10 February 2010.

Fish Dissection – Internal Organs. Australian Museum, n.d. Web. 8 February 2010.

Fuson, Robert H. *The Log of Christopher Columbus*. Camden: International Marine, 1987.

Ganon, Paddy. *Framework Science 7*. Oxford: Oxford University Press, 2002.

Ganon, Paddy. *Framework Science 8*. Oxford: Oxford University Press, 2003.

Ganon, Paddy. *Framework Science 9*. Oxford: Oxford University Press, 2004.

Guitar, Lynne. *History of the Dominican Republic*. Hispaniola.com, n.d. Web. 30 January 2010.

Hagerman, Howard. *Perch Dissection*. n.d. Web. 15 March 2010.

Haney, David. *Captain James Cook and the Explorers of the Pacific*. New York: Chelsea House Publishers, 1992.

Heat-Moon, William Least. *Columbus in the Americas*. New Jersey: Wily & Son, 2002.

Heckscher, Mary. "The Ultimate Fizz." *Science and Children*. December 2008: 24-27.

Hough, Richard. *Captain James Cook: A Biography*. London: Coronet Books, 1994.

Instruction. Virginia Department of Education, n.d. Web. 28 April 2010.

Lew, Kristi. *Acids and Bases*. New York: Infobase Publishing, 2009.

Lew, Kristi. *Chemical Reactions*. New York: Infobase Publishing, 2008.

Livingston, Myra Cohn. *Poem-Making: Ways to Begin Writing Poetry*. New York: Harper Collins, 1991.

McGee, Harold. *On Food and Cooking*. New York: Fireside, 1997.

McGrouther, Mark. *Fish Dissection*. Australian Museum, 16 June 2009. Web. 8 February 2010.

Moeller, Robert Jr. *Biology of Fish*. Cichlid Forum, n.d. Web. 8 February 2010.

Morison, Samuel Eliot. *Christopher Columbus: Mariner*. New York: Meridan, 1983.

National Curriculum. UK Department for Education, n.d. Web. 29 April 2010.

National Oceanographic and Atmospheric Administration (NOAA). *Prince William Sound*. Map. Washington, D.C. 1983.

National Strategies. UK Department for Education, n.d. Web. 29 April 2010.

"Native American Mapping Traditions." *Lewis and Clark in the Illinois Country*. Illinois State Museum, n.d. Web. 23 October 2010.

The Ocean's Tides Explained. Moon Connection, n.d. Web. 3 May 2010.

The Ontario Curriculum. Ontario Ministry of Education, 29 July 2009. Web. 30 April 2010.

Palmeri, Amy. "Making Sense of Data." *Science and Children*. October 2009: 30-33.

Pelta, Kathy. *Discovering Christopher Columbus: How History is Invented*. Minneapolis: Lerner Publications, 1991.

Pickering, Keith. *Columbus Navigation*. n.d. Web. 28 January 2010.

Ray, Katie Wood with Lester Laminack. *The Writing Workshop*. Urbana, Illinois: National Council of Teachers of English, 2001.

Revisiting Columbus and the Indigenous Caribbean. Caribbean Amerindian Centrelink, 30 December 2003. Web. 23 January 2010.

Rickards, Debbie and Shirl Hawes. *Learning about Literary Genres: Reading and Writing with Young Children*. Norwood, Massachusetts: Christopher-Gordon Publishers, 2005.

Schemes of Work. Department for Children, Schools, and Families, n.d. Web. 29 April 2010.

Strickland, Jonathan. "What and Where is the Dark Side of the Moon?" *Discovery: How Stuff Works*. 28 May 2008. Web. 22 January 2010.

Temertzoglou, Ted. *Healthy Active Living*. Toronto: Thompson Educational Publishing, 2007.

"The VELS." *Victorian Essential Learning Standards*. Victorian Curriculum and Assessment Authority, n.d. Web. 20 April 2010.

West, Delno C. and Jean M. West. *Christopher Columbus: The Great Adventure and How We Know About It*. New York: Atheneum, 1991.

Williams, Linda. *Navigational Aids*. New York: Marshall Cavendish, 2008.

"Worldly Ways: Cook Islands." *Benjamin Franklin*. Public Broadcasting Service (PBS), 2002. Web. 22 January 2011.

Index

About the Author

Nadine Slavinski is a teacher, writer, and erstwhile archaeologist with a penchant for blue horizons. She holds a Master's of Education from Harvard University and has been teaching in international schools since 1996. Her son Nicky crossed his first ocean at age four and later completed grades two, three, and four while sailing the Pacific Ocean aboard *Namani*.

Visit Nadine's website *nslavinski.com* to find interesting and informative blog posts, links, and resources. That's also where you can contact her or sign up to receive updates on new content and releases. Her travel blog is *namaniatsea.org*.

Also by Nadine Slavinski:

- *Cruising the Caribbean with Kids: Fun, Facts, and Educational Activities*
- *Pacific Crossing Notes: A Sailor's Guide to the Coconut Milk Run*
- *The Silver Spider* (a sea adventure novel)

Please consider leaving a review of this book at the store you purchased it from. Not only do reviews help other readers judge a book, they also help the title appear more often in Internet searches and thus find interested readers. This is especially important to niche publications like this, so please do write a review, no matter how brief. Thank you!

CPSIA information can be obtained
at www.ICGtesting.com
Printed in the USA
LVHW051538200223
739952LV00005B/410

9 781733 667616